Family Plots

University of Pennsylvania Press
Feminist Cultural Studies, the Media, and Political Culture
Mary Ellen Brown and Andrea Press, Editors

Lisa M. Cuklanz. *Rape on Trial: How the Mass Media Construct Legal Reform and Social Change.* 1995

Margaret J. Heide. *Television Culture and Women's Lives:* thirtysomething *and the Contradictions of Gender.* 1995

Dana Heller. *Family Plots: The De-Oedipalization of Popular Culture.* 1995

Andrea Press. *Women Watching Television: Gender, Class, and Generation in the American Television Experience.* 1991

Family Plots

The De-Oedipalization of Popular Culture

Dana Heller

University of Pennsylvania Press

Philadelphia

Library of Congress Cataloging-in-Publication Data
Heller, Dana A. (Dana Alice), 1959–
    Family plots : the de-Oedipalization of popular culture / Dana Heller.
        p.   cm. — (Feminist cultural studies, the media, and political culture)
    Includes bibliographical references and index.
    ISBN 0-8122-3294-1 (cloth). — ISBN 0-8122-1544-3 (pbk. : alk. paper)
    1. Family in mass media—United States.   2. Popular culture—United States—
History—20th century.   I. Title.   II. Series.
P94.5.F342U655   1995
306.85—dc20   95-13910
                                                                    CIP

This book is lovingly dedicated to my mother, Dorothy Heller, who, unlike many culturally "enlightened" parents of her generation, nurtured my interest in TV sitcoms, taught me the romantic lyrics to popular show tunes, accompanied me to countless movies about alienated youth, and pretended not to notice when I borrowed her novels and "forgot" to return them. Thanks, Mom.

Contents

Acknowledgments

Family Plots: The De-Oedipalization of Popular Culture has been six years in the making. During this period of time I have been generously assisted by various institutions, colleagues, friends, and family. In recognition of this generosity, I would like to acknowledge here those who supported me in the research, composition, and preparation of the manuscript.

The project was partially funded by the Research Foundation at Old Dominion University, which financed a summer off from teaching so that I could conduct full-time research. In addition, the College of Arts and Letters at Old Dominion provided me with grants for travel to the Museum of Broadcasting in New York and to attend the summer session, "Taking Popular Culture Seriously," at the Massachusetts Institute of Technology. Henry Jenkins, who led the session at MIT, challenged many of my assumptions about pop culture in general and the family romance in particular.

I want to thank Patricia Smith, at the University of Pennsylvania Press, for seeing something worthwhile in an early version of the manuscript, and for remaining throughout the revision and production process a source of encouragement and good sense. Moreover, I am deeply indebted to John R. Leo at the University of Rhode Island, a passionate reader, consummate scholar, and loyal friend. His critical insights were a vital force in helping me refine the focus of the argument. Esteemed colleagues, particularly Fred Reynolds at City College in New York and Ed Jacobs and Manuela Mourão at Old Dominion, tolerated my chronic lateness to dinner parties and dished up endless amounts of moral support. My students at Old Dominion deserve much credit for almost always giving me the benefit of the doubt and for waiting patiently while I finished my sentences. Many of their thoughtful contributions and exchanges have found their way into these pages.

Without the confidence and love of my parents, Dorothy and Edwin Heller, I doubt very much this project would ever have been started, let alone completed. Friends, near and far-flung, have courageously expanded my definitions of family and have honored me with invitations to join them in their rituals, gestures deserving of thanks and lush reciprocation. Finally, I want to thank Janice Conard, whose company has enriched every part of my life. Throughout all stages of this book's production I have attempted—with varying degrees of success—to measure up to her high standards of honesty, sense, and mother wit. Lucky for me, there's more work to be done.

*   *   *

The author wishes to thank the following for permission to reprint:

The image on the front jacket cover, "The Nuclear Family," appears with the permission of Laird Mark Ehlert, Maid in the Shade Greeting Cards, 1990.

Sections of Chapters 1 and 2 appear in modified form in "Housebreaking History: Feminism's Changing Romance with the Private Sphere," in *Feminism Beside Itself*, ed. Diane Elam and Robyn Wiegman (New York: Routledge, 1995).

A modified version of Chapter 8 appears in *College Literature* vol. 21, no. 2 (June 1994).

An early version of Chapter 10 appears as "Almost Blue: Policing Lesbian Desire in *Internal Affairs*, in *The Lesbian Postmodern*, ed. Laura Doan (New York: Columbia University Press, 1994). © Columbia University Press, New York. Reprinted with permission of the publisher.

Chapter 11 appears in *Proceedings of the Conference on Film and American Culture* (Williamsburg, Va: The College of William and Mary), and is reprinted with the permission of Joel Schwartz.

Preface

Any book whose title makes so arrogant a claim as this one does ought rightly to offer some straightforward explanation of the author's intent. To begin with, this is not a book about "family values," an amorphous catch-phrase of recent years. Nor is it a book intended to explain pop-sociological phenomena such as skyrocketing divorce rates, latchkey children, deadbeat dads, and so forth. Rather, the goal of this book is to formulate and demonstrate an approach toward contemporary popular culture that may critically account for the transitory condition of American family romance, or the family plot.

My argument, plainly stated, is that family romance needs to be seen as both a cause and an effect of a more widespread project of cultural remapping. Family romances contribute to this remapping process by dissolving a monolithic-oppositional model of domestic space and its corollary, a properly gendered identity free of internal contradictions. While the tendency within contemporary cultural studies is to conceive positively of such subversions, dissolution is not necessarily to be equated with revolution.[1] Indeed, family romances achieve dissolution at their own peril, for in the process they also redescribe their own generic boundaries and historical references, one of the most basic of which is Freud's Oedipus. But how do these "new" family romances critique Oedipal imperatives and cultural norms even as they assert their formal legacy? What specific social and historical conditions have contributed to the self-conscious foregrounding of contradictions such as this, contradictions that are reshaping both the production and reception of family romances?

Throughout this book, I will be at pains to articulate precisely what is so "new" about the kinds of resistance inscribed within family romances of the latter half of this century. As a means of classifying these familial subversions that cut across so much of contemporary popular culture, I propose the provisional term "post-family romance." Admittedly, I do this with a certain degree of hesitation. After all, surely the last thing the world needs is yet another signifier of cultural apocalypse. Hopefully, though, the usefulness of this term will be its historical specificity, its reference to family plots produced within and responsive to new configurations of gender, narrative, and private space from the period extending roughly from the early 1960s to the present.

My argument is that such configurations may be read—and arguably should be read—through a postmodern awareness of the fault lines of family romance, one of the most massively produced popular narrative forms. These fault lines may be said to function as sites of competition and ambiguity based in new understandings of sexual identification, familial structure, and narrative form. These fault lines are also, I believe, foregrounded in contemporary family romances that provide self-reflexive critiques of the family's dynamic inscription within modernity. The title of this book, *Family Plots*, is intended to stress this complicitous function and serve as a reminder that narratives of origins, whether fictional or nonfictional, are first and foremost contrivances. My title also refers to the Alfred Hitchcock film, *Family Plot*, a film that cleverly asserts a betrayal—or burial—of the Oedipal family at the same time that it articulates this family for popular consumption. It is precisely this double or multiple consciousness, a self-reflexive awareness of the conflicts that decenter every attempt to "frame" the family, that helps define new narratives of identity in relation to origin.

Family Plots is aimed at demonstrating the pervasive and multiplex character of a narrative mode that has often been misrepresented as a draconian discursive implement of patriarchal oppression, a policing agent of social boundaries and class hierarchies, or as an unproblematized mass-culture commodity. Of course the family, like the romance that problematizes it, does have significant ties to mass culture as well as the discourses of patriarchal bourgeois modernity. The expression "family romance" was coined by Sigmund Freud, the great bourgeois modernist patriarch himself, in a 1908 essay.[2] For literary scholars, the phrase retains much of the same value that Freud originally ascribed to it as "an imaginary interrogation of origins . . . which embeds the engenderment of narrative within the experience of family."[3] As a popular discursive form, family romances are typically regarded as narratives that communicate to the members of a reading or viewing public sphere a vision of domestic life presumably basic to the representation of legible identity. In other words, the family romance instructs the public as to how it should understand the relations of the private. However, implicit in this act of translation is an act of transposition, an act that demonstrates the mutual dependency of identity and fantasy, mother functions and father functions, the public and the private sphere.

Transposition remains the most instructive feature here, and it points to the commonly held opinion that romance is a wily genre defined by a historical insistence on its own internal contradictions. Today, this insistence corresponds with postmodern debates over the epistemological clarity of such notions as identity, genre, and separate spheres. For critics as diverse as Richard Chase, Janice Radway, and Diane Elam, romance is resistance.[4] But is it? Perhaps it is the family, as much as the romance, that is antiformalistic. And perhaps this antiformalism is not a break from Freud, but rather something Freud recognized and allowed for specifically through an appropriation of the romance. And while family romance may always be primarily concerned with formal excess, post-family romances perhaps reveal a deeper commitment to the production of gender excess and to the cooperative blurring of spatial and gender limits. The result is not the production of a new center of gender identity or cultural consensus, but a multiplication of competing centers that struggle within the narrative and within individual characters as they challenge their own roles within the Oedipal drama.

Several notable efforts to redirect these patterns deserve mention here. These works have had a measurable influence on *Family Plots* by compelling me to define and refine my own arguments in relation to theirs. In *The Mother/Daughter Plot: Narrative, Psychoanalysis, Feminism,* Marianne Hirsch attempts to define a female version or appropriation of the family romance that locates identity not in the daughter's passive acceptance of a castrated mother, but in her active narrative relation to a powerful mother figure. By way of contrast, *Family Plots* does not argue for a new female-centered romance, but rather suggests that any continued reliance on "centers," no matter what their political or theoretical justification, does not allow us to grasp the complex interactions of postmodernism, romance, and gender identity. In *The Novel as Family Romance: Language, Gender, and Authority from Fielding to Joyce,*[5] Christine van Boheemen also places gender relations at the core of her analysis, yet like Hirsch she seems suspicious of popular aesthetics and reluctant to venture beyond the canons of elite culture. In this way, both writers steer romance away from an allegiance with popular culture, lifting romance up onto the shoulders of high theory where we may better see it as a condition of elite culture. Janice Radway's *Reading the Romance: Women, Patriarchy, and Popular Literature* is in many ways a landmark study that takes issue with the Frankfurt Institute for Social Research and its equation of mass culture with fascism and user passivity. Rather, Radway turns our attention to the agency of romance fans, who, she argues, *do* have some say about the kinds of ideological work romance texts perform. In this sense, Radway's research suggests that romance and social change are not necessarily exclusive to one another.

The texts I have chosen for this study have been selected from a wide range of works that I have encountered—whether accidently or by design—over the past five to six years. Some of my interpretations of these works were rehearsed in the classroom, others at conferences, while some have evolved mainly through dialogue with colleagues and friends. However, all of these texts demonstrate, to my mind, the ongoing debate over the possibility of self-formation in the wake of cultural/familial dissolution. They illustrate lingering formal constraints in combination with new ethical/aesthetic imperatives to write across self-concepts and social spaces historically perceived as oppositional and discrete. I have chosen these texts, rather than others, because they allow us to foreground some of the various fault lines of the family, lines along which desires and identifications, like Gilles Deleuze and Felix Guattari's "deterritorialized flows," become mobile and transgressive, moving toward an affirmative practice of familial redescription.

By adopting the term "redescription" to denote the changing semiotics of family romance, I also owe a debt to Richard Rorty, for whom intellectual history as well as the history of the arts is most productively viewed as the history of metaphor.[6] *Family Plots* will attempt to trace the recent history of one particular metaphor through the "realization that anything can be made to look good or bad by being redescribed."[7] Also, by conceiving of the history of modernity as a metaphorical account of the continuous battle between the vocabulary of public nonfamilial space and the vocabulary of private familial space, Rorty defines the discursive playing field of family romance. In Chapters 1 and 2, I will reckon with some of the players—the producers, theorists, and critics of family romance—specifically in terms of the kinds of intervention they invite on behalf of the category of the familial. In Chapters 3 to 11, I will discuss some family romances that have been redescribed in American culture between the years 1960 and 1992. The questions to be explored in my examinations of these texts, which include novels, television programs, film, and home video, focus on the problems of how the family incorporates a metaphorical vocabulary of contingency, irony, and difference into its inherited vocabulary of unity, consensus, and continuity.

Finally, I want to paraphrase Clifford Geertz and admit that "one does not study family romances, one studies *in* them."[8] I can make no claims to critical disinterestedness in having allowed myself five years to concentrate on this topic. And it hasn't always been easy trying to sort out my own family mythologies from the texts I've selected as examples. Post-family romances, like some cultural practitioners, may truly be compelled to "theorize the possibility of their own subversiveness."[9] Still, I hope these readings will signify more than a sidelong glance at my own processes of Oedipal disentanglement. It may be that the fate of family romance, like the fate of cultural studies itself, rests in the hands of producers and consumers attuned to the powers of redescription in an increasingly ironist moment. This ironic playfulness has, in some instances, resulted in family romances structured in terms of mystery or crime drama, freak shows, cybernetic fantasies, or in the words of comedienne Sandra Bernhard, "portraits Norman Rockwell forgot to paint."[10] However, even family romances that would suppress these portraits are unavoidably eccentric, for they are faced with the impossible task of having to remove themselves from a world in which the family is always already positioned as "other" to itself.

Chapter 1
Introduction: Plotting the Family

The terms of the Oedipus do not form a triangle, but exist shattered into all corners of the social field—the mother on the instructor's knees, the father next to the colonel. Group fantasy is plugged into and machined on the socius. Being fucked by the socius, wanting to be fucked by the socius, does not derive from the father and mother, even though the father and mother have their roles there as subordinate agents of transmission or execution.[1]
        —Deleuze and Guattari

I am beginning to realize that feminists need to stop reading everything through the family romance.[2]
        —Jane Gallop

What is a family anyway? They're just people who make you feel less alone and really loved.[3]
        —Mary Richards, from the series finale of
        The Mary Tyler Moore Show

In the *New York Times* on October 13, 1991, novelist Alice McDermott reviewed a photography exhibit entitled *Pleasures and Terrors of Domestic Comfort*. Installed at the Museum of Modern Art, the exhibit featured 153 photographs, all revealing to McDermott "less about the way we live than about the dilemma that faces any artist who chooses domestic life as a subject."[4] A writer noted for her own attraction to this subject, McDermott directs herself to the root of the problem: in their dogged efforts to disavow the myths of happy American family life— myths that had toppled twenty years earlier with the explosion of the feminist movement—artists have established a new, unrelentingly dark image of domesticity. In fact, so great is the pressure on artists to avoid the hint of anything even remotely resembling sentimentality, that failure, despair, cruelty, and boredom have become the markers of a new traditionalism in representing the family.

While the appearance of new literary clichés poses certain difficulties for McDermott, the main issue for her "arises when, in our avid study of what domestic life has failed to be, we lose all sense of how marvelous are the things we ask from it: comfort, sustenance, fond feeling, a base for all excursions into the wide world, a place to be freed from as well as a place to return to."[5] In conclusion, McDermott concedes that what was once a radical shift in artistic sensibility has become a tired convention: the true maverick is the revisionary artist who would dare to challenge the plot against the family and admit that while home may not always be "Ozzie and Harriet," indeed, "sometimes it is."

Notwithstanding the accuracy of these claims for some audiences, I find McDermott's list of familial expectations oddly conventional for a review that would otherwise caution artists against an uncritical adherence to convention. Perhaps McDermott's problem is not with artistic convention per se, but with the revisionary effort to unravel cultural paradigms, an effort that the 153 photographs collectively narrate. In this sense, McDermott's remarks—as well as the three quotations that precede this discussion—offer good examples of the kinds of textual problems that I will be working with in this book. Although they formulate very different views of the family plot, as should be clear from the marked disparity between McDermott's nostalgia for a lost aesthetics, Deleuze and Guattari's avant-garde Freudo-Marxian theory, and Mary Tyler Moore's sentimental sitcom speak, they share some common features. Most striking is a tendency to divest the so-called "nuclear triad" of its dominant status, a move that would appear to challenge Oedipal relations and paternal dominance, as well as the structural separation of public and private spheres, a historical dualism that has significantly shaped family and gender hierarchy in modern Western societies.

McDermott's review can also be read as an apologia, one that registers in her tone shift from culture critic to champion of the much-maligned "Ozzie and Harriet" image of affectionate, white, heterosexual, middle-class domesticity. But what is she apologizing for? One possibility is feminism, tellingly the only social movement to which family myth-bashing is historically linked in the review. In this regard, McDermott's review serves as a good illustration of how family plots perceived as humorless, cliché, or ideologically motivated are summarily attributed to feminism's critique of the family and to the women's movement's efforts to feminize the public sphere. This tendency to pinpoint feminism as the singular source of the family's semiotic martyrdom is, as I will be arguing, historically myopic and reductive.

Of course, anyone who has opened a newspaper, switched on the television, or listened to a political speech in recent decades will be more than familiar with the notion that the American family is in bad shape. This has become something of a standard refrain, echoing across partisan platforms to the right, to the left, and at almost all points in between. The current rhetoric of familial crisis and recuperation may also be said to operate at the level of popular narrative, or as a semiotic network that frames everything from legislative proceedings to commercial advertising to coverage of sports spectacles such as the 1994 Winter Olympics, which one radio commentator drolly dubbed "the Ozzie and Harriet Olympics."[6] More recently, Pope John Paul II proclaimed 1994 "The Year of the Family." In short, it seems that whenever there is an attempt to evoke a sense of national or spiritual unity, we find a family romance at stake.

Nor is this myth-(re)making apparatus exclusive to the realm of law, politics, religion, or the popular culture industry. In academic circles, in those disciplines that continue to constitute, however precariously, the field of the humanities, family has become the focus of much scholarly interest and classroom debate. As a literature instructor, I've been impressed by a discernible increase in literature anthologies and journals centered around family themes.[7] Even the discourse of contemporary literary theory is not immune to this incitement to organize and thematize the family: Mark Poster, for example, painstakingly directs his analyses of structuralism, French poststructuralism, the Frankfurt School, and the general "mode of information" back to the family, as if "theory" itself inevitably means somehow having to wrestle with a "waning institution" that has "abandoned the oedipal strategy."[8]

Indeed, what has the family romance come to mean within the context of our current cultural and critical pantheons, and *how* are these meanings coded and transmitted for a postfeminist, postmodernist age? The premise of this book holds that although the traditional concept of genre may be dying, family romance is very much alive in post–World War II American culture. It cuts across all genres and discourses, insinuating, criticizing, reinforcing, and reinventing itself in all forms of cultural production and consumption. The logic behind the ubiquitous and pervasive presence of what some many consider a minor subgenre is not, as it might seem, that the family is in trouble and culture has organized to save it. On the contrary, the family romance is everywhere because the family itself is nowhere, meaning that the family exists for us no longer as a symbol of cultural unity, but as an embodied expression of cultural redescription. And to this extent, *Family Plots* is necessarily concerned with the much-debated state of "crisis" in which our traditional concepts of culture, genre, and identity currently find themselves.

This "crisis" is often discussed in terms of a radical de-centering of master narratives that had once been able to provide literary scholars and historians with a map to our common cultural terrain. However, as many recent advocates of postmodernist, multicultural, and new historical studies demonstrate, "our" culture is neither whole nor common. The center does not hold, a presupposition that tests our previous notions of what it means to occupy the margins of mainstream culture. Rather than imagining this illusive core as a "Grand Hotel," or unified sphere of elites, some critics claim that we need to develop tools with which to apprehend processes of cultural production and reception as based in multiple centers of knowledge and discourse.[9] Moreover, we need to observe the often subtle ways in which these multiple centers compete with one another for public space and cut across one another in their struggles for legitimacy before an increasingly heterogeneous audience.

Admittedly, not many of us experience this heterogeneity on a day-to-day level, although we certainly may read about it in the onslaught of contemporary critical texts that seek to identify the diverse sources and agencies of fragmentation in cultural production. "Something is happening," intones Jane Flax in her reading of this state of affairs.[10] Notwithstanding the burden of proof, Flax echoes the concerns expressed by countless literary and cultural theorists who point to the current *Zeitgeist* of transformation, a period characterized by plurality, contingency, and a loss of faith in the unifying discourses and epistemologies that helped define the modern period. This recognition of radical change occurring around us may be the only cultural issue on which there is consensus; however, the widespread articulation of "crisis" is itself, I think, sufficient grounds to claim that a disintegrating sense of identity and narrativity is taking place alongside a disintegrating sense of family, and that there may be good reasons for closely examining the relationships among them.

The far-reaching immediacy of these interrelations can be discerned in passing references to the "postmodern turn." The epistemological and cultural shifts to which this "turn" broadly refers have become to a large degree axiomatic within the disciplines of cultural studies, feminist studies, and gender studies. A new generation of scholars in these fields—many of us weaned on poststructuralist philosophies of language and signification—continues to explore and develop methodological challenges to the stability of categories founded on oppositional hierarchies such as masculine/feminine, heterosexual/homosexual, high culture/pop culture, public sphere/private sphere. As we proceed, any boundaries that might have previously served to fix and divide these concepts prove to be fluid and dissolvable. Indeed, we might even say that the "postmodern turn" specifies, among other things, an incitement to boundary-bash, to break down cultural orthodoxies and start fresh with whatever bric-a-brac we may have picked up from the garage sale of modernity.

By invoking the postmodern, I realize that for some I may be opening a Pandora's box, the contents of which seem to obscure rather than clarify the object of inquiry. However, any topic as formally diverse and ideologically charged as family romance requires a critical vocabulary and an analytical practice welcoming of conflict and contradiction, and by most accounts this is precisely what a postmodern aesthetics provides. At its most ambitious level, postmodernism is a historical rethinking of the spatial politics of representation. According to Fredric Jameson, postmodernism's spatial vocabulary of textual production "involves the suppression of distance . . . and the relentless saturation of any remaining voids and empty places, to the point where the postmodern body . . . is now exposed to a perceptual barrage of immediacy from which all sheltering layers and intervening mediations have been removed."[11] In other words, postmodernism insists that we place scare quotes around any attempt to distinguish between public and private space, community and individual consciousness. Identity itself can no longer be differentiated from the relentless flow of contradictory images, messages, and practices that describe the semiotic network we plug into every time we pick up a telephone, sit down at a computer, or obtain cash from an ATM.

Postmodernism's emphasis on a Foucaultian micropolitics, or a politics of location, implicitly denies access to a unified global reality and undermines all imagined utopias of the Enlightenment tradition. The collapse of macropolitical structures poses serious challenges to the kind of Marxian revitalization that Jameson's writings assert. In Jameson's view, such skepticism with regard to all forms of foundational logic constitutes a stage in the development of late capitalism, a logic that registers in the postmodern work of art through the thematics of paranoia and conspiracy.[12] Consequently, the representation of any figuration of totality—socialism, feminism, familialism—becomes within a postmodern aesthetic an exercise in depthless, self-reflexive irony.[13]

Linda Hutcheon's more optimistic read on this aesthetic situation posits the postmodern text as "complicitous critique," a text that both engages and resists possibilities for social change.[14] Adapting Roland Barthes's notion of the "doxa" as the public voice of consensus, Hutcheon argues that in its unrelentingly "parodic self-reflexivity" postmodern art works to " 'de-doxify' our cultural representations and their undeniable political import."[15] Hutcheon, like Michel de Certeau, appears to hold an affirmative view of subversion as "always constrained by a system . . . that allows subversion only along the 'fault lines' (providing 'lines of escape') of the system."[16] However, Hutcheon does not grant this subversive potential to mass-culture artifacts, an oversight that tends to privilege the cultural avant-garde and metafictional experimentation to the exclusion of romance images that inform daily life. However, if we were to appropriate this perspective for popular romance fiction, we might say that to construct family romance is to effectively de-doxify the master narrative of the familial and its substantiating claim to a universal representation of origin.[17] The post-family romance would thus assume the potential to demonstrate that each of us has origins in multiple and contradictory places and situations. This does not mean that the post-family romance precludes the imaginative quest for origin, but rather suggests that we need to retool the concept of origin in accordance with new commitments to locality, plurality, and mobility.

A considerable amount of effort has gone into defining the "postmodern family" not simply as a new-styled institution but as a symbolic system whose ability to confer stable identity, regulate gender production, and police the boundaries of the public and private is—and has probably always been—based in social and cultural contingencies.[18] Postmodern redefinitions of social space, such as Jameson's, have thus fueled revisionist analyses of modern social history that would appear to allow for a clearer understanding of the situational relations among boundariless subjects, delimited social spaces, and kinds of discursive practice.

In recent discussion of the history, constitution, and internal workings of these relations within the bourgeois public sphere, the writings of Jürgen Habermas serve as a central point of reference.[19] *The Structural Transformation of the Public Sphere* is a brilliant and controversial text, one that has sparked debate among Marxists, cultural theorists, and feminists for its rational-critical approach toward recovering the emancipatory potential of the public arena.[20] Habermas analyzes this arena in terms of the two elements that he feels constitute it: discursive forms and modes of popular participation. Critics, however, find his approach problematic in terms of the qualitative restrictions placed on discourse, restrictions that would, once again, devalue if not discount forms and practices of everyday life. In this, Habermas reveals what some critics read as an uncritical allegiance with the Frankfurt School's critique of mass culture. This poses a problem, for if we are to conceive of mass culture negatively, the question is begged: How might society simultaneously achieve both quality of cultural production and quantity of popular participation, especially when the latter would seem to ensure debate over the very definition of "quality"? While Habermas vociferously encourages public debate on such questions, some consider his vision of debate founded on rational discourse—discourse based in communication rather than domination—less liberating and less inclusive than might be assumed. Who decides what counts as rational discourse or as meaningful participation in public debate?

In response, critics have pointed out the gender blindness that afflicts Habermas's discussion of discourse and participation in public debate.[21] This blindness extends to his discussion of the private sphere. While Habermas—and political theory in general—has much to say about forms of domination in the public sphere, forms of domination in the private sphere remain for the most part invisible. Questions of consensus and justice are considered only outside the realm of the familial.[22] This is not to say, however, that the familial doesn't matter for Habermas. The constitution of the familial as the "private" sphere of intimacy and humane subject formation *is* significant, and it develops in connection with an affirmation of consumerism as well as patriarchal dominance in the public sphere. In the literary world, this interiorization of the family becomes woven into novels that "helped to circulate a vision of intimate sentimentality, communicating to the members of the literate public sphere just how they should understand the heart of private life."[23]

The grounding of the familial or woman's sphere and the appearance of sentimental fiction, a discourse shaped largely by the emergence of popular women writers, appear to contribute mutually to the downfall of Habermas's rational public sphere. Nevertheless, gender difference remains untheorized, marginally linked to the domestic and to a type of commodity fiction we might call family romance. But how is the imperative of dialogue and difference, which Habermas aims to resurrect in the public sphere, inscribed within the private? What are the kinds of discourses that have shaped the transformation of the private sphere, the central setting for the traditional family romance? And how does a postmodern, discourse-sensitive understanding of fragmenting social spaces become manifest in popular representations of the family and the familial?

The post-family romance emerges in American culture as early as the mid-1950s when postwar promises of domestic unity began to degenerate with the emergence of an African-American civil rights movement, demographic changes in the American workplace, and the increasing articulation of American middle-class women's discontent with the intensified structuring of their domestic roles. Although this discontent was not brought to widespread national attention until the 1963 publication of *The Feminine Mystique*, Betty Friedan was preceded, as historians of women's culture have shown, by numerous prefeminist expressions of resentment and confusion that were filtered through the popular women's magazines of the mid-1950s. Especially since World War II, observers note, there has been an intensification of the public's colonization of the private, a colonization reinforced by increased technology, advertising, and mass consumerism. However, as Michèle Barrett and Mary McIntosh point out, "just as the family has been socially constructed, so society has been familialised. Indeed, it can be argued that in contemporary capitalist society one dominant set of social meanings is precisely an ideology of the familial."[24]

On this basis, it might seem possible to conclude that the study of post-family romance is the study of the impact of second-wave feminism's leading banner, "the personal is the political." However, the terms of this banner were organized around spatial problematics inherited from nineteenth-century suffragists, some of whom appropriated the late Victorian concept of the "angel in the house" to assure their detractors that women's voting rights would bring the virtues of domesticity outward into the public sphere, to the moral benefit of all. In the mid-1960s, this challenge to a patriarchal separation of spheres found expression once again, not in the promise of moral betterment, but in the deconstructive logic of a motto suggesting that the private sphere was not—and had never been—a unified sphere of consensus, but a field of opposition where psyche and history, Oedipus and ideology, crisscrossed, contested, and mutually constructed one another.

The evolution of such transpositional logic has led to a feminist reconsideration of the subject and her/his historical inscription across spheres reified as complements to the essential nature of men and women. The breakdown of structural metaphors and cognitive boundaries more appropriate to modernist self-definition than to postmodern self-decenteredness is prefigured in contemporary feminism's self-acknowledged overinvestment in the historical stability of the separation of public and private spheres. Feminist studies and gender studies (the latter suggestive of a more rigorous dissolution of identity categories to include masculine, gay, lesbian, bisexual, transgender/sex subject positions) have become particularly alert to this history and its implications for the spatial organization of social relations, institutions, and labor.

But how personal is the political? Where and how do women experience the overlaps and stress points of these formations? Such questions have become the source of serious debate among Western feminist critics, many of whom have sought to identify a universal origin of women's social and economic oppression. By seeming to satisfy feminism's wish to unify its own purposes, the doctrine of separate spheres has fueled the construction of feminism's own totalizing narrative, the result of which has been the erasure of differences among and within women. However, as Linda J. Nicholson points out, there exists within contemporary feminism an increasing recognition "that the divisions between . . . spheres are not as rigid as we are led to believe and that conceiving them in such a manner obscures the realities of women's lives."[25]

Nicholson explains that feminism inherited the terms of this division from eighteenth- and nineteenth-century discourses such as psycho-analysis, liberalism, and Marxism. As industrialization and newly emerg-ing social institutions engendered a growing separation of the family, the state, and the economy, these social theories represented attempts to produce new political alignments of the private and the public. How-ever, these theories also tended to universalize their claims on history, suggesting that all cultures organize themselves according to the same categories and principles that Western culture has fashioned for itself. As Nicholson shows, early feminist thinkers uncritically assumed these categories that severely limit historical analysis by reifying structural dualisms such as public/private and by privileging the notion of unified origin.

Thus, from the nineteenth-century establishment of feminism as a sig-nificant public discourse, feminism has tended to construct the private sphere as an arena of female consensus in opposition to an increasingly multiple and contradictory public sphere. And while many feminists still use this logic for historical analysis, more and more are abandoning these terms along with the concept of origin and a discrete category of "woman." To this extent, earlier feminist analyses that equate the history of the private sphere with the history of "women's" community cry out for reexamination.[26] For even when the private sphere is apprehended as a source of female empowerment, the implicit assumption seems to be that private and public spaces exist as unified and discrete.[27] To counter this assumption, feminism has become more insistent on understanding the contingent character of public-private separations.[28] By recognizing the family's complex interaction with the rest of society, feminists "have begun to develop the means for becoming self-conscious about the very historical forces which have brought modern feminism into being."[29] For this reason, Nicholson argues, contemporary feminism offers the best position from which to theorize the relations of private and public as historically contingent.

Contemporary feminism has indeed become far more self-conscious about the need to acknowledge historical contingency as a feature of all narrative, including its own. However, what Nicholson overlooks in her otherwise comprehensive analysis is the extent to which this contingency is built into the very discourses that feminism has defined itself in oppo-sition to, discourses that intersect with and help shape the post-family romance. In other words, the instability of public and private separations is no more the unique product of a unified feminist perspective than essentialism is the unique product of a unified psychoanalytic, liberal, or Marxian perspective. Certainly, twentieth-century feminism has played a significant role (albeit contradictory and by no means exclusive) in redescribing the gender-specific topography of the family romance. The post–World War II redescription of the family (as a usable symbol of cultural consensus) and family romance (as a usable narrative blueprint) interacts productively yet inconsistently with feminism's development of a historically situated analysis of the private sphere and the meanings produced through its equation with the female subject. But to what extent can feminism be held mainly accountable for the complex "identity crisis" that family romance has been undergoing during the last half century? Not decidedly, it seems, for to trace the trajectory of family romance across so complex a sociohistorical landscape is to acknowledge, as Mikhail Bakhtin does, a fundamental polyphony or plurality of differentiated voices within the space of the novel.

Of course, interpretation also depends on our ability to grasp relations external to these intertextual negotiations, such as the specific interests and purposes according to which an author might consciously structure the family romance, or the specific needs and desires that are fulfilled for the reader who reads or critiques the family romance. Returning to Alice McDermott's review for a moment, the conflation of a unitary feminism and a unitary antifamily romance makes sense when understood as a reaffirmation of modernity's overinvestment in the gender specificity of separate spheres. However, while this study acknowledges the thoughtful agency of producers and consumers, its primary concern is to examine how texts position themselves in the midst of widespread cultural realignment. Family romances produced in these contexts need to be read as fields of competition or as stages on which feminism may be said to compete for the spotlight along with numerous other performers or kinds of discourse. The interactions between and among these discourses, many of them culturally and politically opposed, construct the family plot. Yet at the same time these discourses plot against one another, each wanting to claim the position of narrative authority vacated in the wake of wide-ranging cultural realignments.

David Cooper, author of the controversial book *The Death of the Family* (1970), wrote, "Families are about the inner and the outer." [30] Twenty-five years later, this statement seems naively formalistic, especially insofar as its logic relies on a binary system of meaning that has fallen from grace. However, one way of understanding Cooper's statement in terms of more recent reconfigurations of the family plot is that it locates the family within a signifying apparatus. Here, the family functions as a mediating device, a border patrolling agent in the socially constructed spaces that serve to differentiate and build relations between inner and outer, the feminine and the masculine, as well as successive generations.

These spaces occupied by the family do not denote unalterable structural relations, but rather they are themselves constructed by the various discourses and material practices that attempt to ground subjectivity within the familial. However, as Teresa de Lauretis has argued apropos of gender, the family "is not only the effect of representation but also its excess, what remains outside discourse as a potential trauma which can rupture or destabilize, if not contained, any representation."[31] Family romance has traditionally served to ensure the containment of such excesses as are produced by efforts to represent identity. By contrast, in *Family Plots* I will explore more recent "technologies" of the romance in order to understand the various ways in which family-situated subjectivity is simultaneously constructed and deconstructed. Whereas family romances of the modern era were conditioned by pressures to contain Oedipal imperatives, in the postmodern era we find romances that openly debate the family's status as the psychosocial container of our most fundamental identifications and desires. Instead of family romances that defer to the formal prerequisites of genre, we find romances less determined by specific formal patterns than by a preoccupation with the multifacetedness of representational systems themselves. And indeed, this multifacetedness often leads characters along unpredictable paths toward a usable articulation of "self."

Of course, one of the problems with the paradigm I'm proposing is that it appears to reduce the family to a mere effect of discourse. At the risk of such a reduction, I want to stress that the kinds of discursive and semiotic contexts I'm looking at are marks of broader historical and cultural changes. For example, the year 1975 saw, in addition to the publication of Anne Tyler's *Searching for Caleb* (see Chapter 5), the first organized socialist-Marxist-feminist conference in Yellow Springs, Ohio, which opened large-scale acknowledgment of the political, racial, class, and sexual differences among feminists *and* opened debate over the efficacy of a movement previously dominated by a middle-class ideology of individualism. Rochelle Gatlin notes that this increasing recognition of differences within feminism occurred in connection with "a growing theoretical sophistication."[32] This "sophistication" was becoming evident in literature departments during the latter half of the 1970s, as the introduction of French feminism sparked debate within academia in the United States, creating a newly perceived sense of division between critics who worked within the paradigm Toril Moi terms "Images of Women" criticism and those whose work began to take up questions of linguistics, semiotics, and psychoanalysis.[33]

The ascendancy of theory was indicated as well by the 1975 publication of Josephine Donovan's *Feminist Literary Criticism: Explorations in Theory*, the first volume in feminist literary history to explore from a number of perspectives feminism's new theoretical engagements.[34] Jane Gallop suggests that the text was probably more successful in its declared intention to establish "a point of departure for further development," than it was in addressing the kinds of differences that more recent feminist critics invoke in the face of totalizing or essentializing inclinations.[35] However, Jane Rule's 1975 publication of *Lesbian Images*[36] and an unprecedented outpouring of fiction during the late seventies by African-American women inspired by the civil rights movement indicated an awareness of the contradictions posed by the institutional welcome of women's studies to the university curriculum. At the same time, in the arena of television culture, 1975 saw the premiere of the popular situation comedy *One Day at a Time*, a program about a single, working-class mother, Ann Romano (played by Bonnie Franklin), whose feminist consciousness is nurtured less by theory and abstraction than by material need and "hands-on" experiences with family life and the business world. In short, it is clear by the mid-1970s that the feminist movement can be conceptualized no longer as the field of consensus, but as the foregrounding of negotiations of differences. This social moment registered in women's fiction and literary criticism, both "high" culture and mass culture. In academia, it was discernible not only in the shift from feminist "criticism" to feminist "theory," but in the wider epistemological shift from structuralism to "systems theory" and other poststructuralist paradigms that offered rhetorically impelled strategies of aesthetic resistance to laws of genre and the hegemony of subjectivity.

Throughout these changes and developments, the continued interest in deconstructing and reconstructing family romance as part of our American cultural mythology shows that the symbolic currency of the family plot retains its value even as it continues to undergo reevaluation. American historians, social critics, and literary theorists have recently begun asking if American culture perhaps holds a unique relation to the concept of origin. According to historian Edward Shorter, origins would appear to be less of an issue for American families than European families, who, he claims, experienced far more dramatically the processes of modernization which threatened the European family system.[37] By contrast, the American family was probably "born modern," a conclusion Shorter defends with the claim that Americans lack "time perspective" or strong ties to past generations. In addition, he claims that the historical tendency on the part of American families has always been toward isolation and withdrawal from whatever community life surrounds them.[38] While these hypotheses may help account for the historical myopia that Jameson laments (perhaps American families were not "born modern," but postmodern), Shorter fails to take into account factors such as cultural, racial, and religious differences that have historically distinguished American family life from other national cultures. The oversight also cannot account for the American novel in which we find patterns of familial imagery far more culturally diverse and concerned with issues of racial difference than the traditional European bourgeois novel concerned with the class relations and the dynamics of social obligation and betrayal.[39]

For example, William Faulkner's gothic family romances install racial difference as a trope of familial cruelty and instability, the hidden key to unlocking abject, contradictory identity. In fact, it could be said that the revelation of miscegenation constitutes the structural aporia of the Faulkner canon, or the unraveling of relations between individual and social consciousness. While racial impurity suggests an excess of what the family romance cannot contain, there is an attempt to suppress such contradictions within the romance of southern cultural history *and* the history of romance. In *As I Lay Dying*, this excess is prefigured in the decomposing body of the mother, Addie Bundren, the primary catalyst for each family member's revelation of loss and decenteredness. The construction of Addie's coffin, which she oversees at the outset of the novel, and the family's hapless journey to Addie's family burial ground suggest futile efforts to contain and uphold the formal integrity of identity. Ultimately, these efforts succeed no more than efforts to contain the stench of Addie's rotting corpse, a rather unpleasant reminder to all who come into contact with the coffin of the dissolution of familial embodiment, a dissolution underscored by the absence of any controlling narrative point of view. That Addie speaks to us halfway through the novel, after the literal event of her death, suggests that she may be only figuratively dead.[40] By comparison, one is reminded of Donald Barthelme's *The Dead Father*, who remains throughout the narrative, "dead but still with us, still with us but dead."[41] Similarly, Addie seems to exist in the metafictional margins between presence and absence, an indication that identity has become disembodied simultaneously from language *and* from Oedipus, itself a rhetorical effect. However, in *As I Lay Dying* the traumatic disengagement of language and subjectivity emanates specifically from the mother whose ascertainable position within the Freudian family romance poses a potential threat to paternity and the patriarchal establishment. And indeed, Addie holds the secret of her son Jewel's illegitimacy, the result of her infidelity to Anse. That she is permitted to speak this knowledge only after her death reveals, however, the preeminence of the paternal function even in the face of its illusory status. Paternity remains that which consolidates body and voice, being and its

signification, as is ultimately proven in the revelation that Anse's motivation for making the journey is neither loyalty nor grief, but a new set
of false teeth that await him in Jefferson. Anse's acquisition of corporeal
"wholeness" and his immediate remarriage to the "new" Mrs. Bundren
comically suggest that while destabilization and decomposition permeate the family plot, paternity retains a privileged, albeit precarious,
relation to permanence.

In this century, the reification of an American literary tradition itself
occurred largely in accord with a critical tendency—most impressively
demonstrated by Eric J. Sundquist's *Home as Found*, Richard Chase's *The
American Novel and Its Tradition*, and Leslie Fiedler's *Love and Death in the
American Novel*—to concentrate on the male American writer's ambiguous yet powerfully romantic attachments to Oedipal myths of origin.
Studies of Nathaniel Hawthorne's fascination with dominating father figures, Ernest Hemingway's fascination with dominating mother figures,
and Herman Melville's fascination with philosophies of domination all
offer cases in point. However, I would argue that family romances written in this century, and particularly those written after World War II,
betray an increasing sense of skepticism and resentment toward the
privileging of father-son relations. I have already mentioned Barthelme's
The Dead Father, a metafictional family romance that is not concerned
with the death of fathers per se, but with the exhaustion of our belief
in them as signifiers. What Barthelme's novel suggests, to paraphrase
Simone de Beauvoir, is that fathers are not born; they are made. In
other words, fatherhood is not a biological function but a sociosymbolic
currency, and perhaps we have reached a point in our culture at which
we no longer need to use it. The father function, or the stabilization
of forms of origin and authority, may no longer be viable. And to the
extent that literature has rehearsed these forms, the father narrative
too may have passed its prime and should be retired.[42] This is what the
D.F. (Barthelme's shorthand) realizes himself, at last: that his power
and influence have been limited all along by the signifying potential of
a father romance inherited from all past father romances. The novel
thus addresses a patriarchal crisis, where in a world of contingencies
our only option is to let go of the romances of the past and attempt to
redescribe them, author our own romance. But at the same time, we all
remain limited by history, a history we cannot entirely disavow even as
it forces on us a legacy irrelevant to the world as it currently exists.[43]
While it is tempting to claim that Barthelme's *The Dead Father* attempts to
deconstruct patriarchy, Teresa Ebert points out that the main arena of
Barthelme's contestation with patriarchy is confined to the son's struggle
with the father over the nature of the patriarchal legacy and his place
in it. Barthelme's politics in the novel, according to Ebert, repeatedly

diffuse the possibility of disrupting the basic economy of difference in which men hold power and wield it over women by sexualizing them and marginalizing them.[44] Thus, it would seem that post-familialism of romances like Barthelme's exists in their engagement of a gendered politics of the signifier.

Notwithstanding Barthelme's elite positioning within the emergent canons of postmodern high culture, much of the analysis derived from readings of *The Dead Father* pertains to John Cheever's immensely popular novel *The Wapshot Chronicle*. Here, Cheever presents a sort of apology for Hawthorne, or for the Puritan tradition to which he is reluctantly heir apparent. The novel is a post-family romance specifically posted between the conflictual forces of filial empathy and homoerotic desire, origin and simulacra, transcendentalism and the corporate ethos, New England pastoralism and the new prefab suburbs of the postwar housing development boom. The novel makes us aware of not so much the historical processes by which these dualisms are either strengthened or broken down, but the narrative ceremonies—represented by Leander's journal, an odd incorporation of mundane facts, sentimental flourishes, filial advice, historical fragments, and mythopoetical references—by which we have traditionally invoked the illusion of structure, order, authority. These ceremonies are presumably for the son's moral and cultural benefit, textual occasions that offer small compensation for the fragmentation, feminization, and phallic inadequacy that have shaken the foundations of the Oedipal family.

Modernity's unified organization according to the separation of private and public, female and male, identity and desire, imaginary and symbolic, has traditionally informed representations of family's such as Cheever's Wapshots. However, the changing perceptions of gender and woman's public role, in addition to ongoing explorations into the complexities of sign (re)production and reception, have challenged the value of unity as a privileged logic. Consequently, American culture finds itself at the crest of a paradigm shift requiring no less than a complete reevaluation of the spatial configurations and metaphors with which it has organized narrative accounts of its history and logic. Precursory inscriptions of this complexity with regard to the familial can be discerned in a 1906 literary "experiment," *The Whole Family*.[45] The project was conceived by William Dean Howells, the champion of literary realism at the time, whose vision was to gather eleven other important American authors to collaborate on a novel realistically depicting the life of an average middle-class American family. Before appearing as a novel, the chapters were to be published as a series in *Harper's Bazaar*. Howells and *Harper's Bazaar*'s editor, Elizabeth Jordan, solicited the participation of some of the most popular magazine and fiction writers of the time, among these

Elizabeth Stuart Phelps, Mary E. Wilkins Freeman, Henry James, Alice Brown, Henry Van Dyke, Edith Wyatt, and John Kendrick Bangs. Several writers, including Mark Twain, Hamlin Garland, and Kate Douglas Wiggin (who originally agreed to contribute but later withdrew), declined participation. Those writers who did enlist were each assigned a chapter centering on one of the characters: the Grandmother, the Father, the Mother, the Son, the Daughter-in-law, the Daughter, the Son-in-law, the Little Girl, the Small Boy, the Maiden Aunt, the Young Girl, and the Female Friend of the Family.

The Whole Family's emphasis on female characters and female writers was clearly a reflection of *Bazaar*'s female readership.[46] Yet even with careful attention to audience, enthusiastic editorial sponsorship, and an impressive collection of much-admired writers, the project amounted to a dismal failure. At least, it was a failure for Howells, whose vision of the "whole" family was shattered. According to Alfred Bendixen, whose well-researched introduction to the 1986 text provides historical backdrop, the problem developed out of artistic rivalries that existed among the contributors, particularly between Howells and Freeman. Howells, who wrote the chapter on the Father, saw the project as an opportunity to affirm the principles of literary mimesis through the realistic representation of character. Freeman, who was assigned the chapter on the Maiden Aunt, disagreed with Howell's imposition of literary and social values; she portrayed the Maiden Aunt as vivacious, sharp-tongued, and comical, a character completely out of sync with the genteel, sentimental rhetoric that Howells had hoped to encourage. He was, in short, outraged by Freeman's chapter, in which the Old-Maid Aunt compares the mechanical gestures of a woman darning socks to a cow chewing its cud. Furthermore, she complains about the moral stodginess of her family, their stagnant perception of unmarried women, which she is nevertheless pressured to conform to: "Not a day, not an hour, not a minute, when I am with other people, passes that I do not see myself in their estimation playing that role as plainly as if I saw myself in a looking glass."[47] Other contributors to the project reacted strongly, either favorably or disfavorably, to Freeman's renegade artistry, some taking it as their own license to stray from Howells's prescriptive design and deliver their own interpretations of family tensions and conflicts. In the end, the series was completed and its publication in book form was met with "polite reviews," subsequent to which *The Whole Family* sank out of the literary arena until its reissue in 1986.[48]

What conclusions might we draw from this history, and what does it suggest about the twentieth-century dissolution of the family plot? Apart from the Bloomian analysis of Oedipal artistic rivalries the account cries out for, what seems important here is the discursive battle over who controls the discursive spaces in which the family plot appears. Bendixen's account is telling insofar as it suggests a contest of incompatible understandings of where and how the boundaries of private and public cultural relations should be drawn. In this instance, the private sphere of the family becomes opened to public debate within a magazine designated as woman's public discursive territory. Howells's inability to ultimately impose the values of a "dominant" literary culture demonstrates how fragmented that culture had already become at the turn of the century, and it also shows how various fragments were becoming aligned with gender-specific interests and interpretations.

This gender-culture realignment is reiterated in terms of cultural aesthetics by Andreas Huyssen's claim that woman has historically represented high art's "other." She remains, in this sense, the discursive mark of the low, of a popular aesthetic in contradistinction to which high art defines itself through exclusion.[49] Indeed, modernism has been generally characterized by its self-distancing from and strong distaste for the mutually contaminating forces of the popular and the feminine. In the United States women's association with mass-produced formula fiction has remained historically in flux, albeit pervasive and suspect, from Hawthorne's condemnation of the "damned, scribbling mob" of nineteenth-century popular women novelists, to charges of geriatric mediocrity against Angela Lansbury's television depiction of a sleuthing mystery writer in *Murder, She Wrote*, to moralistic attacks against the postfeminist pop music icon and multimillion-dollar image producer Madonna.[50] Throughout this evolution, family romance has represented another sort of "low" cultural engagement for women writers, an engagement that nevertheless affirms patriarchy's containment of women's imaginative capacities within the private sphere.[51]

However, just as gender studies have reevaluated woman's relationship to language and social space, so too have they begun a reevaluation of woman's relationship to mass culture: Some recent theorists, taking issue with the Frankfurt School's equation of mass culture with fascism and user passivity, are attending more thoughtfully to the user, to the agency of fans and audiences who, many conclude, *do* have some say.[52] Janice Radway's research on the dialectical relationship of female readers to romance fiction has been instructive in this sense, laying the basis for understanding that romance and social change are not necessarily exclusive of one another.[53] The Frankfurt position holds that by reifying "human process," or in this case the processes of familial interaction, mass culture images of family life dominate and contain readers, allowing them no path of resistance to the dominant ideology that governs the production of mass-culture images. Radway's claim is that the romance form, while commonly acknowledged as eliciting readers' complicity with the status quo, also allows for resistance and subversion, if only in the act of reading itself. Thus, there may be, in the representation of family and in the organizing logic of family romance, niches of feminist recuperation and resistance.

Radway successfully questions the assumption that mass culture allows only for passive consumerism in its readership. It is difficult to disagree with her insistence that to see readers as totally helpless and passive and to see texts as totally dominating is to "petrify the human act of signification."[54] People are not total slaves to the text, helpless to do anything but consume their meanings, buy into their political agendas. However, while "the ideological power of contemporary cultural forms is enormous, indeed sometimes even frightening . . . interstices still exist within the social fabric where opposition is carried on by people who are not satisfied by their place within it or by the restricted material and emotional rewards that accompany it."[55] The women Radway interviews say they are not trying to escape from their husbands and children by reading romances. Rather, they read because it frees them from "the psychologically demanding and emotionally draining task of attending to the physical and affective needs of their families, a task that is solely and peculiarly theirs." Ironically, we may consider that reading novels about the family does not so much suggest an overt attraction to family or an over-involvement with family as much as a desire to "suspend temporarily those familial relationships."[56]

To a surprising degree, Radway's research serves as a kind of cultural wake-up call, a reminder that readers' relation to mass-culture forms and modes of production has become in many respects more conflictual than at any previous time in American cultural history. As feminist discourse has helped establish the politicization of the private sphere, the establishment of gender-specific reception theories within cultural studies has taken on significance for readers who feel themselves drawn to spaces where fantasy and reality overlap, or where their private yearnings and their public obligations as parents, children, and lovers merge and redefine one another. In the material and situational act of reading the romance, fantasy begins to transgress its domestic boundaries to establish the generic principle that has been identified as characteristic of both romance *and* postmodernism, historical excess.[57] To this extent, gender studies and postmodernism would seem to have similar objectives in mind, objectives that become powerfully manifest in what I have provisionally termed post-family romance.

From photography to theory, from theory to poetry, from high culture to mass culture, the family romance is undergoing a complex recodification by contemporary novelists, critics, filmmakers, and literary/culture critics. Some of these recodings challenge the constitution of a unified domestic sphere along with the social relations that domestic spaces are traditionally believed to nurture.[58] Some seek to specify and reveal the capitalist instrumentalization of the family romance.[59] Some work to resurrect the Freudian schema.[60] Others celebrate its passing.[61] However, crucially at stake in these various remappings is our waning faith in the concept of unified narrative itself. What is brought to light in post-family romances, however nervously, is that the plot for origin need not inevitably lead us to the discovery or invention of a paternity, the privileged trope of Freud's family romance. Nor does it necessarily lead to the reclamation of an alternative romance centered on a unified myth of maternity. Rather, we may surmise from post-family romance that origins, once decentered or de-Oedipalized, are never neutral, never innocent, but always contextual and relentlessly demanding. They demand that we—as readers and participants in discourse—make choices and constantly reevaluate those choices.

However, the heterogeneity of the domestic sphere does not mean that all discourses informing it have become, in the final analysis, equal partners. It is not my intention to argue that family romance has become the genre to support pluralist familial utopias. As the history of the genre reveals, the splitting or fragmentation of the family sphere has typically been displaced onto a particular familial figure who functions strategically to contain or absolve the threat of cultural dissolution. Since World War II, the concern that mothers, or female characters in general, are overdetermined in this capacity has led to a degree of doubt among feminist critics about the family romance's potential to affirmatively subvert patriarchal literary institutions. Although these doubts are not unfounded, they mainly seem to flow in two questionable currents. The first is a tendency to reject family romance on account of its assumed collusion with biological essentialism, a trait attributed to Freud's vision of the romance. The second belies an adherence to the Frankfurt School critique of mass culture, which, as I've discussed in this chapter, summarily links family romance with a popular aesthetic thought brutally crass, purely commercial, and faithlessly ideological. According to these approaches, family romance can only be read as an exercise in cultural indoctrination and passivity. In Chapter 2, I address the first concern, and the ambivalence produced by "essentialist" readings of Freud, by identifying within Freud's original essay ("Family Romances," 1908) the traces of a post-family romance already at odds with the romance. Indeed, the result of Freud's text has generally been defined as the containment of femininity's threat to masculine authority—a containment central to Freud's theory of male and female subject formation within the bourgeois Oedipal triad. However, I think that "Family Romances" actually demonstrates a greater willingness to admit—in many cases, an outright insistence on admitting—trouble in highly complex ways.

In Chapter 3, I take up television family sitcoms as the popular form perhaps most troubled by the family's allegorical connection to our national capacity to secure cultural consensus. Popular television shows from the late 1950s and early 1960s like *The Donna Reed Show* and *Bewitched* locate the forces of familial "difference" at the secret core of the domestic sphere, forces that would—and often do—upset the status quo even while the family plot is contained within the *mise-en-scène* of television's own uncertainties about its cultural legitimacy. In Chapters 4, 5, 6, 7, 8, and 9, I will consider works of contemporary fiction that retain the family romance as part of their discursive structuring for the purposes of critique, reclamation, and reevaluation. Contemporary film and home video are the subjects of Chapters 10 and 11, the former concerning Mike Figgis's film, *Internal Affairs*, a police drama that provides an occasion to discuss the inscription of lesbian subjectivity within the familial *mise-en-scène*. Next, I will examine the interrelation of family romance, American cyborg mythology, and GOP propaganda as developed in the home video version of the film *Terminator 2: Judgment Day*. My objective in all of these readings is to show how attempts to admit the possibility of decentered, perverse, or illegible identities (within the conventional romance) wind up at cross purposes, thus extending but maintaining the limits of family representations.

Of course, I wouldn't have undertaken this project at all if I didn't believe that romance is very much alive, still able to negotiate the turbulent relations among individual and social "realities." Furthermore, I agree with Stephen Heath that the history of the novel *is* the history of family romance, a history specifically concerned with both the representation and performance of "a permanent crisis of identity that must be permanently resolved by remembering the history of the individual-subject."[62] But it is yet to be seen to what extent this "crisis" remains resolvable. How, for example, has family romance been impacted by our intensified awareness of gender as performance, or as a system of "roles" that can be adjusted, exchanged, or multiply assumed?[63] How has the media foregrounding of issues of race, class, gender, and sexual orientation impacted on the collective fantasy of familial consensus? How has the dissolution of the private sphere and its increasing dissociation from essential female nature problematized the containment of desire and identification within the boundaries of the familial? And how are we to understand the ramifications of postmodern or poststructuralist critical paradigms in relation to popular culture's attempts to ground human experience in a unifying symbology? If there are answers to these questions, they will certainly vary; however, the new post-family romances being disseminated through fiction, film, television, and home video all offer thoughtful and complicated responses to an emergent aesthetics of self-formation, an aesthetics in which subjects are continually displaced by the heterogeneity of a world that one need not leave home to discover.

Chapter 2
Housebreaking Freud

If there is no longer a Father, why tell stories?[1]
—Roland Barthes

In "Family Romances" (1908), Sigmund Freud describes a "peculiarly marked imaginative activity," a fantasy that structurally unifies normative subjectivity and social consensus, while providing a bridge between the terrain of the bourgeois private sphere and the industrialized public sphere.[2] "Family Romances" thus proceeds to describe the culmination of the Oedipal drama, the "latter stage in the development of the neurotic's estrangement from his parents" through which the son struggles to accept the social privilege that is his birthright—paternal authority, or classic phallic masculinity. However, in its service as "the fulfillment of wishes and as a correction of actual life," Freud's family romance does more than consolidate the power of the patriarch (238). Indeed, if anything it stresses the extent to which fantasy may be more "real" than reality in the formation of social privileges and sexual hegemony. By elaborating the stages of familial disentanglement, Freud laid the groundwork for theorizing that the family, like the romance that constitutes it, is poesy—which is to say that it is constructed through a collaboration of ego and history and made accessible to consciousness through the interpretive process.

For Freud, the family was the privileged site of these constructions. Indeed, as Stephen Heath has suggested, it was Freud's essential vision of psychoanalysis to articulate a critical apparatus for an understanding of the family as the cultural catalyst for the relations of private fantasy and public belief. These relations remain for Freud generally formative of "subject coherence," and so to the extent that notions such as "origin" and "identity" have remained more or less unproblematized, family romance has remained the principle paradigm of all narrative activity concerning "the provision and maintenance of fictions of the individual."[3] "Doesn't every narrative lead back to Oedipus?" Barthes meditates. "Isn't storytelling always a way of searching for one's origin, speaking one's conflicts with the Law, entering into the dialectic of tenderness and hatred?"[4]

As Barthes indicates, Freud's family romance sustains one of the central assumptions of modern social theory and metaphysical thought, the belief that "origin—having and knowing the relation to the transcendent beginning—conveys essence, presence, and authority."[5] For Freud, as for the majority of European intellectuals at the turn of the century, these attributes were directly commensurate with the father, the locus of origin. However, Freud's privileging of origin suggests a more significant historical link between paternal function and the collective fantasies that confer value on socially constructed "reality," or what Kaja Silverman terms "the dominant fiction."[6] In "Family Romances," origin does not denote a reality principle so much as a relation to specific narrative occasions. From this perspective, what Freud invites us to consider are the implicit representational strategies by which the family, as private experience, comes into alignment with romance, or historical fantasy. The family romance is thus defined as the interpolation of the individual *in* patriarchal history and patriarchy *in* individual history.

Furthermore, what is problematized in this approach is Freud's theoretical and narrative reliance on dualistic forms of logic that reify, even as they seek to unify, the separate meanings associated with "wishes" as opposed to "real life," individual as opposed to social beliefs, paternal as opposed to maternal functions. One of the central assumptions on which this chapter rests is that the governing opposition underwriting Freud's family romance and its gendered logic is the bourgeois doctrine of separate spheres. This doctrine constitutes a set of organizing assumptions virtually inseparable from the development of social theory and fictional narrative in modern Western culture. And, as I will be arguing throughout these pages, it has been by challenging the gendered reification of the private sphere, or the House That Freud Built, that feminism and gender theory have developed their most forceful reformulations of the family romance.

In part these reformulations have rewritten Barthes's question, which opens this chapter, to read, "If there is no longer a unified story, why speak of fathers?" To be sure, recent feminist critiques of the Freudian romance have tended to underscore the extent to which origins do not precede narrative, but rather proceed from narrative. Much of this criticism is based on the dubious assumption that Freud privileged inside over outside, or instinctual drive over culture. To the contrary, as Silverman has recently demonstrated, Freud was uniquely successful in articulating the important connections between psychic and social spaces.[7] Nevertheless, it must also be noted that despite this accommodation to theoretical models that exteriorize consciousness, Freud is compelled time and time again to return to the patriarchal family romance as the origin of human experience, an investment suggesting that psychoanalytic theory may itself constitute the grandest family romance of modernity. Peter Stallybrass and Allon White have been particularly attentive to this possibility, pointing out that, for Freud, events and influences outside the domestic scene exist ultimately as symbols of the original parental situation. Persons, places, and situations outside the house are valuable to the extent that they lead back inside the house to the primal romance, the main event. Ironically, this division between social spaces allows Freud to conceptualize a split within the human subject, a split that threatens to exceed the limits of a unified, coherent masculine or feminine identity. Consequently, Freud's family romance, like his narrative, "proceeds to suppress the social terrain through which that split is articulated."[8]

Freud's own narrative account of "the liberation of an individual . . . from the authority of his parents" is structured by a split into two parts or stages (237). In the first stage, which is characterized by a lack of sexual motivation, the child's introduction to the outside world, his growing awareness of other social possibilities and conditions, leads him to reconsider his original estimation of his parents as the most powerful and extraordinary beings in the world. At this point, "the child's imagination becomes engaged in the task of getting free from the parents of whom he now has such a low opinion and of replacing them by others, who, as a rule, are of higher social standing" (238–39). Freud's assertion that the child's "low opinion" of his parents will typically result in a desire to replace them with parents of higher "social station" assumes that the subject's most productive and formative fantasies involve the attainment of class rank. To this, socialist feminists have rightly pointed out that Freud's preoccupations with class rank are the product of a particular historical moment, a particular definition of family, and particular cultural biases that Freud himself, as a bourgeois Victorian patriarch, could hardly be expected to transcend.[9] What also needs to be noted, however, is that an emphasis on class structure underscores Freud's insistence that psychological tensions be understood always in relation to cultural tensions, one of the more salient of which, in Freud's instance, was class difference.

Moreover, such preoccupations also suggest the degree to which

Freud is attempting to rethink the romance genre itself across class lines. By appropriating the romance formula, Freud portrays the unmasking of material differences that divide bourgeois and working-class families as the distinctive manifestation of the desires and identifications that produce divisions *within* particular families of either class. In this sense, as Rosalind Coward argues, Freud "uses the distortions operated on the typical romance as the evidence of historical events."[10] Perhaps this is Freud's intent when he suggests that a younger child who wishes to displace his elder siblings and deprive them of their authority within the familial pecking order is especially vulnerable to excessive reaches of the imagination "in a way which reminds one of historical intrigues" (240). History and the family romance thus would appear to mutually establish one another as legitimate narratives precisely at the moment when they can no longer be contained within the respective limits of collective and individual discursive form. As temporal boundaries fail to contain postmodernism, aesthetic boundaries fail to contain romance, thus establishing the condition that Elam identifies as characteristic of both: excess.[11]

I will take up Elam's argument in more detail in Chapter 6; however, we may begin to see here how Freud's phallocentric romance actually anticipates the postmodern turn in subtle and culturally specific ways. As we have seen, subjective fragmentation and imaginative excess are inspired by the child's initial recognition of how fragile the social boundaries are that construct the bourgeois family. The child's awakening to class difference in the first stage of the romance and paternal inadequacy in the second stage is directly related to the production of excessive fantasies within the structure of the psyche. This production is established as the inevitable precondition of subjectivity. However, there is little or no evidence that the structure of the psyche exists prior to, or independent of, the conflictive cultural structure of romance. In other words, contrary to some claims, Freud may not be attempting to romanticize the family so much as to familialize, or domesticate, the limit-breaking potential of romance.

I want to return to this point presently, but suffice it to say for now that Freud's "Family Romances" attempts to formally appropriate romance as the fixed inscription of a mutually productive subversion and recuperation of the bourgeois family with its unifying metaphor of the phallus. However, a problem arises when ultimately the child's attainment of normative identity, his initiation into the dominant social and familial order, is brought about by the very same narrative structure that precipitates his psychic fragmentation and rejection of the social position into which he is born—a rejection marked by fantasies that he is adopted, an orphan, or the long-lost issue of a royal personage. As we shall see, Freud nervously suppresses this contradiction in his account of the second (sexual) phase of the romance. However, as he proceeds through the asexual phase of his development, the subject's romantic fantasies of liberation from parental authority require his dislocation from the ideology of separate spheres, just as his eventual reinstatement within that ideology depends on his creative capacity to subvert patriarchal authority. In this stage, the boundaries between private and public, inside and outside, become fluid and nomadic as the child becomes a site of deferral and competition, a dubiously gendered ingenue of romance.

In Freud's second stage, faith in the unifying powers of the creative imagination takes over and marks "Family Romances" as an extension of the Romantic belief in the alignment of grand poetic structures with (Victorian) structures of masculine subjectivity. In this stage, the child has learned enough about sexuality and sexual relations between men and women to comprehend that "Pater sempus incertus est," or paternity is always uncertain. At this point, argues Freud, the family romance is curtailed: "it contents itself with exalting the child's father" (239). Here, fantasies of maternal infidelity invite the child to reinvent his paternity and, by extension, his social origin. The revenge fantasies of an envious younger sibling take on a distinctive erotic content as well, one that also serves social ends. By imagining his mother's external sexual relations, the child may reveal the illegitimacy of older brothers whose inheritance now becomes rightfully his own. In addition, fantasies of multiple paternity within the family allow the boy child to imagine that his sisters are not really his sisters, but females who may be sexually accessed without fear of incest. However, Freud begins to struggle uncomfortably with the question of how the same contradictory narrative structures that give rise to the boy's fantasmatic rejection of the father subsequently figure in his ascent to the father function. In part, Freud suggests, this can happen because, contrary to what we might think, "the child is not getting rid of his father" in the process of fictionalizing him, but is rather "exalting him." This interesting turn in effect may be explained by the fact that fantasies, for Freud, are never wholly fantasmatical nor wholly ideological. Here, it is worth quoting at length:

We find that these new and aristocratic parents are equipped with attributes that are derived entirely from real recollections of the actual and humble ones. . . . Indeed the whole effort at replacing the real father by a superior one is only an expression of the child's longing for the happy, vanished days when his father seemed to him the noblest and strongest of men and his mother the dearest and loveliest of women. . . . His phantasy is no more than the expression of a regret that those happy days have gone. (240–41)

Thus, the potentially nomadic identity that is produced by fantasies of replacing the real parents with parents of "better birth" is resolved by the child's resituation in relation to "real" memories and "actual" parents. The family romance becomes an "expression" of nostalgia for lost principles of consensus and privilege, principles that are rerouted into the dominant social fiction where they become the catalysts of male homosocial bonds. Finally, the family—and the phallus—is restored as the original locus of meaning, origin, and identity. However, this restoration occurs with discernible discomfort on Freud's part as he strikes a defensive posture for having exceeded the boundaries of familial sentiment, based in domestic relations of consanguity and affect, as well as the boundaries of social consensus, a disaffected arena based on hierarchies of class, gender, and race.

If anyone is inclined to turn away in horror from this depravity of the childish heart or feels tempted, indeed, to dispute the possibility of such things, he should observe that these works of fiction, which seem so full of hostility, are none of them really so badly intended, and that they still preserve, under a slight disguise, the child's original affection for his parents. The faithlessness and ingratitude are only apparent. (240)

Arguably, it is here that Freud's ideology of romance unravels itself, for it seems that an apparitional subject is the only possible product of betrayals that are merely "apparent," but nevertheless constitute and complete the individuation process. The dislocated or otherworldly condition of the subject who successfully navigates the family romance is further underscored in James Strachey's translation. The evocations of "horror" and "depravity" suggest, indeed, that as romance exceeds its own generic limits it dissolves into "other" forms of identity and desire uncontainable within the Oedipus.[12] I believe it is this generic transgression, an open acknowledgment of the monstrous structural heterogeneity that continuously dissolves the romance, as well as the family-situated subject that is foregrounded in post-Freudian family romances.

For example, one might view the film version of Spalding Gray's monologue *Monster in a Box* (1992) as a post-family romance defined by its reluctance to remain within the conventional limits of genre, gender, narrative space.[13] The film remains undecided about its status as family romance in much the same way that Gray remains uncertain about his status as author; the narrative centers on his inability to finish a novel that he's been writing for more than twenty years. Turning to therapy for enlightenment, Gray becomes ambivalent about his role within the traditional psychoanalytic relationship, referring to himself as a "reluctant Freudian." These formal, open acknowledgments of genre and subject displacement—the inability of this text to perform any single, unified function—ultimately produce the post-family romance's cross-transference with another genre, "horror."

"You see," begins Gray, "in 1967, while I was trying to take my first vacation, my mother killed herself. And since then I've written a book about it." The book Gray has been writing for more than twenty years is entitled *Impossible Vacation*. It is 1,900 pages long and "almost finished," according to Gray, although not quite. In the novel, he traces the development of a character named Brewster North, who is much like himself, "a Puritan who can't take a vacation." *Impossible Vacation* is Gray's family romance, his attempt to reinscribe himself into a historical intrigue of his own design, one that would complete the individuation process and free him of his attachment to the maternal sphere. *Impossible Vacation* is also Gray's attempt to purge himself of guilt for having brought on his mother's suicide by testing his independence, venturing beyond her domain in pursuit of thrillingly subversive countercultural pleasures, like "hanging out" at Provincetown. Clearly, Gray's inability to quit working suggests a displacement of the unfinished mother-son business; however, as romance, his work exceeds the individual drama of subjectivity to suggest a displacement of historical narratives that inscribe a Puritan work ethic centrally within Gray's cultural definition of masculine identity. The merger of these displacements multiplies the possible meanings of the film's title, so that *Monster in a Box* refers at once to the novel exceeding its market usefulness (as salable work), the mother exceeding her coffin (to haunt the son), and the narrator exceeding the limits of genre by rejecting containment within the conventional cinematic space of the family plot.

Like *Swimming to Cambodia*, the first cinematic treatment of one of Gray's dramatic monologues, *Monster in a Box* is filmed on an austere stage. Gray sits at a wooden desk with only his huge, unfinished manuscript and a glass of water near at hand. The camera frames him squarely, moving from medium long shots to extreme closeups that amplify and isolate the "talking head" in its most intense moments of discursive performativity. Although free of the conventional settings and visual clues of the family romance or the horror film (domestic space, decrepit mansions, and so forth), Gray's monologue is loaded with parodic references to the classical American horror film.[14] Eerie nondiegetic music plays intermittently in the background. A disembodied heartbeat sounds as Gray recalls his mother's numerous breakdowns, his fervent desire to save her in spite of his equally fervent desire to escape her. Gray recounts his residence at the McDowell writer's colony where he's assigned a cottage named Bates, after the nurse who cared for McDowell while he was dying of syphilis. Here, Gray confronts the horror of writer's block.

However, the nod to Hitchcock's *Psycho* references more than the popular horror style that circulates throughout Gray's family romance. It also invites a consideration of matricide, the son's retainment of the mother's decaying body, and the monstrous inversion of Oedipal desires, all of which Gray gives particular attention to in his working out of "Oedipal themes."

It is while working through these themes that Gray begins to lose the vision in his right eye. He becomes obsessed with the fear of losing his vision, just as later in the film he becomes obsessed with the fear that he has contracted AIDS from a one-night stand with a stage-door groupie that occurred years ago. Like classical horror, *Monster in a Box* is in one sense a dark meditation on the open, diseased, permeable, and vulnerable body.[15] Along these lines, Gray admits that he has "very weak boundaries." His is not the classical closed, seamless masculine body, but a body feminized, open, and penetrable. In this way, the film theorizes the potential relations that exist among postmodern bodies, genders, writing, and genres.

Feminist theory conceptualizes maternity as a monstrous reflection; Gray conceptualizes it as a monstrous text that cannot be contained or unified.[16] Within these terms, the promise of monsters (or monster "theory") has been conceptualized by Donna Haraway as a means of theorizing subjectivity beyond the customary closures that are performed by binary thinking and beyond the social spaces traditionally aimed at dualizing and containing gender.[17] Monsters, as Haraway demonstrates, productively defy individuation in the classical, Freudian sense. The figure of the monster thus holds liberatory potential as a trope of postmodern heteroglossia, an effect of multiple boundary crossings. Like post-family romance, monsters continuously transgress fields of discourse. Accordingly, *Monster in a Box* implicates family romance in horror, as it implicates maternity in every futile effort to construct a unified masculine subject position.

The reluctant Freudianism of numerous contemporary feminist critics similarly stresses the extent to which Freud's theoretical formation of the Oedipal family romance plays ambiguously at the borders of nature and culture. This ambiguity has served social constructivist *and* biological essentialist efforts to interpret Freud's structuring of gendered subjectivity.[18] Still, commentators have tended to insist on locating Freud's theoretical commitment to the family romance either inside or outside of the house. Far fewer readers of Freud are willing to grant that both interpretations of the issue—or neither, depending on how you look at it—are correct. Irresolution, contradiction, and incongruence are the compelling features of Freud's work, and these features become strikingly evident in "Family Romances." Thus, an important task for a postfeminist theory of the family romance involves, in Flax's words, an acceptance of "the existence of these antimonies" and an investigation of "why Freud could neither recognize nor reconcile them."[19] While pursuing this entreaty, I maintain that "Family Romances" works, however murkily, toward the final restoration of subjectivity to the original bonds of consanguinity and affect. This is nowhere more evident than in Freud's final embrace of rational dualistic thinking. Here he exalts those elements of the "real" and "actual" parents who survive in the child's conscious memory, while dispelling the "ingratitude," infidelity, and paternal insufficiency that are innocuously "apparent," mere fantasy. As in "A Child Is Being Beaten" (1919), Freud attributes what the child experiences as actuality to representation; however, at the same time he proposes that the Oedipal family is the origin of both the reality and the fantasy.[20] In short, while Freud flip-flops between psychic romance and social romance in determining the most potent organizing force in the subject's development, the triangulation of bifurcated identifications and desires remains the universal structural experience of the growing child. What we might question, then, is why Freud was unable to limit his investment in the phallic principle and get beyond many of the structural dualisms that tend to reify his thinking.

Freud's irresolute treatment of the origins of the family romance suggests that there is no given or stable commensurability between romance, as a narrative displacement of realism, and patriarchy, as a collection of loosely supportive institutions that require discourse for their communication and legitimization. Thus to speak of "family romance" is perhaps to deconstruct both terms, for while "the family" has been variously used to signify unity, consensus, nature, origin, privacy, nurturance, rationalism, property, labor, and universality, "romance" troubles all of these concepts and asks us repeatedly to question the terms of their use. What Freud's essay shows, perhaps even despite itself, is that there is nothing inherently romantic about the family or, for that matter, familial about romance. Throughout modern history patriarchy has enacted certain distortions on romance, on the one hand appropriating it for its perceived interests, on the other, discrediting it as mere formula or mere "women's writing" when it claims to have no use for it.

So, what happens when phallocentrism maps itself over romance, a narrative mode traditionally associated with the figures and structures of the feminine? Possible answers are articulated in Freud's second stage. Here, both boys and girls take up their official social positions with the recognition of castration. For the boy child, successful passage through the family romance promises compensation for the fear of castration, the fear that motivates all subsequent identifications and object choices. Fantasies, which are "seldom remembered consciously but can almost always be revealed by psychoanalysis" (238), displace the "low" father with the heroic father. Suspicions of paternal inadequacy are eliminated thanks to imaginative faith in paternal dominance. Illusion undoes the Oedipal threat of castration with initiation into the dominant fiction, or collective consensual belief in the supremacy of the phallus.

For Freud romance itself offers a defense of the patriarchal status quo, a symbolic appeal to belief in paternal privilege, masculine superiority, and the intractable social order. Of course, that such faith can *only* be supported through romance is instructive and suggests how shaky these systems of belief have become in the early part of this century. By imaginatively reinventing the father, Freud suggests that the child imaginatively rewrites the history of modernity and by so doing constitutes a more secure basis on which to articulate a coherent masculine identity. In his service to the romance, the father is the lightning rod for those creative and intellectual forces that ultimately liberate the child from his guilty role within the family—defined as a reenactment of historical trauma—and insert him instead into his guilty role within history—defined as a reenactment of familial crisis and resolution.

For the girl child, Freud's "Family Romances" marks the culmination of the process by which castration is incorporated into her acceptance of a social position characterized by lack, passivity, and inferiority. Ostensibly it is this acceptance of her lack that motivates the girl to shift her object of desire from mother to father, with the hope of filling the phallic void with a child of her own womb. However, to the extent that this crucial recognition of castration is "synonymous with the possibility of representation," Freud's family romance becomes synonymous with woman's disenfranchisement from the symbolic order, or language itself.[21] According to Freud, females will experience less intense feelings of hostility toward the father than boys; since females have accepted their castration they have no need to free themselves from its threat. The attainment of femininity thus requires less creative power, so that consequently, "the imagination of girls is apt to show itself much weaker" than the imagination of boys (238). Here it would appear that Freud constructs a rational connection between fear, creativity, masculinity, and authority that requires public consensus for its legitimacy. Femininity, on the other hand, is constructed in relation to loss, imaginative inertia, and authority that speaks for itself despite its containment in the private sphere.

This authority, although theorized as marginal and supplemental, is wholly dependent on language. With the mother's status as "*certissima*" the mother function symbolizes the source of identity that she alone may know, the secret of paternity. Consequently, the mother figures as a site of potential deception, a betrayal waiting to happen. Through spatial divisions that naturalize gender difference, the mother's voice in the public sphere is effectively muted. Ultimately, it is her relationship to the phallus, rather than her relationship to the public sphere, that most matters. Thus the Freudian family romance constructs paternity as the privileged site of origin and social meaning, while it constructs the mother as a voiceless and potentially deceptive enclosed space where mysteries of multiple origin are encoded in a language no one can read.

However, in order for the father to function effectively as a bridge between Oedipus and the socius, there must first be a division established for the child to negotiate. No separation, no father function. For Freud, it is this contradiction, suppressed for the most part within the recesses of the unconscious, that constitutes "normal" adult subjectivity. However, the male child must first perceive this binary split in order to claim his power, just as the female child must perceive it in order to properly divest herself of any aspirations to transcend it. Given Freud's understanding of the crossings that only males can properly effect, matriarchy would constitute a regressive, fragmented state, while patriarchy constitutes a consensual, bonded, fully civilized state.

To be sure, the female child "comes off badly" in this formulation, although this is probably not due, as Freud suggests in "The Dissolution of the Oedipus Complex" (1924), to the recognition that the girl's clitoris is by comparison smaller and inferior to the boy's penis.[22] Rather, the problem lies in the tradition of metaphysical dualistic thinking that would require an opposition of anatomical features in accordance with a symbolic dualism in which relations of domination are structurally unified. The implicit assumption of positive Oedipal logic, that children will identify with the parent of the same sex and desire the parent of the opposite sex, reproduces gender and sexual hegemonies and defines the family romance as the imaginative process by which these hegemonies are positioned for naturalization.

This process has been beneficial for the Enlightenment philosophies of psychoanalysis, as well as Marxism, to the extent that the naturalization of hegemonic relations between the sexes attributes this same naturalness to hegemonic relations between social classes. Freud's essay on "Family Romances" is particularly revealing in this regard, not simply because it gives a name to the genre with which this study is centrally concerned, but because by splitting his own narrative into the same dualistic pattern that he experiences within social and familial relations, Freud creates a hierarchy in which the structurally unified romance of the analyst (or critic) ranks superior to the contradictory, uncritical romance of the people (consumers). However, my sense is that a new reading of the family romance emerges when we shift our attention to examine the compulsion to unify and pigeonhole discourses as well as subjects. Indeed, we may then take such statements as "the whole progress of society rests upon the opposition between successive generations" as saying more about the fear of discursive heterogeneity and cultural chaos than about the diachronic structure of generational conflict (237).

Freud thus makes it possible for us to pry apart the romance from the family in order to observe more closely the historical points at which they attract and repel one another. Recently, this insistence on using history as a guide for prying loose narrative forms and ideological contents has made it possible for feminist psychoanalytic critics to argue that the oppositional structures of identification and desire that define Freud's positive Oedipus complex are by no means natural or essential.[23] Furthermore, by revealing the powerful cultural forces that police representations of family in both theory and fiction, feminist literary scholars have been able to seize the family romance and foreground its contradictory formulations of the gendered subject.

During the pivotal decades of the 1950s and 1960s, the lingering historical trauma of World War II and European fascism demanded a radical reconsideration of theories of the subject in relation to history and ideology. The advent of nuclear technology provided a powerful new metaphor for a fundamentally split and potentially implosive experience of self. Technological developments and new patterns of labor and leisure contributed to this sense of fragmenting self and demanded a complete rethinking of the value of kinship, nuclear family relations, and domesticity. In the United States, the cold war and the ongoing crisis of race relations fed into national hysteria over the family's role in producing national consensus to counter the threat of contaminating social "difference." Subsequently, the emergence of a youth-oriented counterculture sparked intergenerational antagonism and posited the private family as the inevitable site of political and historical turmoil.

From as early as Bronislaw Malinowski's rethinking of kinship in terms of a "series of heterogeneous relationships with distinct social functions," the family had begun to be broken up into its pieces.[24] In 1970, when David Cooper proposed "a destructuring of the family on the basis of a full realization of the destructiveness of that institution," he, like his mentor R. D. Laing, bespoke the structuralist assumption that the family romance could best be apprehended by recourse to familialism, or by a shift from the study of the family as a discrete and natural source of individual psychology to a study of the family as the systemic effect of the individual's assumed roles within the group dynamic.[25] The move represented a shift from a diachronic to a synchronic study of kinship in which history, or Freud's symbolic struggle between generations, was not the central concern.

The Cooper/Laing argument advanced this move in several directions, not the least of which was an emphasis on signifying practices and social consensus as constitutive of familial subjectivity. The constructivist leaning was, furthermore, by no means unique to Laing and his followers, but was only one articulation of a much broader cultural and epistemological transformation, at the heart of which were philosophical questions concerning the validity of representational forms and strategies. Naturally, these questions were of great concern to the evolving feminist movement in the United States, as was evidenced by Kate Millet's *Sexual Politics*, a groundbreaking critique of women's oppression through the mutual collusion of patriarchal politics and literature, as well as by Betty Friedan's attack against advertising's abuse of women's images in *The Feminine Mystique*. In Laing and Cooper, feminist critics of the patriarchal family romance found important allies, not just because they viewed the family as oppressive but because they viewed its oppressiveness in terms of systems of representation, systems not unlike language and literature itself.

Cooper's call for a revolution in family structure *was* a call for a revolution in language and representation. However in issuing such a call he pushed himself to the front of an already-advancing army; a reformulation of the symbolic logic of family romance was well underway and had been for some time to the extent that novelists, critics, and social theorists were confronting new concepts of subjectivity capable of accounting for—or at least acknowledging—Freud's cultural blind spots and tendencies toward biologism. As we have seen, Freud's formulation of the family romance perceives the Oedipal crisis to be the privileged event in human psychological development. The event itself is organized around the central significance of the phallus, its dominating symbol and motor. Paternity is thus understood as the origin of meaning, albeit a contestable origin. It is for this reason that the inscription of subjectivity within the symbolic order requires narrative, a fantasmatic creation, as its proof. For Freud, female sexuality, the impact of the pre-Oedipal mother-child relationship, and the figure of woman in general return to confound the romance formula, defying its logic in ways that Freud himself recognized and was unable to sufficiently address.

One of the most influential figures for feminist revisions of the Freudian family romance has been the French psychoanalyst Jacques Lacan. The notion that human desire and identification are essentially linguistic as opposed to anatomical or biologistic operations is Lacan's chief contribution to an evolving theory of family romance. However, critics of Lacan have pointed out that his work tends to enact a simplistic substitution whereby the universal structure of the bourgeois family is replaced with a far more totalizing structure of language. For Freud the family romance is wholly reliant on the power of the phallus; for Lacan the phallus is wholly reliant on the powers of language, or on the extrinsic operations of a linguistic romance that inevitably intrudes on and splits the human subject. For Freud, identity is founded on the consolidation of the phallus; in the broadest sense, this is true of Lacan's rewriting of the romance as well, however Lacan focuses far more critically than Freud on the extent to which the phallus, as universal signifier and agent of cultural disenfranchisement, remains always a symbol of lack. Indeed, according to Lacan *all* gendered subjectivity is marked by castration. All identity is lack; no one actually has the phallus. Language thus constitutes the great divide whereby the phallus, as public matter, intrudes on and ultimately fractures the private, blissfully narcissistic coherence of the prelinguistic infant.

For Lacan, this fracturing is conceptualized in a lack of commensurability between phallus and penis, terms that Freud tends to uncritically equate. Lacan's rejection of commensurability between the phallus and the penis and his insistence on the cultural construction of gender have had enormous appeal for feminist theorists working to unmask the sex/gender system. Castration, the unavoidable condition of subjectivity, is understood to be an effect of culture, not anatomy. However, the phallus, as the prominent symbol of the Father's Law, remains for Lacan the equivalent of culture, something men would appear to have more immediate access to. The figure of woman remains far more hopelessly consigned to the realm of "otherness." She remains culture's opposite, a signifier of nothing. However, as Flax has rightly indicated, this raises a problem that might prompt one to wonder "*why* the mother lacks the phallus if it is purely a linguistic artifact."[26] Both women and men are marked by castration; however, clearly the consequences of this marking are not the same. To the extent that Lacan does not address this problem, his privileging of the phallus is in many ways as problematic as Freud's, albeit less conspicuous, and may be read as equally permeated with gender bias.

Undeniably, the Lacanian shift from an understanding of identity in terms of anatomical haves and have-nots to identity in terms of linguistic lack and the shift from a discrete and expressive human subject to a discrete and expressive symbolic order have provided feminist theorists with important tools for intervention into the Oedipal family paradigm.[27] Lacan's work has made it possible for feminists to conceptualize the family as a symbolic system founded on the operations of language. However, in his work Lacan represses the conditions, contradictions, and variants that have historically maintained an undeniable correlation between penis and phallus. As Kaja Silverman and Tania Modleski have recently suggested, masculine dominance tends to assert and consolidate itself in and through such disjunctures rather than disappear in the gap between penis and phallus.[28] Language is not a neutral force—even in its absence—nor are its effects on subjects consistent across different societal organizations and historical epochs. Feminists would deny these differences at their own peril, for the diverse operations of language, as much as the diverse articulations of gender, need to be understood as cultural contingencies rather than universal and unchangeable facts. Furthermore, Lacan's emphasis on the binary opposition of signified and signifier is as ideologically charged as the Freudian opposition of public and private, or Lévi-Strauss's opposition of gift giver and gift.[29] Such oppositions, as we have seen, tend to close down rather than open up discussion of gender difference beyond the reification of the Name-of-the-Father.[30]

In her influential essay "The Traffic in Women," Gayle Rubin demonstrates that in the system Lévi-Strauss describes, women are excluded from participation as exchangers in the public sphere, relegated to a position as mere objects of exchange.[31] She argues that it is not a general system of exchange, but rather a systematic exchange of women that establishes kinship relations. The institution of marriage establishes women as symbolic links between family and society, thus positioning them as the foundation on which social organization rests. However, in accounting for the formation of the social field, Lévi-Strauss, like Freud, privileges paternity as the locus of origin. Rubin understands women's oppression not in terms of their exclusion from this field, but in terms of a "sex-gender system," a network of beliefs and practices that naturalize gender and stratify cultural distinctions between gift givers and gifts. Here she provides means for understanding how a conflation of sex and gender facilitates a "natural" consolidation of public and private. She thus perceives the separation of private and public to be an expression of relations of domination within *and* between families; however, the implicit correspondence between language (or coinage) and women, spatial systems and a sex/gender system, tends to overlook the historical specificity of systems, as well as the cultural specificity of the objects exchanged within them. Such logic bypasses the fault lines of power structures by reducing them to binary oppositions of haves (men) and have-nots (women) in a relation in which the latter always reproduces the interests of the former.

In their challenge to binary logic, Deleuze and Guattari have offered one of the more radical redefinitions of family romance.[32] In *Anti-Oedipus*, they argue that desire is never split along the opposed axes of identifications and desire, but is always complexly and simultaneously intertwined with both. The child's identification is never *with* one parent or the other, just as his desire is never *for* one parent or the other. In this way,

Deleuze and Guattari mount a rigorous theoretical attack against the confinement of desire within the field of the Oedipal family romance. The Oedipalization of desire is defined as a psychic function of fascism. Deleuze and Guattari move to deconstruct the dichotomous separation of social and subjective being, and their attendant regulatory regimes, capitalism and psychoanalysis. They proceed to reconceptualize group and individual identity through the method termed "schizoanalysis," a revolutionary and potentially liberating account of a postmodern psychic condition that opposes centeredness, authority, and closed systems, articulating instead an ever-mobile plurality of nonhierarchical desires that are productive and threatening.

In recent critical practices and counter-Freudian moves such as these, subversion tends to be conceived positively. However, Deleuze and Guattari's subversive "desire" is essentialized to the point of obliterating "the specificity of the motives for which they are employed."[33] For instance, in their rejection of a socially articulated, subjectified state, Deleuze and Guattari do not sufficiently take into account that desire, as a historical, social, and psychic field, has been constructed quite differently for men and women, heterosexuals and homosexuals, white Americans and non-white Americans. These historical and cultural "differences" that form the sort of socially legible subject position that Deleuze and Guattari wish to see deconstructed would seem to place some families at a distinct disadvantage in the process of becoming nomadic desiring texts, or "families-without-organs." However, given that the postmodern subject is continually dissolved by the heterogeneity of the world, how do post-family romances respond to the political usefulness of identity categories and at the same time rehearse Foucault's call for an aesthetics of self-formation, a self free of ethical and moral predeterminants, free of modernity's foundational discourses? In such a scenario as this, what does the family romance—long considered the founding fiction of the individual—have to offer? In order to address this question, we need to examine some post-familial contexts and consider the choices they offer.

Chapter 3
The Third Sphere: Television's Romance with the Family

Could the room without a name be evidence of a growing desire to provide a framework within which the members of a family will be better equipped to enjoy each other on the basis of mutual respect and affection? Might it thus indicate a deep-seated urge to reassert the validity of the family by providing a better design for living? We should very much like to think so, and if there is any truth in this assumption, our search for a name is ended—we should simply call it the "family room." [1]
—George Nelson and Henry Wright, *Tomorrow's House: A Complete Guide for the Home-Builder*

If I am right, the problem that has no name stirring in the minds of so many American women today is not a matter of loss of femininity or too much education, or the demands of domesticity. It is far more important than anyone recognizes. It is the key to these other new and old problems which have been torturing women and their husbands and children, and puzzling their doctors and educators for years. It may well be the key to our future as a nation and a culture.[2]
—Betty Friedan, *The Feminine Mystique*

In 1946, George Nelson and Henry Wright named a new household space in accordance with the postwar imperatives of domesticity and family unity. Behind their call for "mutual respect and affection" was undoubtedly a degree of concern about the changing constitution of the public sphere and the impact of these changes on the many women who had entered the work force during the war, as well as on returning GIs in search of employment opportunities. However, Nelson and Wright's "new design for living" constituted more than an enlightened foreshadowing of bureaucratization, economic shifts, and subsequent gender realignments. Their manual may also be read as a cultural manifesto aimed at unifying and spatially recodifying the family romance. Woven into Nelson and Wright's practical "how-to" rhetoric is an unacknowledged wish to contain that network of relations and sentiments long associated with the feminine, to detour femininity away from the public sphere and away from the popular image of a self-sufficient Rosie the Riveter. Waiting to take Rosie's place as representatives of the new feminine ideal were Donna Stone and June Cleaver, television moms who gracefully embodied the values of "the room without a name" in their ostensibly wholesale commitment to domestic space.

Indeed, after World War II, as American women who had joined the wartime work force were encouraged to return to the happiness and security of home, mothers' place within the family structure became a turbulent site of contradiction and cultural upheaval.[3] In 1950, when the popular women's magazine *Better Homes and Gardens* renamed the "room without a name" the "family-television room" it was a sign that efforts to unify the postwar family romance were under siege by the very exigencies of its mass marketability.[4] The marriage of the intimately sequestered nuclear family and its correlative cultural ideal, the television set, indicated that the terms of the family romance's centrality within the private sphere were far less stabilized by femininity's containment within that space than might have appeared judging from popular texts that defined women's essential biological function as mother, wife, domestic caretaker.[5] These terms were, in fact, reconditioned by an increasing emphasis on American women's moral and familial obligation to consume the new technologies that vied with one another to rename the family sphere. Accordingly, advertising strategies were developed to equate the value of household gadgetry with *both* women's responsiveness to family needs and their own needs for self-empowerment. In this way, the industrial development of network television played a major part in communicating cultural ambivalence toward gender and family relationships, even as specific programming attempted to resolve this ambivalence through the image of the "perfect mother" and her logical extension, the image of the consensual American family.

In 1963, Betty Friedan sought to evaluate the impact that contradictions such as these were having on women's lives. In *The Feminine Mystique,* Friedan encouraged readers, in a sense, to remap the political implications of "the room that has no name" over the figure of woman, a move that resulted in the identification of "a problem that has no name." The family/television room was thus redubbed a prison in which hundreds of thousands of American women struggled with inarticulate longings. In this way, *The Feminine Mystique* proceeded to reject the name that had architecturally circumscribed middle-class American women in an effort to raise awareness of their subordination to patriarchy's romance with the family.

In *Make Room for TV: Television and the Family Ideal in Postwar America,* Lynn Spigel documents the mass installation of television into the post-war American family sphere. By 1960, Spigel reports, "almost 90 percent of American households had at least one receiver, with the average person watching approximately five hours of television each day."[6] And although the public response to this sudden and dramatic claim on the family's time and energy was ambivalent at best and at times downright hysterical, television's rapid integration into the structures and conventions of American family life indicated, among other things, the conflictual status of postwar domestic ideals. These conflicts were played out in a series of heated debates that have outlived Newton Minow's "Vast Wasteland" speech to plague contemporary sociologists and legislators alike.[7] How does television impact on children's development and on intimate adult relationships? In which room within the home should the television set be located? How much control should parents take in deciding what and how much television their children watch? In the midst of these debates, television represented, to its advocates, a new entertainment-centered familial unity, and to its opponents, the family's moral and social demise.

In its infancy, American television promised a means of stabilizing such conflict. It presented a forum for relieving public anxiety over the perceived loss of paternal authority and for restoring the family's essential structural wholeness. However, the medium's penetration into the family domain also suggested a new and insidious electronic arm of social regulation *and* control. Historically, one of the television industry's main preoccupations has been the shifting power relations of private and public. Yet somewhere between the two extreme views of television's service to these opposed spheres, television discourse developed into a transmutable and oblique gray area where the market concerns of the state economic apparatus and the regulatory concerns of the state social apparatus overlap with the affectional and nurturant concerns of the ostensibly private family. Television's mediating function has expanded rapidly over the last forty years, at times seeming to take on the dimensions of a third sphere, a separate space where fantasy and ideology overlap to problematize cultural formulations of history in relation to family, and family in relation to individuality. Moreover, television's discursive function has been to probe contemporary thinking about television itself.[8] Indeed, television has grown up alongside the post-family romance, offering itself as an ally (a condition dramatically evidenced in the proliferation of specialized cable networks) and as a marketing ideology, the register of an increasingly pluralized cultural topography. Today, television continues to provide commentary on the changing dimensions of public and private space, thus rehearsing "older questions in a new social environment."[9]

In this chapter, I want to offer some readings of television's historical representation of the post-family romance, its evolving commentary on the dislocations of the domestic sphere, and its tradition of a multi-accentual deployment of gender within that sphere.[10] To some, this may seem a redundant task, especially to those who have come of age watching syndicated reruns of sitcoms and serials from the fifties, sixties, and seventies. Viewers of Nickelodeon, the popular cable channel whose evening programming is wholly dedicated to celebrating "our television heritage," are reminded constantly of the extent to which television's primary historical function has been to provide perpetual commentary on television itself, its themes, conventions, and images. Nick at Nite's tendency to jump from decade to decade, juxtaposing episodes from *I Love Lucy* with *The Partridge Family*, encourages a synchronic as opposed to diachronic method of perceiving television's social meanings. This emphasis on an innate structural coherence, in addition to Nick at Nite's cheeky, pseudo-academic tone with regard to its programming, suggests that family sitcoms are best viewed with a cool, ironic detachment that culturally decontextualizes specific programming while reinforcing viewers' unity of experience and commitment to the dominant fantasies of the television dreamscape. Of course, this decontextualization is largely produced by the self-referentiality of television discourse and through technologies that regurgitate and recodify family plots more quickly and efficiently than any other narrative medium. I mean, why bother worrying about whether Lucy will ever get that big break in show business, or if Laura Petrie will remain forever content to be a housewife in New Rochelle? We know Lucy will be a wacky widow and secretary in her next television reincarnation just as surely as we know that Laura Petrie will eventually "make it" on her own as Mary Richards, an associate television news producer in Minneapolis.

In other words, the tendency in television is to collapse the relationship of history and gender into the familiar gap between the character's "situation" then and character's "situation" now. When the plot situation calls for a fixed opposition of domestic and public space, television commercials implicitly deconstruct the division by inviting viewers at intervals to leap across the divide via consumer activities and an assumed allegiance to program sponsors. However, if there is one thing that contemporary feminist critical analysis underscores it is the fact that such divisions are never negotiated innocently or transparently. Consequently, fifties and sixties family sitcoms—the seemingly bland artifacts of a mythical family heyday—were never so intellectually mined for social meaning as they are today, a worthwhile enterprise when we consider that this "heyday" was itself precipitated by malingering doubts about gender roles and the family's function in an accelerated postwar consumer economy.[11]

Speaking from my own experience as a television fan, I can recall—like so many middle-class children of my generation—being parented, comforted, and at times even reprimanded by network television of the sixties and seventies. Some of my fondest memories are of sick days at home when the television set was brought into *my* room where I was nursed by the sequence of early morning reruns—*Dennis the Menace, Leave It to Beaver, The Donna Reed Show, The Andy Griffith Show, The Beverly Hillbillies, Family Affair.* Today, I am the proud owner of numerous television tie-in products that proclaim my "television heritage" (a Donna Reed wristwatch most valued among them). The product, like the program itself, addresses the cultural desire for a repeated postulation of a perfect postwar nuclear family that baby boomers and post–baby boomers can claim and disavow at the same time, thereby insinuating that we have reappropriated for our own revisionary purposes the ideology of the family.[12] However, it is precisely here that the family romance continues, even in its hypersimulated guise, from the Munsters to the Huxtables to the Simpsons, as we continue to gauge our own participation in the social norm and redefine our identifications with the order of law and the order of fantasy.

Nevertheless, as experts in the field of communications and media scholarship have repeatedly advised, television, by its very nature, demands a materialist frame for critical evaluation. In this sense, television "texts" are most slippery when talked about outside the context of the sponsors who purchase the airspace and the viewer's private space. "It is a truism in the industry that the networks are not selling programs to audiences—they are selling audiences to sponsors. There is hardly a study of television that does not mention this."[13] Maybe the reason this point bears such constant repetition among television critics is because it's so easy to miss. Television, on one hand, offers us a comforting illusion of privacy and autonomy. We seem to be making choices—what to watch, what sponsors to patronize, whether to watch or patronize at all—yet it's so easy to overlook the fact that *we* are what's being sold, our dreams, our fantasies, our fears, our deepest disappointments.[14]

On the other hand, when viewed in a historical context, television instills in us more profoundly than any other discursive form a sense that the binary ideology of separate spheres has vanished and the marketplace has shattered into a multiplicity of spheres—or channels—any one or combination of them capable of penetrating into our living rooms, seeping into the most private recesses of American domestic life. The seemingly pervasive need of critics to reassert television's commodification of its viewers may be a necessary reminder of this thrust, however it also indicates a general intensified awareness among television scholars of the powerful role television has played historically in reshaping our perceptions of a marketable family romance.

In her research on postwar popular media, Spigel spotlights 1954 as the year that saw the birth of an important new term: "togetherness." Its first appearance in the popular women's magazine *McCall's* is significant, Spigel argues, "not only because it shows the importance attached to family unity during the postwar years, but also because this phrase is symptomatic of discourses aimed at the housewife."[15] With the end of the Second World War and the surge of new domestic technologies aimed at the American housewife, television assumed a central role right alongside "Mom" as a unifying agent within the family. It assured women that their true fulfillment could be found in raising children, experimenting with Jell-o mold salads, and overseeing the acquisition of the many new domestic appliances guaranteed to save time and confer social status. It appeared, in fact, that television might mend the family fractured by war and help bring its members closer together. Advertisements anthropomorphized the television set, portraying it as the newest member of the kinship group, an additional child or loving pet. Such images betray the belief in television as the perfect peacetime advocate for a changing economy based on the values of consumerism and family unity.[16]

Oddly, however, the years 1953 to 1955 also mark the period that ethnic family situation comedies such as *The Goldbergs, Life with Luigi,* and *Amos 'n' Andy*—sitcoms developed from popular radio comedies of the 1940s—were last aired.[17] Black family comedy would not return to television until the 1968 NBC comedy series *Julia* offered a perfunctory means of addressing civil rights tensions perpetuated by the absence of blacks on television.[18] However, in the fourteen-year interim, white, non-ethnic, affable, middle-class nuclear family situation comedies such as *Leave It to Beaver, Father Knows Best, The Donna Reed Show, Make Room for Daddy, The Honeymooners, I Love Lucy, Ozzie and Harriet,* and *The Patty Duke Show* became—and for a large part still remain—a staple of network television programming. According to Andrea Press, these humorous and seemingly transparent domestic comedies owe their popularity to an implicit contract they form with viewers. This contract promises to maintain "our belief in the indestructibility and perpetuity of the family, which must stay together if we are to view it week after week."[19] This is indeed a crucial function of the genre; however, as social texts, sitcom narratives are inevitably marked by the complexities and contradictions built into postwar familial ideology. Consequently, while popular television itself cannot transcend ideological boundaries, it does "reflect a desire to simplify terrains of ideological confusion and contradiction within our society." [20]

In 1954, popular journalism's invention of the term "togetherness" and the erasure of racial difference from popular television reinforced the preexisting social taboo against questioning the internal contradictions of the social order. The pressures of acceptance and conformity were concentrated as well in the processes of suburbanization, a phenomenon reflected in the social criticism of David Reisman's *The Lonely Crowd* (1950), Philip Spectorsky's *The Exurbanites* (1955), and William H. Whyte's *The Organization Man* (1956). The American suburbs of the 1950s provided a mecca for the thousands of young families and couples on the move in a period of widely perceived economic prosperity. [21] Perhaps more than the nuclear family itself, the suburbs provided a means of packaging a "life-style"; they were a symbol of hope, promise, and youth in an environment where there was no visible poverty, little crime, and practically no death. Above all, life in the suburbs underscored the value of adjusting the private sphere to the norms established by the corporate sphere, so that all residents within a certain development would dress, vote, educate their children, and spend their money in the same way. An emergent corporate ethos was based on the belief that such group sameness was the ultimate source of individual happiness; however, the belief extended outside the workplace to create a life-style rooted in the negation of differences in the home and family. Whyte describes the evolution of this trend in the case of Park Forest, a community that advertisers originally sold with the promise of inexpensive housing but eventually repackaged with the promise of happiness. "You *Belong* . . . in PARK FOREST! The moment you come to our town you know: You're welcome. You're part of a big group. You can live in a friendly small town instead of a lonely big city. You can have friends who want you" (Nov. 8, 1952). Or this advertisement, which ad agents assembled with the advice of professional psychiatrists: "A cup of coffee— symbol of PARK FOREST! Coffeepots bubble all day long in Park Forest. This sign of friendliness tells you how much neighbors enjoy each other's company—feel glad that they can share their daily joys—yes, and troubles too" (Nov. 19, 1952). [22]

Such advertisements were primarily targeted at women, housewives who remained at home in the suburbs with their furiously bubbling coffeepots during the day while their husbands went to work for the large corporations. Beyond the coffee klatch, suburban women were entreated on a daily basis by television, women's magazines, radio, and newspapers to fill their domestic spaces with new gadgets, furniture, foodstuffs, and so on. Thus, Gatlin argues that the suburbs constructed a "private" sphere essentially for the purpose of permeating it with "market values and corporate authorities."[23] In addition, Gatlin suggests that "suburbanization was as effective as anti-communism and popularized Freudian psychology in depoliticising women's discontent" by effectively trapping women within isolated communities where traditional roles were enforced and where commitment to housework was monitored by both peer pressure and advertising.[24]

Of course, television families of the 1950s like the Andersons, Stones, and Cleavers were already well-situated in well-groomed suburban communities by the time we met them; for many real families—single-parented, working-class, black, Hispanic, Asian, lesbian, gay, elderly—suburbs like Park Forest would have been unreachable, not to mention fraught with social obstacles. Nevertheless, television's naturalization of the white, middle-class nuclear family presumed an audience longing to have its fantasies of familial "normalcy" affirmed by the powers of visual narrative. The precise structures of these fantasies of cohesiveness were not only the subject of television content, but of significant psychological research conducted in the early 1960s by R. D. Laing and colleagues such as David Cooper. Part of Laing's analysis was based on an important distinction between two separate operations, or sets of relations: the "family" and the family. By placing the family within quotation marks Laing makes reference to a reciprocal process of transformation, the aim of which is to unify fantasy and reality. The "family" denotes the family as a "fantasy structure," which persons within the system internalize and then project back onto actual family and work relations.[25] In a sense, the process resembles Freud's stages of "neurotic family romance," whereby the subject resolves erotic tensions through fantasy. However, what Freud understood to be the "freeing of an individual . . . from the authority of his parents," Laing saw as group dynamic in which variant fantasies internalized by each individual member of the family are mapped onto the same system.[26] As these mapping operations became compounded, the family system could become a potentially knotted order of relations. This process, which Laing referred to as the "nexification" of relations, could possibly result, he claimed, in the closing of the family system and its hermetic isolation from the outside world.

Looking back on the process of suburbanization and the quest for consensus, it's possible to imagine that isolation was just as much, if not more, a cause of Laingian nexification than a result. But let's consider a possibility that Laing did not: what happens when variant fantasies within the family system are collectively mapped onto *one* family member, the mother? Obviously, this was not a question Laing specifically sought to explore in any depth; however, if we suspend Laing's uni-fying fantasy of the "family" in order to examine the correlative unifying fantasy of the "mother," what can be learned about the compound map-pings that construct relations within the family? More importantly for the purposes of understanding women's role within the private sphere, what can be learned about the multiple relations which sustain the ideo-logically motivated fantasy of a stable maternal identity? And lastly, what assumptions can be made about the power of television images to assert and destabilize such ostensibly immobile identities?

In order to explore these questions and their textual reverberations I want to look at an episode of *The Donna Reed Show*, an extremely popu-lar comedic series which aired on ABC from 1958 to 1966.[27] I choose this particular program for several reasons. To begin with, *The Donna Reed Show*, in many ways, is an exemplary specimen of the nuclear family situation comedies that dominated American television in the late 1950s and 1960s. It follows almost to the letter David Marc's definition of the sitcom's generic principles that frame comedic incidents within an essen-tially "conservative body of drama," the subject of which is American culture.[28] The humorous situations that ostensibly move the sitcom nar-rative forward thus remain "always a subordinate concern to the proper solution of ethical crises."[29] While *The Donna Reed Show* certainly meets Marc's general criteria, it differs from the traditional family sitcoms such as *Leave It to Beaver* by fixing "mother" at the center of most episodes. Unlike June Cleaver, whose marginal importance to the episodic narra-tive leaves her with little of central importance to do beyond suggesting that Ward "talk to the Beaver," Donna Reed's character, Donna Stone, is both mother and "star." Perhaps it is for this reason that she could afford a side to her character that I like to think of as Donna's "dark side." Not typically, but occasionally throughout the series, she is given moments of indignant resistance to the demands of housekeeping and care-giving. Usually her rebellions result from frustrations she experi-ences over the inequities of the familial gender hierarchy; however it is not the injustices themselves that occasion the humor of the plot, but the predicaments leading either to the inevitable resolution of the problem or to Donna's realization that she has perhaps been overreact-ing a little, although the rest of the family must also reconsider their own behavior on these occasions. As Ellen Seiter observes, it is often these "good-natured power struggles . . . or the 'battle of the sexes'" that makes for much of the humor in family situation comedies.[30] The comedic portrayal of infrequent "challenges to paternal authority," are, of course, inevitably resolved by mother's return to "mother," or to her happy complicity with the proper role. But when one watches Donna Reed closely, this performance seems at times to border on a kind of camp performance—a self-consciously stylized surrender to the social script, a script held in quotation marks by Donna's very insistence on acting it out with a kind of excessive sincerity that never precludes ironic undercuts or wry quips, often at the expense of her character.[31] What makes *The Donna Reed Show* a pleasurable television narrative capable of spanning generations of viewers is precisely this excess of gender performativity, our knowledge of the dark side that threatens to reveal itself, and our trust that in the end Donna will adhere to the script that our collective fantasies of the perfect mother have provided her with.

Such expectations are addressed in an episode of *The Donna Reed Show* that also teases out the oppositional patterns of contempt and idealization characteristic of the postwar representation of motherhood. The episode begins with the opening credit sequence, which even occasional viewers will likely remember. The sequence is structured around a vignette of what viewers may assume is a "typical" morning inside the Stone household. As the orchestrated theme music begins, the shots establish the setting: a tasteful middle-class home. The focus is on a staircase at the foyer, signaling that the Stones's home is spacious and the family is well-off. The actors and their characters are introduced one at a time as each descends the staircase. Donna Reed, the first to enter the frame, smiles toward the camera, looking through it but in no way acknowledging it. The camera remains transparent as she attends to the activity of children and husband as they prepare to exit the front door, thus crossing the boundary separating the cozy inner sanctum of home from the outside world of competition.

By presenting the actors in character, the opening sequence clearly establishes the roles each one plays within the family system. Donna oversees the smooth departure of each family member, distributing bagged lunches and sweaters. In this flurry of domestic activity, the theme music conceals the ring of the telephone, which Donna picks up and then promptly hands to her husband, Alex Stone (Carl Betz). From this image we can surmise the premise of husband's and wife's relationship: Alex holds the essential connection to the outside world. He elicits and responds to calls from the outside. Donna, on the other hand, remains silent, dutifully facilitating these connections, a mediating agent between her husband's need for a refuge and the public's need for his time and expertise.

The opening shots of *The Donna Reed Show* feature its star at the hub of brisk familial activity, however everything she does during the brief sequence is determined by the needs and desires of her husband and children. There is nothing unusual about this, as Press observes that early television mothers are "rarely (if ever) . . . shown to be mature, independent individuals. . . . [They] are consistently pictured almost exclusively in the domestic or private realm; rarely do they legitimately venture into the male, public world of work."[32] Alex Stone is so preoccupied with this public world of affairs that in a subsequent season's title sequence he forgets to kiss his wife good-bye as he and the children rush headlong out the door. In this sequence, Donna turns to face the camera and frowns as she shuts the door behind him. In an instant the door reopens and Alex kisses her. He exits again and Donna remains inside, alone, her family now dispersed. She leans against the door, folds her arms across her chest and sighs contentedly. The day is now her own: the "situation," whatever it holds, may now begin.

This final shot of the opening sequence leaves viewers with both the image of Donna's relentless good humor in the midst of hectic domesticity and of her isolation and refuge within the home. The busy routine of the morning—the frequent opening and closing of the front door during the sequence—emphasizes the gateway between inside and outside, which everyone except Donna hastens to pass through. Although Alex Stone's authoritative demeanor and hurried manner identify him as the paternal breadwinner, his syntactical relation to the children, and his momentary lapse of husbandly affection as he goes out the door, suggest that within the mother's sphere he is for all effective purposes a child himself. Clearly, Donna is "mother" to them all as she coordinates meals, warm clothes, and incoming calls, yet equally clear is the fact that she is a worker, in a sense, employed by them all. In short, Donna Reed's fantasy mother is a unit of indispensable labor power, as much a packaged commodity as the consumer goods sold during commercial "interruptions." Moreover, it is reasonable to say (as Ella Taylor does when she reminds us of Harriet Nelson selling Listerine, in character, between the acts of *The Adventures of Ozzie and Harriet*[33]) that commercials do not actually interrupt anything, but rather consolidate the ideology of consumerism that is the program's ultimate product. *The Donna Reed Show*, like other family situation comedies, constitutes a powerful advertisement for a "life-style" based on precisely this notion of seamless coherence between the world of maternal nurturance and the world of consumer usables: to attain this unity of function is to attain consensus, wholesomeness, nonflamboyant status, self-sufficiency. It is to be modern, yet fundamentally traditional.

Although it is reasonable to surmise, after watching enough episodes of *The Donna Reed Show*, that the images produced by the program reify the private sphere as the sphere of feminine feeling, virtue, and nurturance, my sense is that such readings are misreadings. Donna's devotion to family is, first and foremost, her devotion to work. Her commitment to her husband and family is her commitment, above all, to an employer. Alex Stone is a doctor; he is a professional care-giver; in a sense, what this indicates is that the spheres are not so separate for him, either. There is a mapping of the private onto his public role, and there is a mapping of the public world of work onto Donna's role. The difference is, of course, Donna is neither paid nor publicly recognized for her work. Donna's portrayal as the perfect mother is her portrayal as the perfect worker, happy to serve, the perfect corporate employee. Donna mothers and nurtures with incredible work-like efficiency, solving all problems in thirty minutes with a smile, never a hair out of place: the emphasis within the family is on maintaining a kind of corporate structure in which affections and nurturant relations matter; the familial sphere is thus seen as an extension of the public sphere. And as a result of this emphasis, Donna's realm of influence extends into the public sphere where, in some instances, she holds more authority than her husband.

Consider the following plot: Alex Stone, a successful pediatric physician, is scheduled to present a keynote speech at a professional dinner. Naturally, Donna will attend with him. However, on the day of the dinner Jeff Stone is appointed as a substitute first-string player for a school basketball game scheduled for that same evening. Jeff pleads with his mother to be there in the stands for him. A conflict ensues but is quickly resolved when Donna telephones Alex, at Jeff's insistence, and asks if he would mind if she missed the dinner to go to the basketball game. Always the understanding husband and father, Alex gives his consent. The matter appears to be put rest; however, moments later Mary Stone, the teenaged daughter, receives a letter informing her that she has been selected for membership in an exclusive and prestigious girl's club that she has desperately wanted to join. Her formal introduction ceremony is scheduled for that evening, and all the girls' mothers are requested to be in attendance with their daughters.

The central ethical conflict is thus defined: to whom does Mother most belong? There is pressure from both the children who insist that their events take precedence over all others. Alex does not formally enter into this debate until later in the plot; earlier an emissary from the hospital, his friend and colleague, Woody, "drops by" the house to warn Donna that she will likely jeopardize her husband's career if she misses the pediatricians' dinner. "Now, look, it's more important that you be at that meeting than Alex," he cautions. According to his theory, the wives of doctors play a greater role in shaping their husband's futures in Hillsdale medical society than the doctors themselves. He instructs her to "wear something attractive, but nothing the wives will consider overdressed." Donna responds to each of his directives with a sarcastic remark, suggesting, for example, that she might wear "a bikini with long, white gloves." Woody dismisses her sarcasm and issues the ultimatum, "I'll see you tonight. Tonight." Here we are shown, to borrow Jacques

Donzelot's phrase, the "policing of the family" by an external authority whose narrative purpose is to resolve internal instability.³⁴ Ultimately, the anxiety generated by this scene has less to do with the Donna's quandary than it does with the intrusion of an "outsider" into the sacred family space. Family decisions, it would appear, are a public as well as private matter. Alex's success in the patriarchal medical community depends not on what the other doctors or their wives think of him, but on the wives' mutual assessments of one another and on the social meanings they produce and exchange through appearance, dress, and public demeanor.

An apparent implosion of familial desires ultimately erupts. Alex, Jeff, and Mary battle it out for Mother's company. Pushed to the limit, Donna becomes angry and declares, "Oh, I give up. . . . Don't expect me to behave like mother of the year." She announces her decision to go nowhere with any of them. "I hope you all have a lovely time tonight. As for me, I'm getting into my toreador pants and go shoot billiards." We next see her languishing in bed, reading a fashion magazine and extending a desultory reach toward an open box of chocolates on her night table. The following scene depicts the repentant family as husband and children cautiously approach Donna—the maternal diva—to apologize for their thoughtlessness. They are all now determined to sacrifice Mother's company in order to restore peace in the household and soothe her wrangled nerves. Wives belong *with* their husbands, the children argue. But truly, Alex counters, mothers belong *to* their children. Conflicted and clearly moved by their concessions, Donna asks Alex to take the children "out of here." When they're gone, she asks herself aloud, "Why did they have to be so sweet?"

Finally, it would seem that it is not Donna's lack of a defined subject position within the family sphere, but an ambivalent subjectivity grounded in *both* public authority and a capacity for human sympathy that causes her to experience a change of heart. The climactic resolution of the narrative depicts Donna performing the miraculous task of appearing at all three functions. In the final analysis Mother belongs to everyone, but by her own volition, an act that establishes her as everywhere and nowhere in the family plot. Although she is never shown en route to any locations, we see her arrive in the nick of time at Alex's presentation, then slip out to appear next at Jeff's basketball game—just in time to see him make the winning basket—and subsequently land at the girl's club meeting where her anxious daughter sits dejectedly by an empty chair. Naturally, Mary's face lights up upon Donna's entrance as she joyfully introduces her as "my mother, Mrs. Alex Stone."

The concluding scene is set back in the Stone home. Dressed beautifully in elegant bedclothes—and miraculously still awake while everyone else has passed out from his or her respective activity—Donna silently observes her sleeping family, alone once again. As she climbs into her bed and closes her eyes, she hears—as we do—a symphony of familial voices calling out to her, echoing her name: "Mother . . . Mom . . . Donna." She sighs and smiles peacefully while the picture fades to black.

Several points need to be made. Chief among these is the image of Donna Stone viewers are left with at the end of the episode. The sleeping mother, smiling as her subconscious reproduces the voices that had been driving her consciously crazy during the day's hectic events, suggests that even below the psychic surface—or especially below it—there is nothing to worry about, no repressed conflicts liable to explode, no domestic rebellions stewing. In short, what we see is what we get; fantasy can aspire to offer no more than what reality already offers, so why aspire? Responding to her family's needs is a mother's pleasure, whether awake or dreaming. Such seemingly transparent contradictions are generally at the core of television's efforts to resolve gender instability in the representation of postwar motherhood.[35]

This particular episode also stresses the centrality of food preparation and kitchen table intimacy. The opening scene shows Donna making breakfast and attempting to serve Alex through the newspaper that claims his attention and blocks her access to his plate. Like most television mothers of the period, we rarely see Donna eating much herself, nor do we see her engaged in stressful and laborious housework.[36] Her attentions remain for the most part completely fixed on her family, although her family's attentions remain fixed on events external to the kinship group. As Donna serves eggs, her husband and children remain transfixed, each reading his or her own section of the newspaper. They share an engagement with public discourse, a connection to the external, nondomestic world of affairs, a connection that Donna undermines as she suggests sarcastically to Alex that he cut a whole in the paper through which she might then serve his food.

Jeff Stone enters the kitchen dribbling an imaginary basketball. As he leaves for school, still dribbling, his mother asks, "Well, if you see anyone I know, will you please explain to them what you're doing." The canned laughter that follows her remark plays off Jeff's developing sense of masculine competition, but also reflects Donna's concern that family members—particularly a doctor's family—appear "normal" to the community. Mother's function is to maintain these appearances of consensus; if the community thinks Jeff is nuts, Donna knows she'll likely be the one who takes the blame. Jeff Stone winces at his mother's displays of physical affection. He recoils when she tries to kiss him good-bye, asking if she will always have the authority to do so and demonstrating that he is successfully negotiating the Oedipal passage to male adulthood. Jeff's urgent desire to be chosen by the basketball coach reflects his need for masculine approval, just as Mary's wish to be chosen for membership in the girl's club demonstrates her need for masculine approval, the social status that will grant her access to a distinctive class of available males. While Mary's status will be mediated by the community of young women, Jeff's status must be won directly and publicly on the basketball court where he must demonstrate his preparedness for aggressive action. While Jeff waits and hopes that one of his teammates will break so that he will get a chance to play rather than warm the bench, as he has the past four games, Mary waits to find out whether she will be accepted into the popular clique. The children's similar concerns are constructed differently according to a spatial distinction that metaphorically maintains the separation of masculine/feminine, inside/outside. While Jeff hopes for his chance to perform, to dazzle the crowd in the stands, Mary hopes to be ensconced within the protective shell of the club. The reproduction of masculine and feminine roles ensures that Jeff, like his father, will eventually get *out* onto the court, while Mary will eventually get *in* to the very private, very exclusive sphere of female relationships, relationships that will ultimately help determine her value on the marriage market.

The reproduction of gender categories within the context of the family requires that same-gender members share a special language, or rhetorical currency, that helps constitute gender difference. Entering the kitchen wearing her new dress, Mary confides in Donna her intention to "give one of the boys at school a piece of my mind." The dress, she explains, "gives a woman a certain advantage." "Yes, it does," Donna agrees. Here, the construction of femininity presumes a vulnerable male sexuality that debilitates rational discursive capacities and makes them fair game for intimidation. Rather than positioning herself purely as spectacle for the male gaze, Mary understands that mind and body work cooperatively in the constitution of a feminine subject who wields influence in the public sphere. Later, during the conflict over Alex's habit of reading the newspaper at the breakfast table, Donna warns, "If you aren't careful I'm going to put on my new dress." Alex doesn't understand the meaning of the remark. Donna acknowledges that Mary, her daughter, understands precisely what it means. "I know you're trying to get through to me," Alex admits, "If I could only break the code." To his son, he explains, "Women are sensitive and enigmatic creatures." Surprised and empowered by this definition, Jeff turns to his sister and demands, "Pass the butter, creature." Later, Alex reiterates woman's essential unintelligibility. "You know, sometimes I lose you," he tells Donna. "Is this the inner depth that no woman reveals even to her husband?" In the positioning of woman as mystery, as enigma, as creature, we hear reverberations of Freud's infamous question: "What does the woman want?" The knowing viewer, however, is made privy to the code that male characters find mysterious, threatening, and incomprehensible. Viewers, regardless of gender, are thus invited into identifications with the feminine. These identifications are clearly not based in anatomy, but in the ability to engage and interpret symbolic strategies and codes that baffle Dr. Stone, the medical authority. In this way, viewers—like Mary Stone in her new dress—are given "a certain advantage" over a public sphere becoming increasingly determined by corporate interests.

As speaker before the Hillsdale medical society, Alex Stone figures as agent of the patriarchal medical establishment and its regulatory discourses. He is a master of scientific rhetoric, a spokesman for the medicalization of the family. The subject of Dr. Stone's lecture to the association of pediatricians is "the anxieties of children on their first visit to a pediatrician's office." His message is clear: the anxiety experienced by children on their first visit to the doctor has nothing to do with the doctor and everything to do with the child's mother. It is her overemotional and overprotective response to the situation that upsets the child. Although it may be the mother's intention to protect the child, she has just the opposite effect. The address references Philip Wylie in its emphasis on the destructive effects of overmothering. Here, as in Wylie's attack against American women, smothering mothers are accused of creating a generation of neurotics. Dr. Stone's conclusion, which derives from a former professor of his, wins laughter and applause from his listeners: "Give the baby a lollypop and the mother a sedative."

Alex Stone is certainly not the first fictional American doctor to recommend mastery over women through the administration of drugs, but given our awareness of the historical victimization of women by the conservative medical establishment it is hard to imagine a contemporary viewer hearing this comment without some agitation. The construction of American motherhood as, on one hand, intrinsically nurturant, and on the other hand, hysterical and emotionally overwrought, requiring the intervention of modern medicine, reminds us of the blatant contradiction that is the cult of maternal worship, our inheritance from the Victorian period. To the extent that nuclear family television sitcoms, like all cultural forms, enact a dialogue with such social contradictions, we see the signifying value of "mother" defined by early television as a complex collusion of desires that alternately reproduce and disrupt our traditional sense of the boundary dividing public and private spheres.[37] Could Laing have been thinking of the effects of family television on hapless family viewers when he wrote: "We are acting parts in a play that we have never read and never seen, whose plot we don't know, whose existence we can glimpse, but whose beginning and end are beyond our present imagination and conception."[38] I would venture to guess not.[39] But Alex Stone's admonition to give the mother a sedative clearly demonstrates how the cultural inscription of the Laingian "mother" is a fantasy built not only on the troublesome anxiety of children, but on widespread social anxiety induced by the perceived incongruity of the family and the "family."

In the mid-1960s, as political and social unrest escalated across the nation, anxieties produced over racial, ethnic, and gender difference were nevertheless filtered through television via the popular phenomenon of family sitcoms featuring magical, monstrous, or otherwise weird families. From the unbelievably "normal" families of the fifties, we move to *The Munsters, The Addams Family, My Favorite Martian, My Mother the Car*, and *Bewitched*. These equally unbelievable families composed of witches, ghosts, ghouls, and aliens certainly suggest television's own confusion over the boundaries of social normality, as previously defined.[40] These shows provided an autocritique—something television has mastered over the decades—on network packaging and marketing of the American Dream represented by the socially insipid Cleavers and the Nelsons. In this way, family structure and relation within the private sphere continued to provide a "central allegory for social life."[41] However, at this particular historical juncture these shows needed to be read as allegories of difference, differences that networkers were not yet willing to risk dealing with more directly.

As the civil rights and women's movements worked to shift the axis of legible identity from cultural "consensus" to cultural "difference," the social anxieties that surfaced found a sort of displaced representation in family sitcoms such as *Bewitched*. This series centered on the comic misadventures of a young advertising executive who enters into a "mixed" marriage when his fiancée reveals that she is a witch. The series first aired in 1964 on ABC and throughout its eight-year run developed humorous plot situations around the inside/outside tension that results from Darrin Stevens's need to keep Samantha's heritage of witchcraft a secret. *My Favorite Martian*, another popular program that features an "extraordinary" family, operates according to much the same principle, only in this case the "controversial" relation is an alien uncle from Mars. On both shows, nosy neighbors like Mr. and Mrs. Kravitz (*Bewitched*) and Mrs. Brown (*My Favorite Martian*) threaten the structural separation of private and public sphere, inside and outside the family, by peering endlessly through their shutters or by arriving unannounced with platters of freshly baked brownies, all in an effort to expose the secret they know inheres within the "other" household.

These secrets, which closely resemble Eve Kosofsky Sedgwick's definition of "open-secret structures," may be read as complex metaphors of knowledge that threaten an already crumbling social status quo.[42] For the young, upwardly mobile Stevenses on *Bewitched*, the unspeakable truth that Darrin can only repress by policing Samantha's magical powers is the illusion of masculine authority in the public sphere. Indeed, Samantha is far more effective in the business world than he is, seeing as how she can sell campaigns with a mere twitch of her nose. Thus, for Darrin, the weekly struggle involves how to maintain his precarious masculine position in the bureaucratized public sphere by insisting that his wife conform to the demands of the corporate ethic, even when she is in the privacy of her own home. A good "organization man," Darrin insists that Samantha surrender her privacy and her "difference," thus mirroring the moral dilemma that social critics like Whyte identified as a neurosis of major proportions central to the fifties, a general loss of self for the good of the system. *Bewitched* questioned this consensus-dominated ethos allegorically, week after week, as viewers waited for Samantha to once again disobey patriarchal law and reclaim the power of difference, only to promise Darrin at the end of each episode that she will repress her supernatural "nature" and never do it again. But inevitably, viewer pleasure is produced and reproduced through the knowledge that she will yield to what is natural for her as a witch. She will "out" the family again, thus revealing the essential instability of gender and social space.[43] Later in the series, when Samantha and Darrin give birth to a daughter, Tabitha, the discovery that she has inherited her mother's witchcraft shifts the Oedipal power axis of familial inheritance from father to mother.

Thus the bemoaning of lost masculinity that informed earlier popular nonfiction works such as Philip Wylie's *Generation of Vipers* and Christopher Lasch's *Haven in a Heartless World* are effectively celebrated in *Bewitched*. In its fifty-year history television has affirmed not only the masculinization of the familial sphere but the feminization of the workplace: it has indicated, albeit in uneven and ambiguous ways, that the most important work men and women perform is in the home, and that the most familial, caring relationships are to be found in the marketplace. A recent advertisement for Wal-Mart features testimony from an elderly woman and devoted patron who speaks of visiting her local Wal-Mart when she is lonely or just needs to get out of the house. At Wal-Mart, she is among people who are friendly and helpful. The commercial invites our respect for Wal-Mart, clearly a corporation that places humanistic concerns before net profit. At the same time the advertisement clearly exploits female viewers' fears of getting old, of finding themselves alone without the assistance or support of the young families with whom, and for whom, they once shopped. However, the Wal-Mart shopper finds an extension of those lost relationships in consumerism, a discovery the woman affirms at the checkout counter as she confides, "I've already had three hugs since I've been here."

At their best, such commercial narratives serve as fractured lenses through which, on one hand, we may view the regulatory processes of indoctrination into a mutual ideology of consumerism and familialism, while on the other hand, we view the forces of resistance to reactionary domestic values. This "cultural dilemma" was one of the predominant themes of the television work-family, a phenomenon typical of 1970s television programming. According to Taylor, television work-families like those portrayed on sitcoms such as *Taxi, Barney Miller, WKRP in Cincinnati, Alice, M*A*S*H*, and *The Mary Tyler Moore Show* express, "on the one hand, the yearning for meaning and community in the workplace, and on the other, the fear of the power of corporations and of professionals in corporate settings," a fear that television depicted as "a vague but pervasive post-Watergate mistrust by ordinary Americans of the political and economic institutions that shaped their lives from a great distance."[44]

Premiering in 1970, *The Mary Tyler Moore Show* transplanted the private sphere to the public sphere, where single career woman Mary Richards formed a functional kinship structure while working for a local Minneapolis TV news station. Throughout the series, Mary worries about being thirty, unmarried, and childless, yet the show was emphatically about the possibility of happiness found outside the conventional nuclear family.[45] The workplace is mapped over with many of the typical attributes of the domestic setting: the newsroom becomes the kitchen, the center of familial activity, crisis, and resolution. Here characters hang out, chat for what seems endless hours, make dates over the phone, work out personal conflicts, reveal their deepest fears and yearnings.

In one episode, "Murray Faces Life," a former high-school classmate of Murray's wins the Pulitzer Prize for journalism, and Murray falls suddenly into despair over his lack of professional accomplishment. The plot hinges on the newsroom's handling of Murray's depression and Mary's belief that she must responsibly nurture him back to happiness in spite of her emotional awkwardness and her reluctance to violate Murray's personal boundaries. Repeatedly throughout the series, we see Mary attending to the bruised masculine egos of the underappreciated newsroom staff. With the exception of Ted Baxter, who plays the infantile narcissist kept in check by Mary's maternal care-giving, Lou Grant's paternal dominance, and Murray's fraternal jocularity, the journalistic principles of WJM-TV employees are similarly shaped by her nurturant concerns. Clearly, these are professionals we can trust to bring us the news and report it truthfully. As a newswriter, Murray would never dream of manipulating his audience or falsifying information, no more than

Mary, as associate producer, would ever dream of compromising human relationships for ratings. In spite of his temper and lack of patience, Lou Grant defines paternal authority in terms of loyalty, honesty, and experience.

These "homey" values are reinforced in an episode entitled, "Mary's Aunt Returns," which features Eileen Heckart as Mary's Aunt Flo, an occasional character and seasoned female journalist who enjoys a competitive, albeit flirtatious, relationship with Lou Grant. In this episode, Aunt Flo challenges Lou to a professional competition when a story the staff has been preparing on "a-day-in-the-life-of-an-average-American-family" unexpectedly backfires. The family who has agreed to be the subject of the story announces, midway through production, that they are getting a divorce. Aunt Flo believes this makes the story even better. She argues for incorporating the divorce into the project, shifting the emphasis to show how a family copes with marital breakup. Lou argues for suppressing the divorce and going ahead with the story as originally planned, with the material they've been able to gather. He calls Flo's approach a "cheap exploitation of human tragedy," an accusation with which Flo heartily agrees, adding that all journalism is exploitation of human tragedy. Consequently, Flo and Lou break up into teams, each to produce her/his own version of the story for the station managers to judge. Forced to make the difficult choice between her aunt and her boss, Mary elects to work with Lou while Murray teams up with Flo.

This plot situation, in addition to testing Mary's familial allegiances, also rehearses television's own ethical dilemma over the broadcast of the cinéma vérité documentary series, *An American Family.* Indeed, it is possible that no American television event of the postwar decades conveyed a sense of the performativity of the family plot, the collapse of separate spheres, and the conflation of ideological and psychological production more powerfully than this controversial twelve-part series. Produced by Craig Gilbert and aired on PBS in 1973, the series provoked a number of ethical and aesthetic questions. Were scenes from the Loud family's "real life" taken out of context or edited so as to change the meaning? Did the Loud family react differently to events, and to one another, or were their behaviors in some way influenced by of the presence of the camera and the microphone? Were the Louds performing for an audience? Was the eventual divorce of Bill and Pat Loud a result of the filming?[46]

Whether it was or not, one can easily gauge television's own anxiety over these questions and over its impact on the "reality" of the family by reading between the lines of the *Mary Tyler Moore* episode that mirrors the ethical predicament of *An American Family.* Of course, at the conclusion of the *Mary Tyler Moore* narrative, Lou and Mary's version of the story "wins" final approval and is broadcast. The family is protected from crude public exploitation, the values of privacy and human decency are preserved, and the tensions created by television's ability to construct and deconstruct cultural norms is resolved. However, at the same time, Mary's decision to reject her aunt as mentor and align herself with Lou's journalistic philosophy suggests that these moral choices specifically benefit and preserve an image of masculine authority in both the family and work sphere. Still, the dilemma raised by *An American Family* persists and becomes mapped onto the question of whose text, Lou's or Flo's, is the authorized one: How much of this authority is truth, and how much of it is a fiction created by the editorial/political leanings of the filmmakers/station managers? Indeed, one wonders if in fact family life in the age of television isn't guided or organized by the images of family that we have internalized from its electronic reproduction. Do families think, when they are having a fight, "This isn't dramatic enough," and feel somehow cheated? Do families look to television and film drama for a gauge of how they should act or respond in emotional situations? "To have meaning," says Simon Frith, "emotions must be shaped, and this is as much a public as a private process."[47]

Two years ago I sat before my television and, like two-thirds of viewers nationwide, witnessed the final episode of *Cheers*. The series ended with the scriptwriter making a noble effort to resolve the affairs of most of the central characters. Sam Malone decides to stay in Boston with his barroom family at Cheers rather than follow his long-time romantic interest, Diane Chambers, to California, the land of opportunity and the home of the television industry. Cheers is his home and his job; it's where he belongs and it's where he ultimately decides to remain. However, what interested me about "Cheers: The Last Call," was its striking similarity to another significant moment in television history that took place sixteen years earlier, the final episode of *The Mary Tyler Moore Show*. In both episodes, the ensemble casts are brought together for one last time to share the revelation that what they have established over the years is not just friendship: they are a family. In "The Last Show" of *The Mary Tyler Moore Show*, during the cast's final moments in the newsroom after getting fired, Mary asks, "What is a family anyway?" She answers her own question: "They're just people who make you feel less alone and really loved." The loneliness she refers to is ostensibly the loneliness she feels when she is at home. However, Mary had to come to terms with second-wave feminism and a transposition of the "Donna Reed" image in order to find her family and reinvent television's image of the perfect mother.

Although critics are correct, I think, in citing *The Mary Tyler Moore Show* as an example of television's tendency in the late 1970s to define the work sphere as a viable alternative to—or displacement of—the deconstructed mythology of the perfect family, the burden of unification remains predominantly on the female character who, at the same time, must reckon with feminist pressures to pursue personal fulfillment. This dualism was built into the opening signature sequence of images that shift quickly from the interior of Mary's apartment (where she engages in intimate banter with female regulars, Rhoda and Phyllis), to downtown Minneapolis (where she window-shops and expresses discernible frustration over the cost of meat), to the newsroom (where she embraces the male regulars, Lou, Murray, and Ted, one by one). However, that it is indeed possible to achieve both home and the world is affirmed weekly by the image of Mary exuberantly tossing her tam-o'-shanter into the air.

Yet, we leave Mary Richards, like we leave Sam Malone, contentedly single, biological clocks still ticking. However, unlike Sam, whose ability to remain with his family affirms the need for a strong masculine presence in the third sphere, Mary must leave her family and move on to a new job in the wake of WJM-TV's demise, which may or may not lead to a big advancement in her career. However, as the sentimental Wal-Mart shopper teaches us, a woman's journey out to the public marketplace in search of new forms of personal gratification requires more than a new car or a few hugs, but a negotiation of the limits of familial and market space. Television's romance with the family thus reveals how the conceptual tools of cultural inquiry—or the questioning of private-public separation—are continuously appropriated for the mass marketing and distribution of the family plot.

Chapter 4
The Culture of "Momism":
Evan S. Connell's *Mrs. Bridge*

Almost instantly after India Bridge delivers her firstborn child, a daughter, she asks: "Is she normal?" The question reverberates throughout Evan S. Connell's finely crafted work of minimalist fiction, *Mrs. Bridge.* "Do you want to be different from everyone else?" She warns her son when he rebels against the use of conventional table etiquette.[1] Such warnings reflect the pathological fear of cultural difference that compels the lives of most of the adult characters, especially the female characters, of the novel. Unity, sameness, consensus, centeredness: these are the imperatives of the upper-middle-class, conservative, Kansas City social elite—the only world Mrs. Bridge has ever known. They are also the values Mrs. Bridge tries to reproduce in her three children through a compulsory repetition of performative acts and signifying codes aimed at preserving a cultural tableau of domestic unity, a portrait precariously balanced atop an emphatic shift in the figuration of the Oedipal mother, from a repository image of national productivity and reproductivity toward a repository image of ideological exhaustion, social fragmentation, and cultural redescription.[2]

Motherhood is itself a culturally and historically fluid construct that has served since the eighteenth century as a historical receptacle for social ambivalence and conflict with regard to changes in the institutionalization of childhood, shifting economic patterns, realignments of private and public space, and the scientific reification of human "instinct" and "nature."[3] The emergence of an organized feminist movement in the United States and the evolution of feminist criticism and theory in this century have highlighted maternity's status as a contestatory field, its level of turbulence contingently motored by specific contexts, occasions, or questions that provide a catalyst around which discursive battles are waged.[4] *Mrs. Bridge* builds its maternal critique around the moral and spiritual isolation of the domestic sphere and the structural equation of this sphere with the abstract figure of the American mother and house-wife. Although the novel is set in the American Midwest between the First and Second World Wars, the social issues Connell addresses—sub-urbanization, racism, the feminine mystique, the decadence of the bour-geois family—and the colorless female protagonist whose unexamined life he memorializes bear the distinctive markings of the postwar and cold war era. The novel's publication in 1959 suggests that Connell may have appropriated the modern period in order to displace his critique of emerging postwar, postmodern cultural and aesthetic developments. Indeed, if the Bridges seem somewhat out of place in relation to their setting, it stands to reason that such displacements afford Connell the distance he might have needed to construct this bitter referendum on the grand narratives of white, bourgeois, American patriarchy and its mixture of idealization and contempt toward motherhood.[5]

In this sense, *Mrs. Bridge* may be read as an attempt to deconstruct modernist tropes and cultural fantasies such as the phallic mother, a figure that took on new nuances of meaning in the context of women's increasing participation in the public sphere, and the public sphere's increasing infiltration into the private sphere through the mass media, domestic technologies, and advertising.[6] A massive postwar reorgani-zation of industrial space, which placed traditional masculine roles in jeopardy, produced a plethora of "crisis" texts that sought to transfer the source of conflict from the marketplace to the home, or more spe-cifically in some instances to women and mothers.[7] For example, in 1947, in research that might itself be read as a symptom of cultural post-traumatic stress, Marynia Farnham and Ferdinand Lundberg blamed American mothers for psychiatric disorders that resulted in the mili-tary's rejection or discharge of more than two million men during World War II.[8] Earlier, in 1942, Philip Wylie coined the term, "Momism," a con-dition defined in his diatribe against American womanhood, *Generation of Vipers*. This document sings the litany of indignities cruelly perpetu-ated by American mothers against American men, a species of being all but lost to "megaloid momworship." According to Wylie, American women have morally "raped" their sons and husbands, turned them into "slaves," drained from their spirits all vestiges of an essential masculine barbarism, and pickpocketed them for every cent they're worth. Having escaped the nursery and forced her way to the ballot box, the American Mom has brought upon the male nation "a new all-time low in political scurviness, hoodlumism, gangsterism, labor strife, monopolistic thug-gery, moral degeneration, civic corruption, smuggling, bribery, theft, murder, homosexuality, drunkenness, financial depression, chaos and war."[9]

The "angel in the house," in this context, would seem to have exhausted her period of usefulness in properly signifying cultural balance and wholeness.[10] As a post-family romance, *Mrs. Bridge* addresses this exhaustion by figuring the Oedipal mother as a transitional trope caught between modernism's belief in aesthetic autonomy and a postmodern aesthetic of conflict and loss of agency. *Mrs. Bridge* proceeds to tell the story of a woman who, like the phallic mother, "has it all," but suffers from some nameless malaise, an inarticulate longing, much like the future "everywoman" of Betty Friedan's *The Feminine Mystique* (1963). Connell's novel, which preceded Friedan's critique of the advertising industry's representation of women by four years, anticipates the de-centering of consensual discourses about family, gender, and domestic space and at the same time suggests the cultural emergence of new possibilities for representing the female subject.[11] The full exploration of these possibilities, sanctioned with John F. Kennedy's 1961 Presidential Commission on the Status of Women, is culturally articulated in the figure of the "self-reflective housewife," a figure suggesting both an increased awareness of the obstacles preventing women from full participation in the public sphere and recognition of the ways these obstacles develop in proportion to the difficulties many women were experiencing at home.[12]

Although *Mrs. Bridge* enjoyed a brief resurgence of popularity with the recent appearance of the Merchant and Ivory film adaptation, the novel has never received the close critical attention it deserves. Admittedly, a part of the problem is Connell's minimalist aesthetic, "an effort to reveal or expose by way of negating the real."[13] What *Mrs. Bridge* has to say it generally says with silences, gaps, halting moments of psychic and emotional paralysis in which we see Mrs. Bridge grasping for responses and meanings that ultimately elude her. Connell's stylistic edge is maintained by narrative "sharp cutting," like photographs too closely cropped, so that subjects appear boldly detached from "background, history, even choice."[14] However, choices—or rather, the suppression of alternative cultural formations of subjectivity and maternity within the family plot— are precisely what the novel draws some readers to consider. And I want to suggest that the real difficulty in reading *Mrs. Bridge* is not a lack of information, but rather an explosion of silences that constitute within the text failed attempts to mask the existence of competing maternal ideologies, conflictive practices of production and reproduction, all of which define the post-family romance. The private sphere's inability to suppress these conflicts or contain them within the figure of the mother *is* the crisis to which *Mrs. Bridge* offers a critical response. Connell, in other words, says too little precisely in order to say what, in 1959, had not yet been named: the Oedipal mother, the moral and emotional service center of the family, is a bankrupt trope.

But why is it that such knowledge is communicable only so long as it is withheld? One way of apprehending this paradox is to consider that Mrs. Bridge is a character caught in an excruciating double bind, what D. A. Miller has termed an "open-secret structure." As Eve Kosofsky Sedgwick has argued vis-à-vis Miller's formulation, it is necessary to determine the strategies by which certain textual meanings are "closeted" to the effect that "silence is rendered as pointed and performative as speech."[15] Clearly, this seems to be the case with *Mrs. Bridge,* a text that commands the effects of domestic silence to "collude or compete" with public discourses that become increasingly loud as the novel progresses, discourses that Mrs. Bridge might read about in popular women's magazines but wouldn't dare speak of at home. Mrs. Bridge, in this regard, is a character overdetermined by spatial politics that harness her to epistemological assumptions at odds with her own inarticulate desires. Her mother function—according to the consensual demands of the private sphere—requires her commitment to stabilizing binaristic categories weakened by historical circumstance, categories that construct domestic unity as the "other" to an increasingly chaotic public heterogeneity.

Such structurings of the domestic sphere, like Sedgwick's structuring of the closet, constitute, in D. A. Miller's words, a "subjective practice in which the oppositions of private/public, inside/outside, subject/object are established, and the sanctity of their first term kept inviolate. And the phenomenon of the 'open-secret' does not, as one might think, bring about the collapse of those binarisms and their ideological effects, but rather attests to their fantasmatic recovery."[16] In *Mrs. Bridge,* the structural opposition of private/public and its coextensive assignment of compulsory gender roles remains partially fixed as a result of numerous sustained open secrets, secrets whose names are never spoken: sexism, racism, homophobia, class indifference. On one hand, the emergence of feminism's second wave, the civil rights movement, the movement for homosexual rights are deferred by the narrative's historical positioning; on the other hand, the novel anticipates the incitation to admit cultural difference and fragmentation precisely in its insistence on deferring it and displacing it. Thus, the novel challenges and at the same time recuperates the cultural status quo, forming a flash point of confluence where discursive possibilities are positioned to collide and compete with one another, while conserving yet questioning our cultural fantasies of familial unity and consensus. In this sense, *Mrs. Bridge* is a narrative true to the Freudian formulation of family romance, a cultural allegory of patriarchal loss and recuperation. However, the novel also literalizes the meaning of "bridge," as it connects the family romance to new cultural situations and historical inscriptions that demand its reconsideration. Thus, the novel re-aestheticizes the Oedipal mother as an abject figure, not of power or powerlessness, but of inconsequence in a world where immanence, continuity, and coherence—all values attributed to her—are no longer the reliable givens of cultural life and familial representation.

For example, in a section of the novel entitled, "Very Gay Indeed," Ruth Bridge, the eldest daughter, comes home for an unexpected visit from New York City where she lives in her own apartment and works as an assistant editor. Mrs. Bridge is proud of her daughter's new sophisticated, independent character, yet she worries over the fact that she and Ruth seem to have nothing to say to one another. In passing conversation toward the end of her visit, Ruth mentions to her mother that one of her coworkers is homosexual. "Just what do you mean, Ruth?" Mrs. Bridge asks.

> "Why, he's gay, Mother. Queer. You know."
> "I'm afraid I don't know," said Mrs. Bridge.
> Ruth could not tell whether her mother was serious or not. The idea of her mother not knowing was too incredible, and yet, thinking back . . . and after a long probing look into her mother's eyes, Ruth knew her mother was speaking the truth. This realization so shocked her that she said coldly, "Then it's time you found out." Feeling cruel and nervous and frightened, she continued, in the same tone, "I'm very fond of him, Mother. One morning he brought me a dozen long-stemmed roses." (218)

This passage addresses the complex intersection of "momism" and homophobia, as Mrs. Bridge's closeting in a society that preserves her lack of sexual knowledge, her ignorance of sexual difference, is juxtaposed alongside Ruth's outing of a coworker with whom she apparently shares more camaraderie than with her mother. Further indicated here is the daughter's resentment toward her mother's "lack" of multiple knowledges, a form of castration that renders Mrs. Bridge unable to produce judgments or promote differing values since she has no idea of what the oppositional alternatives are. Still, Ruth's introduction of a homosexual narrative into an otherwise "uncontaminated" heterosexual narrative space suggests that the familial sphere that Mrs. Bridge occupies is being opened to reinterpretation.

Perhaps as a consequence of this openness, Mrs. Bridge often has the funny feeling that she is being watched by outsiders. She experiences the vague sense that her life is a public performance, and that her performance is being critically inspected by neighbors, friends, and acquaintances. However unwittingly, she has mastered the art of "voguing" long before the drag balls that Jennie Livingston documents in *Paris Is Burning*.[17] However, unlike the ballroom walkers, Mrs. Bridge is unaware that her identity hangs between scare quotes. Her dissociation from her own parodic practices and the family's collective denial of her refusal to accept responsibility for her aesthetics of self-formation finally alienate her children to the point of hostility and indifference. As she watches her son grow into a cold and distant young man, Mrs. Bridge has the dim recognition that "she had lost his love, she knew not why" (208). Ruth Bridge, when asked by her lover if she resembles her mother, snaps, "She's my sister's mother!" (222). And sister Carolyn, who seems the most destined of the three children to emulate her mother, bluntly insists that "no man is ever going to push me around the way Daddy pushes you around" (251).

"Daddy," or Walter Bridge, is a successful Kansas City lawyer who spends most of his time at the office. When at home he occupies himself with the newspaper. Connell's portrayal of Walter Bridge, largely unrealized until the 1969 sequel, *Mr. Bridge*, is of a conservative, rigid, and emotionally inarticulate patriarch whose word is law. "Don't let me catch you whining," he warns Douglas, when he complains that the church basketball coach plays favorites. "This country operates on the principle that the more industry and intelligence a man applies to his job the more he is entitled to profit. I hope it never changes" (207). As a husband, he is equally "principled" and given to opulent displays of his entitlements, many of which take the form of ostentatious gifts to his wife: a Lincoln, an ermine coat, a diamond necklace. Embarrassed by the attention such extravagant gifts elicit from the community, Mrs. Bridge is relieved when for her forty-eighth birthday Walter simply takes her out to dinner at the club, whereupon he proudly announces that they will soon be embarking on a six-week tour of Europe. Mrs. Bridge's surprise is quickly offset by an incident that juxtaposes the cultural violence of their marriage with the natural violence of an approaching midwestern storm. While the Bridges are dining, the steward stops at their table to inform them that a tornado has been seen heading directly toward the country club and they had best take shelter in the basement with the other patrons until the danger has passed. Refusing to look up, Walter Bridge says, "I'm going to finish this steak" (161). The winds begin to howl, and soon everyone has evacuated the dining room except for Mr. and Mrs. Bridge. Mrs. Bridge looks anxiously at her husband. He looks around the room for more butter; Mrs. Bridge jumps up to grab some from an abandoned table. The lights go out and they remain:

It did not occur to Mrs. Bridge to leave her husband and run to the basement. She had been brought up to believe without question that when a woman married she was married for the rest of her life and was meant to remain with her husband wherever he was, and under all circumstances, unless he directed her otherwise. (163)

As Walter Bridge continues to eat, his wife listens abstractly to the sounds of the tempest rushing toward them. "Well, that must be the tornado," she offhandedly remarks:

She spread her napkin in her lap again although she had finished eating; she spread it because when she was a child her parents had taught her it was impolite to place her napkin on the table until everyone had finished, and the manners she had been taught she had, in turn, passed on to her own children. (163)

This section entitled, "Tornado at the Club," suggests in its very title the interconnectedness of the socially opposed forces of nature and culture. Mrs. Bridge's apparent lack of a self-preservation instinct is darkly comical, not so much because she is so indifferent to her own safety, but because the encroaching forces of nature ultimately prove to be no match for the forces of nurture, as Mrs. Bridge indicates when she reflects on the familial preservation of proper napkin habits rather than on the potentially life-threatening storm. As if Walter Bridge had successfully called its bluff, the tornado dissolves into the sky, but not before it renders absurd any adherence to the belief that nature commands power or compels gender. Also rendered absurd are the gallant images and gestures associated with the bourgeois idealization of modern romance and the egalitarian marriage contract. Although materially a "good provider," Walter Bridge gives nothing by way of affection or validation of his wife's emotional and physical needs. Thus, Mrs. Bridge learns that "while marriage may be an equitable affair, love itself [is] not" (3). This inequity bothers Mrs. Bridge most when she later realizes that Walter has managed to forge a close, mutually affectionate relationship with the children while she has failed to win their love and friendship. She is "struck by their easy companionship, as though they had gotten to know each other quite well when she was not around" (157). Sensing a kind of conspiracy in their comfort, Mrs. Bridge is drawn even more deeply into her silence and isolation, never realizing that it is precisely this perpetual sacrifice of self that makes it impossible for her children to know her.

Mrs. Bridge demonstrates that the culturally ambiguous representation of postwar motherhood, like the conditions of the closet itself, are performances "initiated as such by the speech act of a silence—not a particular silence, but a silence that accrues particularity by fits and starts, in relation to the discourse that surrounds and differentially constitutes it."[18] Such "fits and starts" accurately define Mrs. Bridge's frequent failed attempts to speak, to name her problem. These advances toward and retreats from asserting her individuality are reflected in the structural composition of the text. The novel is assembled in narrative bits—fits and starts. The text is composed of 117 sections, or microchapters. Each chapter is systematically numbered, titled, and framed to create the effect of looking at a family photograph, a moment frozen in time and space. We see Mrs. Bridge indoctrinating her children into the rules of proper etiquette, attempting cross-cultural self-improvement via hobbyism (she takes up Spanish lessons with a learn-at-home album kit, but loses interest after the second lesson), taking painting lessons, perusing *The Tattler* (a Kansas City society magazine), dining at the country club, chitchatting at friends' cocktail parties, throwing her own cocktail parties, traveling abstractly through Europe (in the Louvre, it occurs to her that all tapestries, Greek vases, and mummies look exactly alike), attending meetings of the Ladies' Auxiliary, delivering instructions to the maid, gossiping, worrying about what others are saying about her, and doing charitable work for the poor (while assisting in the distribution of secondhand clothing, Mrs. Bridge wears protective gloves).

Thus, as in Sherwood Anderson's *Winesburg, Ohio*, a text whose meanings are also determined by its structural fragmentation, there can be traced in *Mrs. Bridge* a reiterated emphasis on the fear or failure of those moments that offer the greatest promise of human contact, of touching hands with another human being. From an aesthetic standpoint, what matters to both Anderson and Connell is the gravity of the moment itself. For Alfred Kazin, Anderson's revelation that "the true history of life is but a history of moments," bespeaks the modernist *Geist* in a self-styled aesthetic manifesto, distinctly public yet at the same time distinctly private in its very reliance on the illumination of sudden, individual perceptions.[19] Kazin explains: "For if 'the true history of life was but a history of moments,' it followed that the dream of life could be captured only in a fiction that broke with rules of structure literally to embody moments, to suggest the endless halts and starts, the dreamlike passiveness and groping of life."[20] *Mrs. Bridge* inherits this philosophy of form, specifically redeployed here as a means of testing the traditionally unifying structures of domestic fiction and family romance incapable of accurately conveying the social and psychological deformities perpetuated by women's entrapment in the private sphere.

When her own children have grown and left home Mrs. Bridge puzzles over what to do with all the leisure time her husband has worked hard to provide for her. Juliet Mitchell's observation that "the 'freedom' of the housewife is her isolation" appears overdetermined as we read about

Mrs. Bridge floundering about the house looking for something to do.[21] "Could she explain how the leisure of her life—that exquisite idleness he had created by giving her everything—was driving her insane?" (224).

She could not. When Mr. Bridge dies unexpectedly of a heart attack while at the office it is his secretary who phones to tell Mrs. Bridge the news. Her response is as emotionally vacant as the "thank you's" she politely delivers to friends and neighbors offering their condolences. Indeed it becomes especially clear with Mr. Bridge's death that husband and wife have lived together as virtual strangers. It even strikes Mrs. Bridge as odd when she receives a letter from her son, suggesting that he knows far more about her marriage than she ever did. "My dear Mother," he writes, emulating the old-fashioned salutation that his father had often used in letters. "My father loved you above all else, and if he was apt to be rude or tyrannical it was because he wanted to protect you" (266).

Protection, in the Bridge family, means above all *silence*. And like members of the family, readers must comply with the silences that structure the relationships between family members. Connell's minimalism is suggestive of the extent to which familial and textual silences are collusive in forming the code that holds this family together. In this way, the Bridge family is intimately structured by the secrets it keeps, by the untold truths that inhere within its system. Unlike Toni Morrison's *Beloved*, a novel also centrally concerned with defining kinship structure as discursive, as the sum total of stories told about itself, *Mrs. Bridge* examines kinship as discursively organized by those stories not told, by a resistance to certain types of narrative that would emerge to redefine women's status as cultural producers and consumers.

A section of the novel entitled "Tower," wherein we read of a conflict between Mrs. Bridge and her son, Douglas, provides a further gloss to this call for redefinition. In a vacant lot nearby their house, Douglas erects a spectacular tower of trash. By following the garbage truck on its daily run through the neighborhood and by grabbing anything he can get, Douglas accumulates an impressive collection of material: "brass curtain rods . . . a roll of electrician's tape and a bent skillet . . . a hatchet with a splintered handle, a cigar box full of rusty nails, a broken fishing rod, several lengths of clothesline and wire, coat hangers, bottles, two apple boxes, an old raincoat and a pair of worn galoshes, a punctured inner tube, some very old golf clubs with wooden shafts, the cylinder from a lawnmower, springs from an over-stuffed chair, and . . . a mildewed leather suitcase" (65–66). With the refuse and waste of consumer-mad suburban life held together by a stolen bag of cement, Douglas constructs what we now might recognize as urban art nonpareil, a monument (like the famous Watts Towers) of bricolage, detritus, and the material incoherence of a mass or popular aesthetic that modernism rejects.[22] And much to Mrs. Bridge's horror the tower continues getting bigger with each passing day. When she finally goes out to have a look at it, she is alarmed to discover that it's as solid as rock.

The tower continues to grow and soon becomes plainly visible to all the neighbors, most of whom are mildly amused by the spectacle. Mrs. Bridge becomes increasingly concerned, but in spite of her veiled insinuations that the tower has become a nasty eyesore, Douglas will not dismantle it. When a neighbor suggests to Mrs. Bridge that the tower of garbage is, for Douglas, a symbolic form of protest, she is moved to action. Calling upon the authority of the local fire department, she has the tower dismantled. From the moment Douglas comes upon the rubble of his creation, his relationship with his mother is forever changed.

Douglas's tower serves as an important allegorical occasion within the development of the narrative's key themes. Resistance to the heterogeneous glut of commodities and the appropriation of these commodities for the purpose of countercultural expression is suggested in Mrs. Bridge's dismantling of the tower. Accordingly, the novel is concerned not so much with the unified expression of subjectivity, as in the traditional *Bildungsroman*, but with the dismantling or deconstruction of the discursive structures that support traditional groundings of (masculine and feminine) subjectivity. Similarly, we witness over the course of the narrative the undoing of Mrs. Bridge's expectations and hopes; gradually, her dreams are shelved in the form of books once loved but no longer read because of the deep disappointments they remind her of. The processes of family interaction become increasingly entangled with processes of anesthetization and denial, until Mrs. Bridge can no longer separate them. Consequently, as the narrative progresses, Mrs. Bridge, instead of becoming fuller and more familiar to us, seems rather to recede into the empty background, so that her image blurs and we see her less and less clearly.

Mrs. Bridge extends Carol A. Kolmerten and Stephen M. Ross's examination of the ways in which "narrative constitutes as well as portrays the fictional American family in which men cluster around a female perceived as an innocent but hollow center."[23] This "hollow center" that the wives and mothers of Connell's novel sense at the core of their being is revealed by Mrs. Bridge's friend, Grace Barron, when she asks, "Have you ever felt like those people in the Grimm fairy tale—the ones who were all hollowed out in the back?" (256). By posing this question, Grace Barron takes an enormous risk. She gives voice and substance to the "anonymous evil" that Mrs. Bridge has felt in fleeting moments but has learned to ignore. Grace's refusal to learn this lesson and her rejection of compulsory female passivity are indications that she chooses to live outside the boundaries of social consensus. And, like modern heroines such as Kate Chopin's Edna Pontellier, Grace pays for this choice. One evening, at a cocktail party, Grace has a few drinks and becomes angry and outspoken. She condemns American fascism, launches into an account of notorious historical injustices, and rails against everything from censorship to the violation of the treaty of 1868. The evening is politely put to rest; however, shortly after the party Grace's son is refused membership in a high-school fraternity. Then her husband loses an important account at the bank where he is an executive. When Mrs. Bridge receives a phone call informing her that Grace Barron has committed suicide she decides that nothing can be gained from any further discussion of the matter. In a letter to her daughter she writes that Grace Barron has died from eating bad tuna salad.

Although Mrs. Bridge says nothing when Grace Barron asks her if she has ever felt hollow inside, the opening sentence of the novel establishes her as a woman mysteriously lacking a self, vaguely bewildered by the fact that she has never felt fully comfortable with her name. "Her first name was India," the novel begins. "She was never able to get used to it. It seemed to her that her parents must have been thinking of someone else when they named her" (1). Indeed, this unusual name hardly seems fitting for the perfectly ordinary Mrs. Bridge. However, this displacement unwittingly defines the pattern of her life; as the narrative progresses we find that it hardly matters what her name is or whether she feels it suits her. Mrs. Bridge is, after all, a wife, a mother, a daughter, and a woman who experiences identity only to the extent that others have imposed one on her. This condition is constantly reinforced by Connell's use of her married name: she is referred to always and only as "Mrs. Bridge." In this regard, the naming of India Bridge may well be perceived as an act of colonization perpetuated by patriarchal structures of female domination; however, the insidious allusion to literary rituals of self-naming, that is, Melville's Ishmael, suggests that while the masculine rite of self-naming may represent an act of self-empowerment in the American literary tradition (even Ellison's Invisible Man chooses his state of namelessness as "covert preparation for overt action"), woman's naming remains largely a case of passive objectification. The names of other female characters, such as the independent poet Mabel Ong (may belong?) and the empty Grace Barron, also seem more like verbal puns than self-proclaimed subject positions, even despite their efforts to forge some sort of genuine communication within the artificial atmosphere of the Ladies' Auxiliary.

The choice of the name "Bridge" may also constitute a play on words insofar as it implicates the mediating function of the family as a kind of border patrol, a socializing agent whose task it is to construct a moral and economic bridge between the private and public spheres. The name connotes the regulatory practices that are herein literally meant to span, or effectively bridge, the generations. The passing on of values from one generation to the next, the conscious effort to preserve family identity, and the reproduction of an ideology of family life are all implicit in the name India assumes when she marries Walter Bridge. However, the ironic implications of her married name, her disenfranchisement from patriarchal inheritance, become apparent as Mrs. Bridge continues to misconnect with her family. She moves toward them, then nervously retreats, always missing opportunities to communicate to the children her own inexpressible longings for affection and love. Instead, she can only regurgitate "words of wisdom" gleaned from ladies' magazines ("It is as easy to grin as to growl"), aphorisms that to her mind convey the foundational truths on which happy family life is built.

The first part of the novel documents the education of the Bridge children and the construction of the ideology of The Family. Through our reader's engagement with the text, we become involved in this process of indoctrination; we are invited to learn—as Ruth, Douglas, and Carolyn do—the language of the family, its specific signs and symbols. Indeed, as Annette Kuhn argues, "the family form . . . is crucial in providing the conditions for certain kinds of entry into the Symbolic."[24] Proper table manners, for example, may be understood as constituting a poolable form of currency, which, like language, indicates one's participation in a class-structured system of exchange. At the same time, however, "proper" etiquette is instilled as a great equalizer, a way of asserting the cohesiveness of internal class relations, which are naturalized through the repetition of even the smallest signifying gestures.

Indoctrination into class and gender roles plays a large part in determining these relations. When Ruth Bridge looks back on her early childhood, she remembers innocently taking off her bathing suit at the public swimming pool and running naked as arms reached out from all directions to catch her. But what she most vividly recalls is the expression on her mother's face and the screams that issued from her own mouth when she was finally recovered. The trauma is implicated as the source of Ruth's adult attitude toward sexuality, as she rebels against the dictates of bourgeois modesty, reclaiming her sexual independence by dressing like "a chorus girl," carrying on casual affairs, and demonstrating a fierce antagonism toward her mother's sexual naïveté. As for her son, when Mrs. Bridge discovers Douglas in the sewing room staring meditatively at the dummy of her own body, she quickly stashes it in the attic trunk. With this, Mrs. Bridge initiates the Oedipal standoff between mother and son. His sexual curiosity disavowed, Douglas becomes increasingly secretive and begins constructing covert linguistic and representational spaces that limit maternal intervention. He adopts street slang, dirties all his mother's guest towels and feigns ignorance when told that they're for guests, and boasts of having been "depantsed" by a gang of boys who routinely steal the pants off select neighborhood victims. "I simply can't understand why they would do a thing like that," Mrs. Bridge muses to herself. Douglas explains, "They just felt like depantsing somebody . . . and I was on the bottom, that's all." "That'll do!" Mrs. Bridge interrupts, apparently agitated as much by the thought of her son on "the bottom" as by the homoerotic subtext of the episode (30–31). When Mrs. Bridge discovers in Douglas's room a hidden magazine with pictures of naked women, she reflects sadly, asking herself where she went wrong. Then she burns the magazine in the incinerator and the matter is never spoken of.

Constantly, the Bridge children insist on producing a progressive sexual openness, on probing Oedipal hierarchies, whereas Mrs. Bridge insists on reproducing structural silences. As readers, we are made privy to the counter knowledges that are nevertheless constructed within these silences. Still, Mrs. Bridge is set on turning every multi-accentual situation into monolithic meanings. Readers observe the frustration of her children as they learn to bury their perceptions of the differences that inhere within these meanings and cultivate the family currency of silence. They must learn not only to deal with the content of their mother's closets, they must also learn to read the repertoire of duplicitous messages that constitute their mother's structure of induction. For example, charitable donations and acts serve for Mrs. Bridge as a consolidation of her own position in the upper class. Thus every Christmas the children are rounded up into the car and taken to the poor section of town where they deliver a decorative gift basket to an address provided by the newspaper. Douglas Bridge despises these yearly visits although he doesn't know why. He only knows that he must participate so that he wouldn't "grow up thinking he was better than someone else" (7).

Similarly, a series of episodes illustrate Carolyn's adoption of her mother's barely contained racism. As a child Carolyn looks forward to every Saturday when she plays with Alice Jones, the daughter of the black gardener who works next door. At first, it pleases Mrs. Bridge to see that the children are not at all aware of the difference between them; but as their friendship continues she becomes concerned and so gently begins to engineer their separation. This is done behind her daughter's back, by letting Alice know she is no longer a welcomed guest for lunch, and by dissuading Carolyn from attending a party at Alice's house because the neighborhood she lives in is "mixed." Mrs. Bridge consoles herself with the knowledge that "time would take care of the situation," and, in fact, Alice Jones's weekly appearances soon stop.

When she becomes an adult, Carolyn stuns her mother when she complains that "the niggers are moving in" to the neighborhood where she and her husband have settled. Mrs. Bridge reflects for a moment, considering that:

On the one hand, she herself would not care to live next door to a houseful of Negroes; on the other hand there was no reason not to. . . . She had never known any Negroes socially; not that she avoided it, just that there weren't any in the neighborhood, or at the country club, or in the Auxiliary. There just weren't any for her to meet, that was all. (253)

The simplistic causal connections with which Connell implies Mrs. Bridge's responsibility for Carolyn's racism, Ruth's sexual promiscuity, and Douglas's emotional woodenness are strategic weapons of a mom-bashing family plot, as are the all too familiar clichés with which Mrs. Bridge absolves herself of any part in influencing the decisions her children make as adults. Nevertheless, her denials have a chilling effect in the context of all the other missed opportunities for connection and dialogue that come and go throughout the narrative.

Yet, there are the rare moments when Mrs. Bridge wavers on the verge of something akin to spiritual revelation. In the section entitled "The Clock," one of the most poetic passages of the novel recounts an instant when Mr. Bridge, sitting quietly in the living room with Mrs. Bridge, asks if she heard the clock strike. Suddenly she is overcome with a powerful sense of time's passage and of her own critical investment in a history far more uncertain and paradox than any she had ever imagined. Looking back on this moment, she realizes how close she had come to apprehending "the very meaning of life, and of the stars and planets . . . and the flight of the earth "(105). The moment passes. She replies to her husband, "No, I don't believe so," and returns to her domestic obligations. Yet, it is moments such as these, I believe, that compel readers to stay with Mrs. Bridge in hope that she might be genuinely engaged by such destabilizing instants.

However, the novel ends with a cynical reaffirmation of her paralysis and isolation. While trying to back her Lincoln out of the garage to go shopping for Irish lace antimacassars, the engine dies and Mrs. Bridge finds herself trapped in the automobile, wedged between the garage partition and the wall. She wonders for a long time what to do. Her husband is dead and her children have left her. Finally, Mrs. Bridge understands that she must engage someone's attention, somehow, or remain imprisoned forever in her luxury automobile. The novel ends with her tapping on the window, meekly calling, "Hello out there?" But nobody answers. The image smacks of a popular 1950s domestic cliché—the cultural contours of which intersect with *Bye Bye Birdie* as well as Sylvia Plath's tragic

suicide—the housewife consumed by her modern, industrial accoutre-
ments. Connell's decision to end the novel at this moment also probes
the American romanticization of the automobile as a gendered symbol
of American freedom and mobility. The scene emphasizes once again
the extreme isolation and uselessness of the Oedipal mother, an isolation perpetuated by a postwar ideology of social class consensus. In the
final moments of the novel, Mrs. Bridge is forced to confront this situation, and readers are left to wonder how she will manage it. We are given
little reason to feel optimistic: Mrs. Bridge's ultimate physical entrapment seems the logical conclusion to the emotional and psychological
inertia she unwittingly embodies throughout the text.

In a section entitled "Leda," this escalating condition of inertia is
examined when Mrs. Bridge signs up for painting classes at a local art
school. During one of these sessions the instructor suggests that the
class paint a subject from mythology. The only mythological legend
Mrs. Bridge can recall is Leda and the swan: "She proceeded to paint
a small, zinc-white swan and a Leda standing stiffly erect, with hands
behind her back and ankle-deep in water because hands and feet always
gave her trouble, and she clothed Leda in a flowered dressmaker bathing suit not unlike her own" (104). Like almost all of Mrs. Bridge's pleas
for help, this indirect assertion of her immobility and defenselessness remains unheard. When the instructor comes by to examine Mrs. Bridge's
Leda, he is silent for a long moment and then comments that the lake
is too blue.

His dismissal of the actual subject of the painting—the mutilated
woman wearing a floral print bathing suit—is reiterated several scenes
later. After talking with a friend who has gone into analysis, Mrs. Bridge
begins to sense that she is ill and unhappy and might benefit from professional help. After many evenings of putting it off, she finally musters
the courage to tell her husband of her decision. Keeping his eyes fixed
on the evening newspaper, he offers some remarks on the stable price
of Australian wool. Then, glancing up at her for an instant, he replies
"nonsense," and the subject of psychoanalysis is never mentioned again.

The deep mistrust of the psychologization of the family, a position
developed by social critics from Max Horkheimer to Christopher Lasch,
is represented in the above exchange through the juxtaposition of contrary discursive practices situated both inside and outside the family
space. The gendering of these practices sets the feminized "private" vocabulary of the psyche and the "self" against the masculine "public"
vocabulary of international social and market relations. In this particular instance, the privileging of the latter (stable commodity structure)
over the former (unstable emotional structure) tends to trivialize the
feminized internal sphere and results in the immediate dismissal of per-

haps the only open acknowledgments of the possibility of refashioning the self that Mrs. Bridge ever makes.

The taboo against self-examination in this context points to the fact that there is nobody within the family system whose designated task is to legitimate mother's needs or desires. Twentieth-century definitions of family function have increasingly emphasized the family's nurturant role, and while women have remained largely responsible for providing this nurturance, post-familial romances increasingly portray mothers as rarely getting back the investments they make or the affection they are routinely expected to deliver. I submit that Connell's aestheticization of the Oedipal mother suggests that material critiques of Oedipalization and its devaluation of the mother through a conflation of her meaning with a consensual, unitary private sphere may be best effected by texts that recuperate *and* subvert the image of mother dissociated from her own desire.

In his study of family structure, Talcott Parsons differentiated the mother's expressive role inside the home from the father's instrumental role outside it. The above scene from *Mrs. Bridge* discursively mirrors the unequal valuing of these roles in the syntax of family relations, but further suggests that patriarchal hegemony is decentered by the rhetoric of psychic fragmentation, which, in the postwar and cold war era, posed a significant threat to the separation of expressiveness and instrumentality as natural extensions of "fixed" feminine and masculine roles. Nevertheless, the separation is deconstructed by the paradox implicit in the patriarchal ideology of the family, a paradox that both materialist and psychoanalytic theories of the family agree on. The domestic internalization of capitalist market relations is mutually dependent upon the projection of Oedipal relations onto the sphere of industrial production. Consequently, one of the primary objectives of the patriarchal family—alongside the separation of property relations and private relations—must be the unification of property relations and psychic relations, a conflation ominously manifest in the final image of Mrs. Bridge hermetically sealed in the object of her desire.[25]

The conflation is granted a more positive representation in the figure of Harriet, the maid. For a steady salary, she offers Mrs. Bridge what her husband does not: devotion, interest, and respectful obedience. In "The Search For Love," Mrs. Bridge sits at the dinner table with Mr. Bridge and longs for him to offer some reassurance of his affection. He is unable to respond, and in her nervous embarrassment, Mrs. Bridge accidently steps on the floor buzzer, "with the result that Harriet soon appeared in the doorway to see what it was that Mrs. Bridge desired" (77). In a subsequent chapter, Mrs. Bridge eavesdrops on a "flirtatious" phone conversation between Harriet and a Mrs. Porter who attempts to seduce

Harriet away from the Bridge family. To Mrs. Bridge's relief, Harriet rejects the offer, adding that her employers "'could not precisely survive too well'" without her (79). Set against a domestic tableau of homosocial bonds between women, these scenes demonstrate how Harriet's nurturant value might blur any effort to separate or isolate economic or labor relations and relations of affect, erotic attachments, and emotional exchanges. Harriet's significant role within the family plot mitigates Mrs. Bridge's sense of isolation, but more importantly multiplies the codes available in any given reading of the text so that the compulsion to unify domestic relations is met with race, class, and sex-specific alternatives.

Without doubt, such images make it possible to redefine the Oedipal mother as an effect of specific economic and gender relations, and this redefinition may be counted among the contributions of *Mrs. Bridge* to the post-family romance. But is the post-family romance concerned with the transformation of the Oedipal mother within the family plot, a figure marked by idealization and contempt? Or is it concerned with the transformation of the society that needs and constructs her? In part, it remains the task of an emergent feminist social critique to address ambivalence toward the Oedipal mother. However, feminism will also be required to examine its own tendencies toward maternal idealization and contempt, thus acknowledging its dependence on the very society it would transform.[26]

Chapter 5
Rules of the Game: Anne Tyler's
Searching for Caleb

"Games" form a family.[1]
—Ludwig Wittgenstein

Anne Tyler's novels pay close attention to the formal details and abstractions of the family plot. Her protagonists are often portrayed as family-centered eccentrics, men and women complexly defined by their struggles against the forces of familial attachment and separation. Tyler is a prolific and immensely popular fiction writer whose work has precipitated a considerable amount of scholarly criticism. Perhaps because she is a female writer whose audience is perceived to be largely female, the vast majority of this criticism is gender-inflected, centering on questions of female identity and feminist ideology. What's less apparent in these discussions, however, is that popular constructions of identity and ideology, like the family romance itself, have become increasingly discourse-sensitive and multitendentious. Rather than interpreting Tyler's protagonists as the gendered effects of historical and social contradiction, the usual procedure has been to treat her fiction as mimetic, or as quirky reflections of the basic problems and concerns that "real" women actually face: the quest for coherent selfhood, the search for a balance of autonomy and attachment within marriage, the need to embrace yet at the same time disengage from the expectations and demands of parents and children.

To be sure, women do face these concerns; "identity" assertions have played an important part in the historical evolution of feminist literary criticism, particularly where readings of the family romance are concerned. However, these assertions acknowledge neither the diverse range of feminist methodologies, nor the racial, sexual, and class differences that currently underwrite feminist textual discussion. In the case of Tyler's critics, an exclusive focus on heterosexual desire in family romance, a tendency to conceptualize racial difference—when it enters discussion at all—as a generic structural dualism, reduces the question of gender to bland categorical conflicts of female versus male, sameness versus otherness. Ironically, many of these readings rehearse cultural hierarchies that in other contexts marginalize popular fiction *and* women writers, thus suppressing their respective claims to discursive legitimacy and influence in the public sphere.

Even deconstructivist approaches to Tyler have overlooked this particular problem. Mary F. Robertson, for example, makes the case that while binary logic has traditionally governed family romances, Tyler disrupts and, in a manner of speaking, deconstructs these conceptual limits through a consistent blurring of boundaries that neither eradicates nor sustains dualistic thinking.[2] While the dialectic practice of deconstruction and feminism may function as a valuable form of resistance to master discourses, a way of insisting that we listen to historical differences within and beyond texts, Robertson's assumption seems to be that a deconstructed binarism constitutes a successful feminist subversion of family romance, a *fait accompli*, regardless of the social or historical context in which these moves are made.[3] There is, in other words, a lack of explanation as to how or why Tyler's conceptual blurring should empower her female characters who often seem just as interested in recuperating traditional gender roles and family values as in figuring forms of rhetorical resistance. If, indeed, an essential ingredient of female-positive discourse is a rejection of the "hypostatization of category differences," it seems curious that Robertson would begin her analysis with the assertion that "novels about family can be divided into two groups," a hypostatization that sanctions the very kind of dualistic logic she subsequently applauds Tyler for overthrowing.[4]

Perhaps the question of dualistic blurring that Robertson rightly locates needs to be granted a greater complexity and historical specificity within the framework of contemporary family romance, including Tyler's. To neglect this complexity may be to run the risk of compromising the institutionally cooperative aims of liberal feminism *and* the decentering strategies of radical feminism by falling too complacently into line with the uncritical assumption that blurred boundaries between private and public, or autonomy and attachment, produce transformative critiques. Quite the contrary, my sense is that Tyler's blithely ambiguous resolutions of her female characters' quests for stability and her emphasis on the possibility of achieving identity based on a balance of family and self offer meanings as potentially up for grabs, relativistic in the very sense that postmodernists such as Jean-François Lyotard would hope to circumvent by insisting on the difference, locality, and singularity of the language act as opposed to the sort of pluralism that sees all acts and all representations as equally valid. Simplistic inversions of hierarchical logic that place feminine over masculine or self over family move us no closer to a happy marriage of feminism and family romance.[5]

Robertson's appropriation of deconstructive logic reflects a broader dehistoricizing tendency within feminist theory that predominated during the height of the Reagan-Bush era's threat to women's social, economic, and reproductive rights. Similarly, Anne Tyler's fiction and her eccentric families operate to the exclusion of specific historical reference points while relying almost entirely on the terms of a hermetic selfhood driven by familial relativism, ambiguity, and inversion. Of course, within these terms historical significances are deeply embedded. John Updike and Mary Ellis Gibson have both discerned metaphysical rather than material forces underlying Tyler's systems of signification.[6] Gibson argues that "a careful reading of Tyler's recent work suggests a philosophical coherence and depth residing in aptly chosen domestic details."[7] Here Gibson acknowledges that public discourses inhere within the traditional private sphere of the family, but what are we to make of her impression of a structural "coherence" that emanates from the relations of particular units of signification within the domestic realm? My sense is that Gibson, like Robertson, is engaged in a particular kind of theoretical language game in which history coheres under the presumption that philosophy and domesticity speak a common language or that they follow a general economic rule of exchange through which all details become valuable precisely because they are exchangeable. Again, by effecting coherence through an insistence upon the philosophical familialization of the domestic setting, the critic reproduces the illusion of a unified construct that would relegate difference to a reading less "careful" than the kind Gibson urges.

Frank W. Shelton's 1984 critique is the final and most blatant example of undifferentiated judgment with regard to Tyler's cultural significance.[8] Opening his essay with some observations on the author's personal life, he quotes selectively from Tyler's 1980 article, "Still Just Writing," in which she allegedly addresses the question (in Shelton's words): "how can she be wife, mother of two, and housekeeper, yet still be a prolific writer?" Shelton goes on to splice together his own words with quotations from Tyler, explaining that while Tyler sets aside a portion of every day for writing, "the rest of the time is for family, children, 'real life.' " Shelton notes that "far from resenting the demands her family and children have made on her . . . time with family and children nourishes her emotional roots." [9] And while, indeed, Tyler's fictional representations of women's conflictive emotional obligations to the family may be largely influenced by her own experience as both a mother and a successful author, one wonders if Shelton's repeated reference to Tyler's "family and children" occurs because of their extraordinary service to Tyler's imaginative capacities or because they assist in the advancement of Shelton's own family romance, a pseudo-liberal narrative that subtly undoes the threatening potential of women's writing by conflating their creative and procreative functions. Moreover, by amplifying his own critical voice at the expense of decontextualizing Tyler's, Shelton obscures the more complex dynamics of the popular writer's ambiguous relation to the domestic sphere. He plays patron to the notion that "just" writing means "mere" writing (given such accents, might "still . . . writing" lead to still birthing?), especially when weighed against women's "real" fulfillment in having children and working for the family.

Thus the family is defined as a recuperative trope for the Victorian "angel in the house," a figure of philosophical coherence offering redemption from the chaos and disorder of the outside world. But here's the problem: While Tyler's fiction provides fodder for the argument that women's public and private labor are not mutually exclusive, her novels seem to offer little for rigorous discussions of representational difference within the family romance. Furthermore, it seems that academic commentators are partially responsible for this construction of the author and her works. This may be speculation on my part, but perhaps the situation reflects the anxiety of literary professionals who, in the wake of institutionalized feminist theory and debates over the continued existence of gender and sex bias in the academy, must continuously reassess relations to work and family, private and institutional life. Perhaps the tendency to seek out and simultaneously nullify deconstructive potential in Tyler suggests that we remain unsure about our commitments to indeterminacy and difference within a profession where pressure still exists for us to make sound, unambiguous judgments about literary value. Perhaps the dual tendency to radicalize Tyler and domesticate her speaks of our nervousness about the possibility of being perceived as too committed to changing gender roles in the public sphere or not committed enough, too protective of the family or not protective enough. Perhaps the antidote is a theoretical environment where textual ambiguity could mean, for those who equate indeterminacy with meaninglessness, never having to say you're sorry.

Having defined my position as speculative, I'll go a step further and admit that for the purposes of my own readings of Tyler's *Searching for Caleb* (1975), I have imagined that "just writing" refers less to the sense of frivolity that Shelton evokes than to a sense of justice and fair play. Perhaps "just writing" is writing that adheres to the rules of language and exchange that govern the family, although not to the exclusion of relationships that would disrupt those rules and allow for their re-description. What one might draw from this process of redescription is an absence of discursive unity that makes possible the narrative articulation of transgressive or renegade subjectivities. This understanding, drawn from Jean-François Lyotard's dialogue with Jean-Loup Thebaud in *Just Gaming*, leads to an assumption more or less implicit throughout this discussion: Gaming is a fact of post-family romances such as Tyler's.[10] Her "genetic comedies," to borrow Updike's phrase, often focus on individual family members' strategic efforts to contest the rules and meanings that inhere within a seemingly closed binary system of emotional relation and exchange. In novel after novel, Tyler stages the conflict whereby sons and daughters struggle to separate their fortunes from their families', to invent new moves within rigidly defined familial paradigms. I've chosen to discuss *Searching for Caleb* rather than one of Tyler's other family novels because to my mind it is the work that most effectively argues that the modern, bourgeois family romance is not the only game in town. This position, demonstrated through comical rhetorical conflicts and narrative inversions that deny the Oedipal family's claims to centrality and consensus, is maintained in *Searching for Caleb*. The novel suggests that only by actively seeking out difference, or multiple gaming contexts, does one arrive at a just determination of origin.

In *Searching for Caleb*, Justine and Duncan Peck are first cousins who marry against their family's wishes and strike out on their own, abandoning the ancestral seat in Roland Park, an affluent suburb of Baltimore where generations of Pecks have remained. Determined to escape this fate, the couple move out in the country where Duncan plans to raise goats rather than join the family law firm, Peck and Sons, as is the tradition among Peck men. Among those relations Justine and Duncan leave behind is their grandfather, Daniel, the family patriarch. Daniel is a model Peck who suddenly assumes a life mission when he determines to locate his long-lost brother, Caleb, a free-spirited lover of music and travel who disappeared without explanation in 1912. Daniel enlists Justine's help and eventually moves into Justine's household, where the conduct and form of day-to-day life are as different from Roland Park as could be. The plot unfolds around their cooperative efforts to track down Caleb with their only clue, an old photograph taken around the time of his disappearance, showing Caleb with his beloved fiddle. As their efforts lead them down one dead end after another, Justine assumes her grandfather's urgency as the search for Caleb becomes increasingly bound up with her own need to define herself and her marriage outside the context of the Pecks, an agoraphobic clan who huddle together in smug isolation from the rest of society.

"All our misery comes from the length of our childhood," says Daniel Peck.[11] With these words Daniel expresses a sentiment uncommon among the Pecks, although his granddaughter Justine experiences as well this sense of a sinister force that penetrates the hearts of children who remain too much and too long at home. As a little girl, Justine fears imaginary bearded men who, she believes, lurk underneath chairs and tables waiting to grab her; yet at the same time Justine remains a willing captive of the theory these whiskered patriarchs symbolize, that the only people who can be trusted are other Pecks. Indeed, as in later works such as *Dinner at the Homesick Restaurant*, the family in *Searching for Caleb* envisions itself as a closed system against which certain family members plot their paths through life, in defiance of their role within the system. The Peck family is, above all, opposed to outsiders, to otherness, to the nonlogical, to differences. They shun anything unfamiliar, which is to say that they reject anything that is non-Peck. The individual members of the family, male or female, are defined either by their furious resistance to changes in the family system or by their rejection of permanence of any kind, an obsession that drives them back to the clan even more forcefully than they left it.

This insistence on restoring all meaning to the site of the family romance is complicated when we consider the opposing factions of the Peck family as incommensurate discourses struggling to redefine the genre in terms of its own precedents, excesses, and exclusions. In this way, the text—like the family itself—becomes a play of intertextual struggle, the purpose of which is to keep the narrative alive while it dissembles and reshuffles its own conventions.[12] The process is far more mediated and much less a matter of individual creative will than Freud's Oedipal engagement between fathers and sons or Harold Bloom's literary struggle between "strong" and "precursor" poets.[13] Yet neither is the process utterly patrolled by anonymous external principles as Pierre Macherey suggests.[14] Rather, the goal is to transgress the limits of inner or outer influence, to defer all final judgments with regard to closing the question of genre. Given this objective, Lyotard's theory of judgment is useful in imagining that texts may contain both representable and nonrepresentable genre elements, all of which simultaneously attempt to articulate the text's similarities and differences to related texts.

By extension, we might imagine that the Peck family, or any family positioned within the post-family romance for that matter, consists of both representable and nonrepresentable identities, both of whom pose a perpetual threat to one another's sense of justice, subjectivity, and origin. This relation, or *differend*, poses a disruption within the familial system by keeping the system open to the extent that the differend is kept alive. In a language game, for Lyotard, the differend is defined as "a dispute between at least two radically heterogeneous or incommensurable language games, where no one rule can be invoked in terms of which to pass judgement, since that rule necessarily belongs to one language or the other."[15] For Lyotard, justice is produced not by observing the rules of a language game, but by playing at the very limits of what the game allows. By occupying the margins of master discourses, by testing and destabilizing the rules of the games by which they operate, a self-conscious refashioning of form and truth takes place. New games and new possibilities of just communication evolve in a context that is always local and contingent. In a sense, Caleb's disappearance constitutes the fault line at the limits of family romance, a flash point of tension between two incommensurable games being played among the Pecks. These games are the language of the law, or stability as represented by the Roland Park Pecks, and the language of the carnivalesque, or indeterminate subjectivity as represented by Justine, Duncan, and to some extent by Daniel, who eventually changes camps in order to facilitate the search for Caleb.

As they assemble, disassemble, and reassemble throughout the novel, the Pecks form a unifying contradiction in each other's lives, a point of departure from which there is apparently no escape. The family is never an answer to the question, "Who am I?" It remains a question that some family members would close down, while others would prefer to leave open-ended, never allowing the issue of individual roles within the family to become a finalized concept. According to Lyotard, all language games enact a similar "distribution of roles" that are incommensurate with the "roles" effected by the various narratives that compete within the language game. Consequently, all players within the language game occupy and define multiple positions. This meaning of "roles" is understood by the younger order of Pecks who see themselves as adaptable and nomadic rather than fixed by tradition and consensus. The roles assigned by gender, itself a contestable discourse at the time of the novel's writing, is likewise opened to doubt and reconfiguration within the terms of "role playing." That Peck men flock unquestioningly to the legal profession is a reminder that the family is committed above all to the preservation of its own laws and its own language. However, Justine's very name and her quest for Caleb are reminders that differences need to be kept alive and acknowledged within the system so that justice is never final, but always and only achieved in motion. And as the hermetically sealed structure of the Peck clan is invaded by this knowledge from within its own ranks, the family appears less like a single entity dictating proper character and more like a locus of transaction, an open system that proposes—in opposition to itself—a new set of assumptions about relations between and among family members.

Searching for Caleb is thus recuperative, on one level, as a language game that, in its populist celebration of the individual within the family system, expresses at the level of romance narrative a certain degree of nervousness about the possibility of social and epistemological difference. However, it does not seek to resolve the importance of these issues in women's lives, nor does it propose criteria with which to judge the redescription of attachment or autonomy as forces central to female development. One of the messages to be derived from the text is that women's role within the family must be left open to discussion and debate. Indeed, what marks Caleb (a figure of feminist resistance, as I will argue presently), Duncan, and Justine as differends, threats to the family, is that they require competition, indeterminacy, and difference in order to thrive; however, their difference can only be granted value from within the institution of the family itself. Thus, if a family's shared language sustains the context from which the representability of individual subjectivities are won and lost, it seems reasonable to surmise that "family" itself denotes a contestable field for the negotiation of various styles of engagement with the world.

Justine's search for a new configuration of self in the outside world develops alongside her prescience, or what she describes as her ability to detect changes coming in other people's lives. One evening not long after Duncan and Justine move to the country, Justine experiences a vague yet disturbing premonition. "Something terrible's going on at home," she tells Duncan. "Something terrible is always going on at home," he replies (120). On her hunch, they drive immediately to Roland Park. Something "terrible" *has* happened: earlier that day Justine's father, Sam Mayhew, was found dead of a heart attack. Stricken with grief, Caroline, Justine's mother, strays out onto the main road and is killed when she walks directly in front of an oncoming car.

Back at Roland Park, Justine roams around the house in a guilt-ridden state of shock and realizes that every item, every detail of domestic life she sees before her is meaningless until placed in the context of a much bigger picture. "Now as she cruised through the darkening house she was aware of how everything here was attached to everything else. There was no such thing as a simple, meaningless teacup, even" (125). Like the jigsaw puzzles that Duncan pores over endlessly, their family, Justine realizes, is a closed system composed of units that gain meaning only through connection with other units. By redescribing her connection to this system, it is implied that Justine has deeply offended her parents and all the other pieces of the household, their overarching value.

In other words, by spatially and socially abstracting themselves from Roland Park, Justine and Duncan do not so much attempt to establish an alternative closed system, a discourse separate from the slippery network of family communications, but rather they open the Peck system up to destabilizing currents—paradox, parataxis, paralogism—which the young couple experience even from a distance as "an endless advancing and retreating." Justine and Duncan refuse to install a telephone; mysteriously one day a "gift" telephone arrives to be installed by and billed to Peck and Sons. Letters and invitations to Sunday dinner arrive daily in bunches from Justine's mother and great-grandmother, each one subtly aimed at provoking some casual meditation on Justine's failure as a daughter. Doubting her decision to separate, Justine makes the reciprocal moves that assist Caroline in consolidating the symbolic foundation of the Pecks' structure of kinship. She nervously reads and rereads each letter searching for some stable meaning, even when Duncan gleefully points out to her that all the notes contain phrases "with double and triple and quadruple meanings" (117). The multiple meanings at odds in the family language system constantly unravel one another in a whirlpool of relativism, precluding the possibility of fixing the code long enough to form even a temporary judgment about what people think or about where they stand in relation to one another.

At the same time the multiple meanings produced by the family's letters present a challenge that Duncan finds hard to resist. He makes the next move of the game. In a postcard he writes, "Dear Ma . . . High!" While Duncan's own ambiguous message, a reference to smoking marijuana, is intended to mock the conservative, prudent values for which the Pecks stand, he achieves this ironically, by demonstrating his mastery of the very grammar through which the family attempts to effect the structure of an insular and wholly unified familial identity.

Anne G. Jones has argued that in the union of Duncan and Justine, Tyler depicts a marriage that occurs "safely within the family."[16] But what is she suggesting they are safe from? The implication seems to be that Duncan and Justine are safe from the general threat of genetic "difference," and that they have achieved a kind of purity in their genealogical similarities. However, Duncan's insistence on marrying Justine despite her father's violent disapproval and the rest of the family's vague dismay takes the Peck emphasis on self-sufficiency to an extreme that demonstrates that difference *is* sameness's excess, its point of collapse. Compounding the irony of their incestuous engagement is the question of its legality, which the male Pecks, all lawyers of the incestuous firm Peck and Sons, are forced to ponder. Although the marriage breaks no statutory law it nevertheless challenges the cultural law of exchange, which, according to Lévi-Strauss's structural analysis of kinship systems, consolidates the collective identity of the family and confers individual identity on its male members through a symbolic act of differentiation that simultaneously unites and distinguishes nonrelated clans. By refusing to participate in this economy of difference, or, in other words, by seeking difference-in-sameness, Duncan consolidates a subversive identity that appears to shatter the structural dialectic of inside/outside on which the family is founded.

The apparent threat of a radical identity-in-sameness is expressed in Justine's father's refusal to grant the cousins permission to marry. "Don't you see why you're doing this?" He asks Justine. "It's merely proximity, the two of you had no one else, *no* one in this family has anyone else" (106). However, this should not be confused with an attempt to undermine the patriarchal order by deconstructing its binary logic. Rather, the sanctity of masculine bonding, along with the value of women as objects of exchange, is held open for discussion in *Searching for Caleb*. The marriage of Duncan and Justine represents neither the closing off of the Peck men from exchanges with the outside world nor the successful unraveling of masculine social privilege. What their marriage does amount to is a reinscription of those exchanges and privileges that Lévi-Strauss identified as tantamount to masculine subjectivity—along with the dialectic pattern that both differentiates and binds—within the gaming structure of the insular clan. Duncan's proposal to Justine grants the male members of the Peck family an opportunity to effect the social negotiations required to unify familial identity. The reason this can occur at all is because sameness, like difference, does not precede these negotiations but follows from them. As differend, Duncan is no more related to the Pecks than he is to any other family in Baltimore, that is *until* he performs the linking ritual that establishes his relation, as well as the genre of the text: family romance.

For Lyotard (in Bill Readings's words), "a genre supplies a rule for linking phrases, for selecting one phrase to link rather than all the other possibilities."[17] Genre is thus established by a series of linked phrases, although how these phrases get linked remains contingent on the particular occasion and purpose for linking in the first place. In other words, there is no universal law for linking, although linking itself is an unavoidable activity. In Tyler's case, we can note that play with the social rituals of linkage parallels play with the structures of generic convention. This comes as no great surprise considering the heavy emphasis in the novel on the metaphor of games, systemic breakdowns, and the recycling of previously incompatible configurations of play. For example, Duncan's conflictual involvement with the family is made manifest in his deep love of puzzles, particularly those that require, by definition, one person to solve them. He is addicted to solitaire, preferring games that require "hours and days of deliberation and strategy and intricate plotting" although invariably he loses and has to begin a new layout (269). As he becomes increasingly depressed, he takes solace in a 1,200-piece jigsaw puzzle depicting "Sunset in the Rockies." He has no problem constructing the puzzle frame, but then he becomes utterly immobilized, unable to do anything except move random pieces aimlessly around the center. In another instance, Duncan entertains himself by composing a list of all his favorite words, each one estranged from any meaningful context.

Paralleling Duncan's difficulty with puzzle construction are his difficulties in assembling any kind of legible social identity for himself: Although he believes he has successfully analyzed the bewildering contradictions of Peckism, in fact he understands only the external forms of its signifying postures. Referring to his own wife and child, Duncan insists, "This family is not a closed unit" (171). However, the heterogeneous possibilities of linkage remain a mystery to him. He is unable to form links not proscribed by the fabricated rules, the precut, predetermined mode of order. Just as the frames of Duncan's puzzles are defined by the lack on the inside, his status as the family rebel is not the self-determined identity he would like to think he has independently forged, but rather remains contingent on his relation to the system he supplements, a system made more varied and more open to transformation by his resistance to it.

The paralyzing double, triple, and quadruple messages the Pecks send through the mail on prim cream-colored stationery keep Duncan and Justine on a string and at the same time let them believe that they are free to do as they please. Duncan believes he can see the game for what it is, although he is compelled to play if for no other reason than to show off his mastery of the terms, for indeed they are his rightful inheritance as a male Peck, an interpreter of the law. Justine, however, is drawn into the vortex of unresolvable contradiction because, as a female, she has always defined herself in terms of familial attachments and believes it her function to accommodate others, "to see all sides of every question" (310). While Duncan positions himself solidly on the outskirts of family interplay, a point from where he perceives Peckism to mean a perpetual unraveling of itself, a limitless language game that constructs "family" as a potentially open-ended process of displacement, Justine is discursively installed at centerfield as one of the displaced signifiers over which Duncan and the Roland Park Pecks deliberate. "When [Duncan] pointed out for her the meaning beneath their words, the sharp edge beneath their sweet, trite phrases, Justine pointed out the meaning beneath *that* meaning, and he would have to admit some truth in what she said" (153–54). Justine embodies the possibility of change and social transformation in her propensity to visualize multivoiced meanings at once. Not surprisingly, however, the sheer multiplicity of potential positions from which to act often leaves her feeling immobilized.

Nor is it surprising that Justine should be drawn to fortune-telling. In preparation for running a fortune-telling booth at the high school bazaar, Justine for the first time encounters Madame Olita, who teaches her the rudiments of palmistry and card-reading. In the course of their interview, Madame Olita informs Justine that she has the markings of a superior fortune-teller and should perhaps consider telling fortunes professionally. Years later, when a deep, unexplainable sorrow overtakes her, Justine seeks out fortune-tellers again for an answer to the question: "If your palm predicts a certain future, is there any way you can change it?" (131).

As she wanders about town hoping to discover whether her fate is sealed, Justine seeks assurance that she might yet break free of Peck-induced paralysis, decide her own destiny instead of passively waiting for it to be decided for her. By having her palm read and her cards interpreted, Justine aims to discover whether family romances are permanently inscribed or always in the process of being written and rewritten. To her dismay, the answers she gets indicate that identity, like genre, is a closed and unchangeable system. "What is written is written," she is told. "Man does not avoid the future." "There is no escape" (131–32). Not until she relocates Madame Olita does Justine catch a glimpse of hope. "You can change your future a great deal," Madame Olita instructs her. "Also your past. . . . Not what's happened, no . . . but what hold it has on you" (135). This is not so far from Lyotard when he says, "to link is necessary; how to link is not."[18] The central conflict of Justine's character is thus defined not as a struggle to free herself from the family but as a struggle to redefine her mode of connection, to understand the specific occasion for which attachments need to be judged and enacted. It is this process—taken case by case, link by link—that is constitutive of identity. In this way, romancing the postmodern family may be understood to require a redescription of the Freudian grand narrative in terms of the differend, of divorcing our notion of identity from the question of truthful connection to the law. The difficulty lies in accepting that identity can still function as a position from which to act, from which to judge, while we remain open to instability, contingency, and fluidity. Nevertheless, this is affirmed when Justine reads Alonzo Divich's fortune to say that he should *not* sell his business. At the conclusion of the novel, when Justine decides to join Alonzo's traveling carnival, we realize that she *has* been moving, acting, and predicting her own fortune all along.

For Justine, arranging, rearranging, and interpreting the cards is a way of actively recreating the self. While Tyler suggests that for Duncan solitary games such as puzzles, cards, and the autodidactic accumulation of trivial facts offer a means of keeping human attachments at bay, she indicates that for Justine reading the cards may be the one way she can learn to politicize the personal or balance her desire for connectedness with her desire for distance. In both cases, the seemingly innocuous pastimes of Duncan and Justine provide serious mirrors for meditation on the spatial topography of gender that both Justine and Duncan seek to expand in their public interactions as well as through their marriage to one another. The fixed separation between the home and the marketplace, an essential Peck distinction, is radically undone, for example, when Justine brings clients into her home to have their fortunes told. While she turns her home into a public marketplace, Duncan turns a marketplace, his antique store, into a home filled with a vast assortment of old-fashioned domestic tools and gadgets.

Fortune-telling, for Justine, represents a radical bid for liberation from the self-reified structure of relations that confers origin and identity through the naturalization of its own signifying practices. In a sense, fortune-telling gives Justine permission to reinterpret the past through a formalized process of discursive transformation. Justine learns from Madame Olita that her function is *not* to provide an authoritative account of the future, but to construct interpretations based partly on a semi-intuitive method that acknowledges that fortune, like family, is fragmentary and always in process. Its meaning resides in the gaps between a prescriptive and inscriptive reading of the cards. Madame Olita advises, "You must think of these cards as tags. . . . Tags with strings attached. . . . The strings lead into your mind" (136). In other words, she suggests that the fortune-teller's narrative meditations are not formed by preexisting units, or pieces of meaning, but that these units are themselves constantly renegotiated, case by case, through the intervention of the "teller." In this way Tyler contrasts the powers of legal precedents, or the Peck profession, with the socially disreputable powers of female chicanery, or fortune-telling, and seems to find the latter a more fluid and liberating practice of familial and individual imaging.

Consequently, there seems to be something of a suture formed between the notion of a plurality of language games and an essential female capacity to embrace indeterminacy. This is suggested in the revelation that Justine's most valued familial inheritance is the deck of cards that Madame Olita passes on to her at the conclusion of her lessons. That Madame Olita inherited the cards from her own mother establishes the matrilineal connection absent in the Peck clan. Madame Olita, however, is more than just a mentor or spiritual guide to Justine; she shows Justine how to make her own income and manage a business, just as the Pecks would have done for Duncan had he entered the family firm in Roland

Park. Most importantly, perhaps, is that Madame Olita's kinship claim on Justine is a claim motivated by choice as much as destiny, a claim conditioned by a judgment.

However, Justine soon learns that inheritance is double-edged, and the cards are both a gift and a curse. The pressure of knowing that strangers rely on her for advice and judgment is, Justine realizes, immense. As the dry cleaner who works downstairs from Madame Olita explains, what's wonderful about fortune-tellers is that "they take full responsibility. What more could we ask?" (132). To Duncan, Justine admits, "I don't want to be *responsible* for people. For telling them who to marry and all" (140). Until this point in the narrative Justine has never been able to take responsibility for even her own decisions, let alone other people's. All her life she has been swept along by the will and determination of others, pulled in one direction or another depending on the stronger force. When Justine asks Madame Olita why it is that she sometimes has glimpses of the future, Madame Olita explains, "People who have led very still lives can often sense change before others can" (139). "My life isn't still," Justine replies, although her designated position within the Peck family structure as the common accompaniment to others' ventures and quests—rather than a seeker of meaning in her own right—has effectively immobilized her and has rendered her incapable of taking decisive steps in any direction. Tyler suggests that when Justine accepts Madame Olita's cards as her inheritance, she initiates a process of motion that neither her marriage to Duncan, her assistance in her grandfather's search for Caleb, nor her ministrations to mother and aunts could accomplish. By becoming a professional "reader" she takes control of the interpretive act and of public meanings. The point, according to Tyler, seems to be that to interpret one's fortune is to change one's fortune; to interpret one's connection to family is to change forever one's connection to family. Consequently, by becoming an interpreter of the cards, Justine becomes equipped to prepare herself—as well as her clients—for the possibility of radical difference.

For Justine, the disappearance of Caleb Peck represents the event that initiates such change. For Daniel, on the other hand, Caleb is someone who has never changed, nor does Daniel seem to realize the extent to which *he* has been changed by Caleb's disappearance. Daniel's search for Caleb gives expression to his wish for things to remain always as they are, a wish befitting his definition of heaven as a moment frozen in time, "a small town with a bandstand in the park and a great many trees, and I would know everybody in it and none of them would ever die or move away or age or alter" (198). That such immutability is possible only in the world of art suggests that the search for Caleb may not be a search for a person at all, but rather a quest for a narrative structure capable of preserving the collective myths that constitute the past.

But can imaginative structures ever be held in common? Apparently not, since all the Pecks seem to have embraced different ideas about who Caleb actually was, or is, and why he should be found, or not found. Unanimous interpretation or consensus within the family is not only impossible, Tyler suggests, but impossibly comical. As the novel progresses it becomes clear that Caleb is a fictional creation not only within the individual thoughts of the characters but within a wider system of cultural belief as well. If Caleb is restored, some Pecks believe, then so will the destabilized hierarchies of class and race so crucial to Peckism be restored. However, Caleb's love of fiddle music, his easy companionship with the servants of the house, and ultimately the discovered circumstances of his disappearance provide frequent reminders of the contamination of the bourgeois class by desires associated with the lower classes, with the pleasures of the body, and with inelegant, popular tastes.

The search for Caleb is itself a language game, a sort of psychofamilial Mad-Lib in which everybody gets a chance to complete the passage describing the consequences of Caleb's disappearance. The search for Caleb is the search for a missing document in the Peck family archives, a document that each family member has had to invent for herself or himself. However, as Daniel reaches his old age he determines to know the authoritative version of the story without which Peck history can never be considered complete nor the future secure. While the search for Caleb gives purpose and order to Daniel's life, for Justine the search begins as just another chance to play the role of the servile granddaughter, a chance to be pulled in directions for which she needn't necessarily be responsible. It isn't until Daniel Peck dies that she inherits his mission and decides to learn the truth about Caleb for herself.

Ultimately, the truth Justine arrives at is a truth about no one other than herself: Justine's participation in the search for Caleb and the constant moving around that has entailed teaches her that what she values most is transience and difference. This realization leads to her employment with Alonzo Divich's traveling carnival, a position requiring her to become a vagabond like Caleb, always on the move. The carnival, it is suggested, will provide Justine and Duncan with a social and economic base. And yet, like Caleb, who left Roland Park to pursue music for the love of music itself, Justine joins the traveling carnival not for the opportunity to tell fortunes but for the love of motion itself and the never-ending process of renewal and redefinition that travel invites.

Amplifications of the Bakhtinian carnivalesque in recent cultural studies affirm the reading of almost all carnival images as eruptions of a potential for social revolution.[19] However, an insistence on remaining at the limits, like Lyotard's insistence on a "justice of multiplicities," may be more relevant in understanding the appeal carnival life has for Justine. "Justice," Lyotard writes, "does not consist merely in the observance of the rules; as in all the games, it consists in working at the limits of what the rules permit, in order to invent new moves, perhaps new rules and therefore new games."[20] Carnival work, in this sense, represents work within the limits of what the rules will allow. Duncan, for whom Justine secures a position as carnival mechanic, is similarly located at a point of unraveling although he remains obedient to the laws of kinship and damage control. As mechanic, he may continue to "fix" things, ironically his most Peckish trait. However, Duncan's job is to maintain technical order in a world of necessary disorder to stabilize that which is by definition unstable. Justine and Duncan salvage the family, and the family romance, through the perpetual displacement of its form.

But the most important connection between Justine and Caleb is that despite their desires to be free of the familial obsession with consensus, neither can fully relinquish their loving attachments to home as origin. The text reaffirms these attachments by emphasizing the literal and symbolic importance of strings in the novel. Justine, it is often said, goes places only when pulled by human ties. Paradoxically, it is these ties that condition the need for freedom and create the opportunity for freedom through motion. Equally paradoxical is the eventual discovery that although Caleb's family reputation is as a runaway, a maverick who managed to extricate himself from the clan, he has, in New Orleans, garnered a reputation as "Stringtail Man," a strange fiddler literally tied by a long rope to his best friend, a blind black guitar player named White-Eye.

According to Jones, in his newfound identity as "Stringtail Man," Caleb rejects his tie to the Peck clan and "celebrates the union of difference, as his relation with White-Eye most clearly shows."[21] Indeed, Caleb succeeds in redefining family through a mutually reliant and supportive interracial relationship with a fellow musician, however it is also significant that Caleb forms this caring lifelong commitment with a partner of the same sex. The existing criticism on *Searching for Caleb* generally omits this point, perhaps because Tyler provides no basis for speculation on the nature of the intimacy that the two men share; however, it seems reasonable to say that their relationship is not, as Jones implies, the embodiment of ultimate difference, but rather, like Duncan and Justine's marriage, an insistence on remaining at the limits of sameness and difference. Of course, Caleb never marries, yet I think that the union of White-Eye and Stringtail Man represents a marriage of sameness far more genuine than does the union of Justine and Duncan. The gender infractions of this unconventional marriage notwithstanding, the strength of their bond, which is ultimately what leads the private investigator, Eli Everjohn, to Caleb's address at the nursing home, raises a very important question: If it is not closeness and familial symbiosis that Caleb rejects when he leaves Roland Park, then why does he leave and what is it that he so longs to escape?

If there is an answer to this question it lies ultimately with Sulie, the Peck family's longtime maid and a figure of mediation between the language of the bourgeois household and the language of the city, its temptations, its music, all the forces that lured Caleb away from stuffy Roland Park. Sulie, like so many domestic "servants" in contemporary family romance, becomes a powerful figure in her capacity to represent what Freud would not fully consider: the dissolution of the private sphere and its continuous dislocation through difference.[22] However, what distinguishes Sulie from the maids of the Victorian family romance is that she functions not so much as a window onto the lower class or as a symbol of sexual knowledge, but as a holder of missing information that the Pecks have remained blind to, although Sulie has lived with them for years. Ultimately, Eli Everjohn, a hired detective and another family outsider, learns from Sulie the truth of Caleb's disappearance, a lesson that places Sulie at the center of the Peck family's history in spite of the social hierarchies of race and class that organize her relation to them.

Tyler's status as a contemporary Southern writer compels any definition of "difference" in the novel to include questions of race, Faulkner's historical aporia. As heir to this legacy, Tyler constructs Sulie, whose very name carries resonances of a system that objectified black women as contradictory figures of sexual exoticism and displaced maternal need. Sulie is the keeper of Caleb's secret, a secret she withholds ostensibly to protect Caleb and because it never occurs to anyone to ask if she knows something. A triple outsider whose invisibility is compounded by conditions of blood, race, and class, Sulie necessarily affirms antithetically the unity and consensus of the Peck family. As a paid servant, she can be dismissed, but only at the expense of the history that remains repressed throughout the novel. Her long-term mutual commitment with her employers gives her a certain power over the Pecks. However, her construction in terms of social marginality allows her to keep a secret that impels the narrative and sustains the romance.[23]

Caleb's discovery by Eli Everjohn results in his recuperation and a rather disappointing visit with Justine and Duncan. Not long after his arrival, Caleb escapes from his family a second time, this time with their full knowledge and understanding. "Let him get a little head start . . ." Duncan pleads with Justine as they prepare to give chase. In the end, they let him go; Caleb's thank-you note, which all Pecks are taught to write and send immediately following any social visit, arrives promptly in the mail. This seemingly contrived "move" on Tyler's part succeeds in comforting Justine as she recognizes that even the legendary family outsider, Caleb, is lost in "that secret language which, perhaps, all families had" (289). When Justine translates Caleb's note into *her* language, it assures her that although she may leave her family behind, a part of them will continue to determine the forms and structures of her identity no matter how far to the limits she pushes herself. This represents fulfillment of Justine's quest, and the beginning of another. She chooses a link, makes a judgment, and determines that she and Duncan will join Alonzo's traveling carnival.

Part of the difficulty in reading *Searching for Caleb* within a feminist framework is that the novel is clearly recuperative on some levels. Tyler seems to believe that we *are* destined or fated to buy into the myth of the unified family, its structural permanence in our imaginative lives. As Caleb's final note assures us, we are bound to negotiate the boundaries of ourselves and articulate our needs and desires with the forms that we have inherited. Even Justine and Duncan betray an uncritical commitment to a process whereby differends are written out of the family romance. When they express disenchantment with the drab, colorless husband their daughter has chosen for herself, she delivers the most damning accusation of all: "The two of you are as closed as a unit can get" (179).

Perhaps the popularity of *Searching for Caleb* is due in part to the fact that it is one of Tyler's best efforts to register discomfort with the prescriptive patterns that universalize and consolidate Oedipal logic and female acquiescence. For me, the pleasure of reading *Searching for Caleb* is in discovering at the novel's conclusion that it is, after all, the post-family romance that holds open the differend, the repressed relation that makes history available to multiple reinterpretation. Justine need not become a feminist for this; however, her family must be conceptualized as a field of rhetorical debate, a testing ground for all the possible links, moves, and phrases that never actually fix the subject, but keep her just.

Chapter 6
Father Trouble: Jane Smiley's
The Age of Grief

> I am annoyed that we lack a history of fatherhood.[1]
> —Thomas Laqueur

Feminism today is being widely reconceived in terms of gender studies, a field that some practitioners claim promises a more culturally comprehensive and theoretically sophisticated analysis of gendered subjectivity.[2] To be sure, men's studies and lesbian and gay studies have opened major pathways for exploring the fluidity of desires and identifications, the instability of sex/gender categories. The challenges and questions raised within gender studies have helped mitigate tendencies toward feminist "essentialism," a discrediting charge these days and one that would challenge polarizations of "female" and "male" as discrete social, psychic, and sexual categories. Theorists argue that by uncritically relying on the stability of identity categories that are, in fact, historically and culturally inflected, we are apt to overlook the multiple differences that construct relations between, as well as within, subjects in specific social contexts. Recently, this move has raised questions about the context of the family and, more specifically, feminism's traditional focus on theories of "motherhood." Accordingly, men's studies have begun to invite reconsideration of the category of "fatherhood" as it, too, is a social construct, one that has often been marginalized within feminist narratives on history, psyche, sexuality, and the family.[3]

Some feminists, however, have expressed concern that the new interest in "men's studies" encourages, or is itself part of, an antifeminist backlash. Such arguments suggest that "male feminists" and analyses of the current "crisis" of masculine subjectivity tend to bypass historical patterns of white, male privilege by incorporating or, in more extreme instances, effacing altogether feminism's traditional focus on the category of "woman," with all its attendant instabilities and contradictions.[4] The complaint is not unique among established academic feminists who see within certain critical responses to postmodern gender contingencies a conservative move to usurp the place of women's studies, installing in their stead a lament for the decentered male subject. Along these lines, Jane Gallop reminds us that "criticism can ambiguate and complexify gender in literary texts to the point that literature, once again, appears to be beyond the cruel binarized oppressions of the world."[5] In other words, feminists are worried that the shift from "women" to "gender" runs the risk of erasing from literary history women's political struggles to undo the cultural devaluation of women's "work" in the private sphere, as well as their efforts to gain a foothold in the public sphere of rational discourse. Ironically, of course, it *was* the grass-roots feminist political coalitions of the 1960s and 1970s (movements that granted a conditional, although by no means unproblematic, "sisterhood" to women based in the common experience of cultural devaluation) that ultimately made possible the more recent historical reevaluations of the fluid boundaries of gender and social space and helped redefine gender as the performative effects of socially constructed contradictions that one may choose to alternately display, exchange, abandon, subvert, and so on.

However, Gallop issues a direct warning to academic feminists who would continue to rely on the discursive trope of family romance. "If we are going to understand our relation to the academic institution within which we think and teach and speak," she claims, "we need to recognize its specific dynamics which are obscured in the recourse to familial metaphor."[6] While reading this statement, two thoughts occur to me: First, while an overdependence on the metaphors of familialism may indeed exacerbate the specific tensions that have long existed for women within the professions, academia not excepted, Gallop's entreaty to "stop reading everything through the family romance" runs the risk of resituating professional women *and* men within an institutional cloister where not only is the personal *not* the political, but the popular is *not* the political. Second, it seems that family romance and the ascension of institutionalized men's studies are perceived as antifeminist collaborators, a connection that strikes me as particularly problematic for anyone involved in the project of reassessing popular culture and its representation of paternity. Indeed, how can we invoke our "authority to call the ideology of high culture into question," as Gallop encourages that we do, without recognizing and to some extent recuperating the themes of family romance, themes that remain central to the organization of mass and high cultural forms?[7]

The fictional terrain of Jane Smiley promises fertile ground for the consideration of such questions and problems as are raised by the inter-relations of feminism, men's studies, and popular culture. Smiley is a writer whose popularity has increased significantly with the success of her award-winning novel, *A Thousand Acres*. Although her work remains, for the most part, uncolonized by literary critics, her fiction has been consistently praised by reviewers who note her portrayals of "ordinary" American families and her ability to articulate the eloquent dimensions of familial love.[8] In this chapter, I will argue that in her 1987 novella, *The Age of Grief*, Smiley urges us to think about the father's erasure from the family romance in relation to the cultural redescription of paternity and masculinity.[9] She achieves this, in part, through the unlikely trope of modern dentistry, which serves as a strategic indicator of a cultural breakdown in gender legibility and a correlative displacement of pater-nal identity. Ambivalence toward castration and its paradigmatic reso-lution through the containment and marginalization of the feminine is demonstrated through a blurring of the boundaries traditionally sepa-rating domestic and work space, nurturant and wage-earning familial functions. Furthermore, the novella openly questions the gendering of discursive genres. In *The Age of Grief*, romance—the discursive realm of family melodrama and feminine affect—collides and intersects with real-ism—the discursive realm of ordinary social exchanges and masculine rationalism.

The postfeminist political implications of the latter intersection are explored by Sasha Torres in her illuminating analysis of the popular 1980s television series *thirtysomething*.[10] On the one hand, the creators and producers of *thirtysomething* adamantly claimed to have rejected popular melodramatic convention in favor of a new kind of tasteful domestic realism. On the other hand, Torres argues, the series centers on the con-ventional issues of contemporary melodrama, chief among these, "the constitution and consolidation of family."[11] Thus, in its unapologetic appeal to yuppie audiences, *thirtysomething* inconsistently aligned family melodrama with bourgeois aesthetic standards less defined by feminine affect than by masculine impassivity. In other words, the program dis-placed femininity at the very site of classic femininity's inscription, the domestic sphere. However, as Torres demonstrates, the underlying issue here is "not the repudiation of family melodrama, but rather the renego-tiation of domestic melodrama's boundaries to encompass male subjec-tivity, too."[12] Thus, Torres notes the program's "melodramatic tendency to collapse a socio-political 'outside' onto a familiarized and domestic 'inside,' " or, to phrase it another way, the program addresses a representational crisis of male subjectivity through a redescription of the private sphere that is alternately suspicious and envious of the feminine.[13]

To invoke the "ordinary" family is to invoke a trope of class consolidation, a move that appears indiscriminately to invite salutary identifications that maintain a Victorian faith in the authority of a patriarchal status quo—a preservation of rightful descent and inheritance. And when we further consider that the father, as history's model agent of transmission, continues to be installed textually as the effective embodiment of cultural authority, "ordinariness" also becomes an ideological reinforcement of compulsory heterosexuality. In short, as an "ordinary" narrative mode, family romance would seem an unlikely candidate for redescriptive cultural intervention.[14] Indeed, the "ordinary" family, or its invert, the "extraordinary" family (that becomes ordinary by virtue of its ability to demonstrate that *all* families are extraordinary[15]) would seem to support the dominant history of an all-pervasive Oedipal structure by sustaining its primary image of unity, by repressing the contingencies of chaos and historical flux, and by naturalizing the white, middle-class, patriarchal family, its universal value along with its inviolable durability.

However, recent shifts in traditional thinking about identity, history, and representation suggest that there is more to the ordinary than meets the eye. Gender studies (with its stress on the historical inscription of women, queers,[16] and nonphallic men as marginal to ordinary forms of public discourse), late capitalism (with its emphasis on the legitimization of certain ordinary forms of subjectivity through the consumption of mass-produced goods aimed at satisfying highly "individualized" desires), and postmodernism (with its stress on contingency, locality, and difference as the antidotes to ordinary unifying narratives) reveal that the ordinary is an instrument of oppressive, regulatory practices. The "ordinary" family thus invokes a particularly suspect mode of representation, a kind of language use that assumes a natural commensurability with a democratized, objective reality. In this way, aesthetic deployments of oppositions between the "ordinary" and the "extraordinary" become politicized at the level of writing itself. It is this opposition that Stanley Fish challenges in his famous attack against positivist linguistics, "How Ordinary Is Ordinary Language?" Insofar as it denotes an opposition to literary language, ordinary language, according to Fish, is a term deployed to "designate a kind of language that 'merely' presents or mirrors facts independently of any consideration of value, interest, perspective, purpose, and so on."[17] The claim that language is capable of such correlations is, Fish ascertains, "a far-reaching one, because to make it is at the same time to make claims about the nature of reality, the structure of the mind, the dynamics of perception, the autonomy of the self, the ontology of literature" . . . and a number of other precepts that poststructuralist and postmodern critiques deign to question.[18]

Fish's aphoristic assertion is that the distinction between ordinary and literary language leads inevitably to impoverished readings of both. He suggests that we are somehow richer if we forgo making the distinction. Rather, it must be understood that when one subjects ordinary language to purely formal description one trivializes the human factor to the extent that literary language—the sphere in which the *human* in the *human*ities belongs—becomes trivialized as well. For Fish, formalistic descriptions of ordinary language uphold the illusory notion that language exists separate of human or historical quirks, mysteries, and contingencies. On the other hand, Fish is himself confident that *he* can escape these contingencies when he describes the failings of formalists who refuse to see what he quite willingly sees, simply "that *there is no such thing as ordinary language*" (italics Fish's).[19]

Now we turn to Diane Elam, who sets the terms of her argument by citing an OED entry that equates romance with "a narrative that . . . documents events 'very remote from ordinary life.'"[20] On the other hand, at the level of common experience, mass market paperbacks promise to transform romance into narrative events so ordinary that anyone might experience them. Taking this contradictory definition as our cue for the moment, it seems possible that Fish's argument boils down to a complaint that formalist critics have milked the romance, or the "extraordinary," out of ordinary language and have coldly packed it off to the sphere of the literary. According to Elam, it is here in the literary sphere that romance becomes "a signature of postmodernism," while according to Fish, the literary becomes instantly undermined by the now undiluted category of ordinary language to which it is opposed. While Elam traces a love affair between postmodernism and romance based on the common feature of excess and a shared concern for the blurring of spatial boundaries, Fish laments that the very paucity of ordinary language ultimately spills over into its opposite, thus dousing the flame of love's language across the boundaries of the ordinary.

If all this seems hopelessly contradictory, let's briefly consider the positioning of these critics within, or between, the spheres they negotiate. Elam is clearly a champion of romance, which by her own definition suggests that she is a champion of the figure of woman within the postmodern and the postmodern within the figure of woman. Theirs is an equal partnership that registers most saliently in a sort of eruption one might call romance. Politically speaking, feminism, like romance, is that which exceeds the limits of representation to become the "other" to history and/or any notion of ordinary representation. Another way of telling this story might begin with the proclamation that postmodernism begets romance through marriage to its other, feminism. Elam thus positions herself as the narrator of a family romance, of sorts, a genealogy best understood by examining the intersubjective discursive claims of postmodernism, feminism, and romance.

Meanwhile, to paraphrase Fish's claim, the instrumental (public) function of ordinary language, when opposed to the metaphorical or affective (private) functions of literary language, does romance a severe injustice through the institution of a binary opposition. The power of the ordinary looms large, Fish admits, although it ultimately trivializes its own claims to privilege right along with its opposite. Thus, when one challenges the efficacy of ordinary language one, in a sense, challenges the efficacy of the boundaries that divide language *users* into two groups: the normal and the deviant; the ordinary and the extraordinary; the realists and the romantics. Fish endorses the humanist view that "the purposes and needs of human communication inform language and are constituent of its structure," no matter what the content, intentions, or style.[21] However, by ascribing to the constitution of linguistic structures the intersubjective negotiations of the public sphere, Fish champions the very division he ostensibly wants to undo. On one hand, Fish is right: there is no such thing as "ordinary" language to the extent that there is no such thing as completely value-free, assumption-free language. However, there is a lurking sort of relativism here that seems to deny the existence of a type of language—a system of metaphors, tropes, and values—that has historically been thought appropriate to the masculine sphere. If there weren't, how might we discern a difference between, say, the Declaration of Independence and Gertrude Stein's *The Making of Americans?* Fish has no qualms about erasing the line that arbitrarily divides ordinary language from literary language, but in doing so he draws firm lines around the category of subjects—Radway's romance readers, for example—whose needs and purposes ostensibly play a significant role in creating the structures of public discourse.

The problem with Fish's argument is his failure to acknowledge that these categories of language, in addition to his own dismissal of them, have powerful gender implications. Thus, he replaces one set of oppositions for another, for when Fish dismantles the boundaries of historically defined language categories he uncritically calls into question the historical needs and purposes of the people who helped give these categories meaning and weight. A better way of posing Fish's question might be: Whose interests are served by the separation of ordinary and literary? It is certainly arguable that the division suits the needs of an economic or intellectual status quo, but it's also possible that as Fish critiques the positivist error of taking "human values" out of language he is actually referring to the crime of taking "deviant" or feminine values out of the privileged language of masculine objectivity and efficiency. Ordinary language is language that allows for the exercise of a certain kind of realistic, lawful, objective subjectivity. According to Fish's own formulation, if indeed "ordinary" language is constituted by the needs of those people who use it, and if the people who use it require that their language be objective, unambiguous, linear, lawful, and without deviation from established linguistic principles, then to what particular subjective needs is that language providing a response? Fish leaves it at that; however, to raise this question is to invite consideration of what Kaja Silverman terms the "phallic standard," a kind of representational logic that supports the presumed "naturalness" of Oedipally defined male subjectivity and its equation of power with the phallus.[22] However, as Silverman is at pains to demonstrate, there are some forms of masculinity that openly defy paternal succession and thereby express ambivalent, if not contemptuous, regard for Oedipal politics and patriarchal culture.

Smiley's *The Age of Grief* delivers a powerful meditation on the formal complexities of cultural transience, the wages of emotional "work," and the price of building domestic fortresses in the sky to insure against the erosion of romances that remain contingent on the historical forces reshaping masculine subjectivity. David and Dana Hurst are dentists who fall in love while attending dental school. They endure a highly competitive courtship, marry in spite of their very different professional "styles" (Dana claims to love routine; David yearns for drama), and open a thriving joint practice. They have three daughters, Lizzie, Stephanie, and Leah, respectively seven, five, and two years old. Among the advantages of the Hursts' two-income, affluent "life-style" are a huge mortgage, a weekend cottage in the country, and the best available child-safety and health-care precautions. For David, however, caring for a family has come to mean creeping "fearfully from potential accident to potential accident (124)," while safety has resulted in tyranny by the emotional and physical demands of routine, both inside and outside the familial sphere.[23]

Ironically, David recalls that there was a time when he and Dana courted danger. In dental school, when he first met Dana, she would sit on the handlebars of his bicycle as he went speeding recklessly downhill, sans brakes. Years later, Dana admits that she had been a little frightened of David. In turn, David admits that he had deliberately *tried* to frighten her because she was smarter than he was. However after ten years of marriage, David confronts the possibility of dangers far more serious than the bicycling antics of his graduate school days. As parents, David and Dana are certain that danger stalks them, watches them through the windows, waits for them to let down their guards for one second. Danger is "a big word in the family vocabulary," David reflects, "a dangerous word" (199). It begins for the Hursts at the moment of conception and continues throughout the process of gestation. David explains, "Each of our fetuses has negotiated a successful but harrowing path through early bleeding, threatened miscarriage, threatened breech presentation, and long labor" (125). Thus poised for disaster, David writes himself into the "maternal" drama of gestation and birth, defining his paternal presence within the female body as a co-guardian against the threat of a too-early separation from the womb.

The *Age of Grief*, much like Silverman's impressive study of subversive masculine identities, opens with the observation that the phallic standard has waned. "Dana was the only woman in our freshman dental class, one of two that year in the whole dental school," recalls David Hurst of his wife. "The next year things changed, and a fifth of them were women" (121). David's recollection of his wife's position at the front of a sudden surge of women entering a profession once dominated by men resonates with a mixture of anxiety and pride over the prospect of a transformed public sphere of scientific knowledge and debate. David recalls how a biochemistry professor habitually turned to Dana during his lectures to ask if she understood the material, the presumption being that if she (female) got it then so did everyone else (male). However, Dana is a biochemistry major, fiercely competitive, and destined to graduate third in her class. The male students, who quickly garner a reputation for being unusually poor in biochemistry, feel betrayed by her unfailing comprehension and by her indifference to their wishes to keep up with her.

Thus, the narrative begins with an account of gender displacement that exposes masculine insufficiency and feminine aggressiveness. Yet this is also the beginning of a love story, the recognition of insufficiency presumably triggering David's desire for a woman who seems remarkably self-sufficient, unshakable. Later, David reflects back on the decades of the fifties and sixties and says that "nothing has really changed at all, except the details" (128). Given the significant record of cultural change that sets the tone for the narrative, we may conclude that gender is a mere detail of historical narrative, a detail that nevertheless carries as much meaning for David's place in history as for Dana's, and for the entire Hurst family. Indeed, David seeks a new figuration of what it means to be a man and to be a father, yet at the same time such Oedipal tinkering threatens his only known legible role within the family romance.[24] As a representative of what Silverman might call "ideological fatigue," or loss of faith in "classic masculinity," David resists a certain preemptive definition of male fatherhood.[25] Yet that resistance also occasions a sort of strategic self-disavowal, or a loss of "realistic" grounding within culture's scripting of male participation within the family.[26] Consequently, the lines between reality and fantasy become less and less clear to David as he works to denaturalize and displace Oedipus.

The dangerous process of recoding Oedipal masculinity is introduced through David's suspicion that Dana has fallen in love with someone else. Although David's governing point of view prohibits readers from knowing for sure whether his perceptions are accurate, he informs us early on that Dana's feelings for him and her relation to their children and their work are different somehow. His doubts are seemingly intensified by the absence of traditional separations of work and family space. David and Dana practice dentistry together as well as live together; they are both business and domestic partners. This destabilization of boundaries is further complicated for David by the fact that Dana seems to manage the back-and-forth without any difficulty, while David's fear of intimacy with patients and fear of losing his family begin to spill into one another. This confusion becomes harder for him to conceal as he grows more certain of her infidelity. At the same time, Leah, the two-year-old, suddenly rejects her mother's attentions and develops a fiercely exclusive attachment to her father. "She would take her oatmeal only from me," David explains. "Only I was allowed to dress her. . . . Dana, forgetting herself, happened to kiss her on the forehead, and she exclaimed, 'Yuck! Ouch!' and wiped the kiss off" (132). Amiable enough at first, Dana and David indulge Leah's "crush," however the intense rupturing of the mother-child bond soon leaves Dana demoralized and David embarrassed. "She loves you," Dana rationalizes. "It won't last" (135). Sheepishly, he attends to his daughter's desire that he be constantly in her sight, while Dana withdraws unseen into the family backdrop.

The narrative follows David's clumsy efforts to go on with the daily emotional, psychological, and material work of family life in view of his baby daughter's entrance into the "classic" family romance and in spite of his own sense of fraudulence as well as a growing certainty that Dana is planning to leave him. When he thinks about it, he has no proof of Dana's infidelity and no idea who her lover might be. A marked absence of pronoun reference in these speculative passages leaves the sex of Dana's lover open; here, it is important that David's scenario of betrayal is framed by his inability to recognize himself in Leah's adoring gaze. David's misrecognition of "himself" within the familial *mise-en-scène*, his resistance to it, his ambivalent attitude toward the possibility of his own castration, result in a transformation whereby David himself becomes the "other," a gender differend within the "representational system through which the subject is accommodated to the Name-of-the-Father."[27]

At a critical point in the narrative, this transformation becomes manifest in David's cross-identification with a figure who epitomizes masculine loss and insufficiency, a patient named Slater. Slater is an angry and desperate man who, according to his own account, has lost everything—his job, his wife, his self-respect—all of the various conditions that support classic masculine identity and father function. Slater claims that he is mistrustful of doctors, yet he is unable to stop pouring his heart out to David who reluctantly tolerates his patient's disturbing fits of self-pity. One day, Slater flatly refuses David's dental services, yet offers to pay for his time if only he'll talk and listen to him. Throughout these sessions David struggles to remain aloof and separate, advising Slater that he had best perform only the dental services he is trained to provide. However, when Slater leaves the office, David sorely misses him. At home with his family, he begins to feel that Slater has invaded his body, taken him over corporeally. He recognizes that he and Slater share the same sorrow, the same loss, and he is no longer able to restrain himself from calling out his rage: "Everything's more fucked every day," he announces to Dana in front of the children. "I could kill you" (174–75). Stunned, the children stare down into their dinner plates. Dana bursts into tears.

In this scene, David violently rejects castration at the very moment of its assertion. He thus presents himself as the deformed object of a disillusioned familial gaze. The family is called upon to witness and acknowledge the spectacle of male lack and "otherness," a spectacle reserved in the Freudian family romance for the figure of the mother. For his wife and daughters, who painfully avert their eyes, this spectacle of paternal insufficiency is unwanted, yet unavoidable if they are to transform their own diminished roles within the Oedipal legacy. Thus, rather than reading David's outburst as a sadistic assault against the family (the abusive father trope), or as the revelation of a world that might be better off without fathers (the absent father trope), I submit that David's "acting out" of the trauma of loss might also be read as part of the struggle toward reconceptualizing masculinity and affirming castration within the family romance.[28] In this instance, David's outburst (and Dana's tears) may be occasioned not by his identification with Slater, but by his unacknowledged desire to relinquish the external position of the paternal wage-earner and redefine paternity as more gender inclusive, including also the bodily work of birth-giving. Slater stirs in David a heightened awareness of his body's vulnerability to alien takeovers. Indeed, it is difficult not to compare David's odd sense that Slater has invaded his body with the female mother's likely sense of bodily invasion by the life that she carries. In this way, David's pronouncement that "things" are increasingly getting "fucked" would justify us in wondering whose position David is most envious of, a potent female or a wounded male. The answer is, I believe, both, insofar as both figures stress resistance to a restrictive phallic fatherhood and suggest an acceptance of castration as a necessary precondition of masculine redefinition. Taken in this context, David's opening reference to the shifting position of women within the traditional structure of the dental school parallels David's own shifting position within the bourgeois family romance. David's sudden inability to recognize himself within the structure of his marriage, his unfounded obsession with Dana's "affair," and the sense of fraudulence that his daughter's Oedipal transference of desire produces within him are symptoms of a "crisis" of faith that exposes masculinity as masquerade and the dominant cultural reality as romance. The historical bolstering of male subjectivity through the gendered organization and division of social spaces and discursive formations—barriers between private and public, realistic and romantic representations—is thus radically revised in Smiley's novella. It is these forms of loss that are implicated by the title, as David explains: "I am thirty-five years old, and it seems to me that I have arrived at the age of grief."

It is not only that we know that love ends, children are stolen, parents die feeling that their lives have been meaningless. It is not only that, by this time, a lot of acquaintances and friends have died and all the others are getting ready to sooner or later. It is more than the barriers between the circumstances of oneself and the rest of the world have broken down, after all—after all that schooling, all that care. (154)

David's climactic revelation of the collapse of "barriers between the circumstances of oneself and of the rest of the world" isolates the moment when "identification may actually function as mechanisms for circumventing or even repudiating the dominant fiction, whose privileged term is the phallus." [29] In this sense, David Hurst becomes yet another modern American Job, questioning his paternal legacy in terms that challenge, in this specific instance, not only the primacy of the Oedipal family but the representational laws that construct the family as a reality effect, a trope of unity and permanence supported by the symbolic privileging of the phallus.

Indeed, as he gives himself over to grief, David embraces those articulations of a masculine identity that disrupts the laws of coherent signification. He rejects those articulations that effect social unity and familial consensus. As Freud demonstrated, the interlocutions of the body and culture form the foundational logic of family romance, so that to place one of these terms in jeopardy is, indeed, to jeopardize them both and, beyond that, the dominance of patriarchy.[30] Analogously, in *The Age of Grief,* David marvels at the thought that while the body and culture are transient, "teeth outlast everything."

> Death is nothing to a tooth. Hundreds of years in acidic soil just keeps a tooth clean. A fire that burns away hair and flesh and even bones leaves teeth dazzling like daisies in the ashes. Life is what destroys teeth. Undiluted apple juice in a baby bottle, sourballs, the pH balance of drinking water, tetracycline. . . . In their hearts, most dentists are certain that their patients can't be trusted with their teeth, but you can't grieve for every tooth, every mouth. (137)

As a dentist, David Hurst has more than a casual interest in the connection between the inviolable structure of the tooth and the illusory structures of paternal sufficiency. Undoubtedly, one of the structuring rituals of modern bourgeois childhood involves the child's initiation into mastery of his own body via mastery of the forces of decay, loss, and humiliation that might result from inattention to, among other things, the teeth. Certain behavioral and hygienic precautions become part of the psychic range of fantasy and abject fear upon which subjectivity is conditioned. As Foucault has demonstrated, such deployments of the body—images internalized through the admonishments of parents, society, and a network of discursive products—constitute the formation of the subject within a web of contradictory identifications. The task of the family is not to prohibit or punish the child's inevitable interest in his bodily potential, but to manage the terrain of desire and stimulation in cooperation with education, medical, and psychiatric professionals and in accordance with an ideology of immanence. Here, the body becomes a center for surveillance, a locus of power subject to interpretation by a ubiquitous network of alliances that may become activated in the smallest details of bodily management.[31] Certainly, not the least of these details is oral hygiene and the notion that our teeth express certain truths about ourselves, about our knowledge and experience of the body.

As we mature, images of heterosexual romance steeped in the promise of economic affluence, eternal youth, and sexual gratification foster a similar adherence to the laws of Oedipal alliance that consolidate "normal" masculine subjectivity. The modern association of hygiene with sexual monogamy, and the more recent panic over exchanges of bodily fluids, the intensification of bodily boundaries in the wake of HIV and other sexually transmitted diseases, now inform the specific technologies of marriage and kinship so that in popular films such as *Fatal Attraction,* for example, we see that even a tiny "slip" in marital fidelity can lead to demoralization, horror, and devastation. In addition, media exploitation of rising concerns over divorce rates, working mothers, and absent fathers has lead to a general skepticism regarding the "health" of the family corpus. Bourgeois identity, it would seem, has been particularly vulnerable to a fetishization of durability, a project that becomes powerfully, albeit anxiously, manifest in cultural representations that seek to equate perpetuity with classic masculinity.[32] Such connections work in collusion with cultural efforts to resurrect faith in the unity of the family, so that ultimately it would appear that Oedipal masculinity itself, like teeth, or like the family, should outlive us only provided that we attend to it meticulously and seek regular checkups with "health" experts.

David's faith in proper dental care represents his only defense against loss—loss of love, loss of one's children, loss of authority. Dentistry symbolically reinforces belief in order, repetition, and the conventional professional practices by which masculinity is consolidated. Unlike the dentists' office, the Hursts' home embodies the conflicting forces of chaos and dissolution; it is an environment infected by lack and compromise. Its surfaces cannot so easily be kept sterile. David's wish that the domestic sphere could be mapped over by the order and neatness of the dentist's office is, he complains, generally taken as an indication of something askew in his psyche:

People would be offended if dentists weren't as clean as possible, but they hold it against us. On television they always make us out to be prissy and compulsive. If a murder has been committed and a dentist is in the show, he will certainly have done it, and he will probably have lived with his mother well into his thirties to boot. Actors who play dentists blink a lot. (121–22)

David's satirical reflection on popular culture's representation of dentists as feminized and compulsive suggests his resentment of the specularization of paternal inadequacy, an image that he will gradually come to embody over the course of the narrative. It is probably no coincidence that among the domestic details Smiley evokes are references to the television program *Family Ties*, which the Hursts enjoy watching, and *Tootsie*, a film about an out-of-work actor who finds work and romance by masquerading as a woman. David's attention to these texts and his discomfort with the cultural inclination to display the neurotic tendencies of dentists indicate his estrangement from his own authoritative "roles" as doctor, husband, and father, but, beyond this, indicate his sensitivity to the notion that masculinity is itself conditioned by these roles and by masquerade. It is this awareness that separates David from his own father who referred to his children as " 'the kids,' in a slightly disparaging, amused tone of voice that assumed alliance with the great world of adult men, the only audience he ever really addressed himself to" (133). While David struggles to sustain his own alliance to this world, he worries that his performance is transparent and he begins seriously to question his ability to support a correspondence between his "self" and the world of "real" men he ostensibly participates in. "What did I think I was doing on that first day of dental school?" (150). Comparing men of his generation to men of his father's generation, he muses, "I don't know anyone who calls his children 'the kids.' It would be like calling his spouse 'the wife,' not done these days" (133). Similarly, "the family" in *The Age of Grief* is no longer superficially bound by any social code that would distribute legible identity only in relation to the all-possessing father.

In the early stages of the narrative, David relates the story of a patient who, after fifteen years of avoiding dentists, tries to relieve a toothache by going out to his toolbox, retrieving a pliers, and pulling out all of his teeth one by one "with only some whiskey to kill the pain."

Pulling teeth takes a lot of strength and a certain finesse, one of which the man had and the other of which he lacked. . . . Teeth are important. Eskimo cultures used to abandon their old folks in the snow when their teeth went, no matter how good their health was otherwise. People in our culture have a lot of privileges. One of them is having no teeth. (122)

Once again, the drama of male lack is conveyed in this passage, which demonstrates the narrator's central association of dental health and phallic health, or conversely, tooth loss and castration. However, two important terms in this instance are "finesse" and "privilege." David's pointed distinction between the clumsy, brutal self-mutilation of the toothache patient and his own status as a man clearly possessed of "finesse" and cultural privilege can be sustained only so long as he discourages conversation with patients and denies his connection with them. As we have already seen, these measures collapse with Slater; however, even before he meets Slater, David appears both repulsed and fascinated by the gaps, lacks, and absences that threaten the conflation of masculinity with Oedipal paternity.

David prefers that all of his patients remain silent during their appointments and refrain from talking about their personal lives. "Patients feel as if they ought to make conversation," he complains (123). However, for David, functioning effectively in his authoritative role means keeping the boundaries of self and other intact while working with teeth as technical abstractions, "senseless, mindless objects" entirely separate from the hidden thoughts and emotions of the patient in whose mouth they reside. Similarly, David's idea of effective fathering requires a fastidious account of the abstract elements and minutiae of family life: grade-point averages, hourly wages, monthly payments, meals, the time of the day, the day of the week, the MPH on an automobile speedometer, numerical readings on a thermometer, the chronological ages of the children, and the benchmark performances—first steps, first words, and so on—that signal their attainment of each normal developmental stage. Like dental X-rays, these are the empty signifiers that effect the unity and durability of the family. However, increasingly David sees beneath the literal surface of these signs and senses the gaps, conflicts, and inconsistencies they mask. As a dentist, father, and even as a narrator, David constructs spaces—open mouths, material shelters, blocks of silence—as he resists asking Dana any questions about who she's seeing. At one point, he recalls considering a career in architecture, thinking how nice it would be to feel "the way lengths of wood, hammered together with lengths of steel, created a space that people either wanted or didn't want to be inside of" (150). *The Age of Grief* is about David's discovery that relations of collective space and individual space are far more deeply interconnected than he thought, and that creating a safe space is no guarantee that those who share it with you will want to remain there, or that they will remain uncontaminated by the outside.

"Ideally, then," writes Tony Tanner, "marriage offers the perfect and total mediation between the patterns within which men and women live."[33] As Tanner has demonstrated, the figure of the unfaithful or adulterous wife is a historical incarnation of destabilizing social forces that threaten the legible opposition of these patterns. Tanner's *Adultery in the Novel: Contract and Transgression* traces a connection between a specific kind of sexual act, a specific kind of social organization, and a specific kind of narrative occasion. He identifies at the heart of the European novel a central concern with adultery and its dangerous encroachments upon the power of the father. As a symbolic act, adultery—and by extension, the woman believed to have committed the transgression—represents a renegotiation of the boundaries between private and public, bourgeois and working-class principles, masculine and feminine identity.

In *The Age of Grief*, Dana remains throughout the narrative more or less a stick figure, a responsive column of energy rather than a substantially developed character. The adulterous woman, in this context, demands that we concern ourselves less with threats to bourgeois unity than with the misrecognitions of masculinity that precede her necessary construction as a precondition for paternal redescription. The adulterous woman, as moral differend, sustains an open dialogue between realist and romance modes of representation, thus dismantling the conventional discursive assumptions on which rational male subjectivity depends. Furthermore, in *The Age of Grief*, Dana's alleged role as adulteress is rendered irrelevant by contrast to David's role as imaginer and perpetuator of this "betrayal." Dana's adultery matters most as a classical projection of David's own sense of having betrayed "the great world of adult men" by his resistance to culture's limiting definition of masculine identity.[34] In other words, it is the dissenting male, and not the dissenting female, who serves as a narrative trope of cultural decenteredness. And while Tanner's adulterous woman may be a figure society would rather not admit exists, in Smiley's world, she is a figure on whom patriarchy depends for affirmation of its own inherently subversive longings to abandon its consensual privileging of Oedipal paternity and "light out" toward a liberation from these restrictive roles.

This longing for liberation has been noted by Joseph A. Boone, who locates in the classic nineteenth-century American quest romance the recurrent fantasy of an all-male world that arguably says as much about cultural misogyny as it does about a desire to reinvent masculinity by circumventing a sexually bifurcated society.[35] However, in *The Age of Grief*, and more generally in the post-family romance, male characters enact this quest among females and *within* the domestic sphere, where traditionally the male has been absent. These domestic "frontiers" provide for the male character new literal and metaphysical obstacles, new problems in confronting the unknown. Consider, for example, David's response to his marital crisis. He avoids any confrontation that might lead to Dana's clarification of whether she is or is not, in fact, having an affair. Here, it's worth asking why David resists clarification. Is it because he is afraid of finding out that she *is* having an affair, or because he is afraid of finding out that she *isn't?* In a sense, he has more to lose from finding out that she isn't, for as long as he can sustain their silence on the matter, he can maintain, for all social purposes, a more or less unified self-image.[36] David recognizes that this silence is itself supported by the social contract of marriage: "I have found that there is something in the marriage bond that deflates every communication, skews it toward the ironic middle, where man and wife are at their best, good-humored and matter-of-fact" (138).

In the novella these ironic middle spaces are invariably framed by what Judith Butler designates as "interval[s] between the acts," temporal and spatial breaks "in which risk and excess threaten to disrupt the identity being constituted."[37] Interestingly, the more David and Dana direct themselves toward the "ironic middle," the more their daughters move out toward the extreme margins where excess "enables and contests every performance," and where emotions are openly and often violently revealed.[38] Lizzie vomits, literally pouring out her insides for public display. Leah promptly steps in the puddle, trailing her sister's vomit throughout the house. In this way, an open acknowledgment of the decaying barriers between inside and outside, image and reality, overwhelms the compulsory restraint of the orderly adult world.

Or at least this is what Smiley suggests by her use of influenza as a trope for the eruption of repressed social and psychological conflicts that render the Hursts, in turn, sick to their stomachs. The antagonistic forces of paternal misrecognition are dramatized by an invasion of the flu epidemic, which systematically strikes everyone in the house. "The great family reunion" is David's euphemism for the malaise, as he observes of his wife and children, "The family patients have their characteristic styles of illness" (177–78). One by one, each member of the family manifests the physical symptoms of flu, takes to bed, and demands immediate attention. Stephanie, the middle daughter, develops a dangerously high fever that requires an emergency trip to the hospital. Before Stephanie takes ill, Lizzie, the oldest daughter, is stricken with incessant fits of vomiting; not surprisingly, she is also the daughter who suffers from crippling stomachaches when the tensions between David and Dana reach their most severe. David takes her to the pediatrician for her stomach and looks on sheepishly as the doctor calmly suggests that Lizzie's problem is likely psychosomatic. "Every feeling is in the body as well as in the mind," he intones (147). David is stricken with guilt; however, this negation of the body/mind dichotomy signals the collapse of David's resistance to the possibility that he has staged his own psychic disappearance from the family plot. The sicker he becomes, the higher his fever, the more he rejects any illusions of self-mastery. "I lay back on the carpet, on the floor of the organ that was my house, and felt my family floating above me, suspended only by two-by-fours as narrow as capillaries and membranes of flooring" (183). As his delirium increases, hallucinations afford David a kind of ecstatic loss of boundaries and proportions that relieve him of the paternal function and thus allow him to relinquish all claims to collective reality or belief in masculine wholeness.

Says David, "There are many moments in every marriage that are so alike that they seem to be the same moment, appearing and vanishing, giving the illusion of time passing, and of no time passing, giving the illusion that a marriage is a thing everlasting" (184). After a weekend disappearance, Dana returns to David and the children, but there is no talk of where she has been and no talk of whether or not she'll stay. Her return to the family holds no guarantee of redemption, no "healing touch" that "will restore the wounded male subject to his former potency."[39] Routine is simply reestablished, and in the end it is largely these two conditions—consensus and repetition—that constitute the practical continuity of family and paternity, the romance of love's permanence. However, these conditions remain contingent on submission to the vagaries of language, a matter that further points the way to Lacanian speculations about masculine identity and its effect through language, the symbolic law that often corresponds in feminist analysis to the Law of the Father.

Indeed, as the symptoms of David's castration trauma coincide with Leah's rejection of mother and her romance with father, we might question the extent to which David regards language as adequate to his vision of fatherhood, his corporeal love and his nurturant longings. Leah's crush on David signals the onset of a love affair that would, in numerous feminist accounts of psychoanalytic theory, ostensibly diminish the female subject and signal capitulation to the Father's Law, her acceptance of cultural lack. According to gender-deaf readings of Lacan's family romance, these capitulations are the misreadings that constitute all human subjectivity, male and female, thus founding social consensus on a void that will productively unveil itself at moments of historical as well as personal trauma. However, what does it mean for men's studies and future histories of fatherhood that maternal betrayal, or its imagining, is represented—even within feminist narratives—as both the cause and the effect of a masculine quest romance within the private sphere? Perhaps, as Tania Modleski recommends, we still "need to consider the extent to which male power is actually consolidated through cycles of crisis and resolution, whereby men ultimately deal with the threat of female power by incorporating it."[40]

However, when David Hurst begins to see his expressions and vocal intonations reflected back in Leah's babyish attempts at conversation, he wonders if the mystery of desire is an effect of her specific capitulation to him, or if all language is an illusory granting of love. "Are these imitations of our gestures?" he asks. "Or does the language itself carry this burden of mystery, so that any speaker must express it?" (137). *The Age of Grief* offers us no easy answers but urges us to consider the myth of paternity's linguistic coherence and bodily disenfranchisement at the very site of the body's traditional maintenance in the home and the world. Perhaps then we may see that fatherhood, like dentistry, is getting "smaller and smaller," like "little machines. Itsy-bitsy pieces of cotton. Fragments of gold you can't pick up with your fingers" (126).

Chapter 7
"A Possible Sharing": Ethnicizing Mother-Daughter Romance in Amy Tan's *The Joy Luck Club*

> I look at their faces again and I see no trace of my mother in them. Yet they still look familiar. And now I also see what part of me is Chinese. It is so obvious. It is my family. It is in our blood. After all these years, it can finally be let go.[1]
> —Amy Tan, *The Joy Luck Club*

Amy Tan's first novel, *The Joy Luck Club*, ends with a transformative image of maternal reclamation and displacement. Jing-mei Woo, the American-born daughter of Suyuan Woo, recently deceased, arrives in China to be reunited with her long-lost twin half sisters. Forty years earlier, while fleeing the city of Kweilin during the Japanese invasion, Suyuan Woo was forced by lack of food and physical strength to abandon the baby girls on a roadside with hope that someone would rescue, feed, and shelter them. Years of subsequent searching turns up no information regarding the fate of the twins. Only in the 1980s, after Suyuan has moved to America, remarried, and raised a third daughter, is an address for the twins discovered and confirmed. Unexpectedly, however, Suyuan dies before she can contact them. At the behest of her "aunties" and "uncles," the three other Chinese families who make up the Joy Luck Club, Jing-mei (or June, her American name) is invited to assume her mother's seat at the mah-jongg table. Here, she is told the story of her mother's lifelong search, and she is given $1,200—from the joint account the Joy Luck families maintain—to fulfill her mother's wish.

On the level of popular romance, Jing-mei Woo's visit to China appears to bring the narrative full circle, harmonizing East with West, the past with the present, the mother's quest romance with her daughter's family romance. In actuality, however, Jing-mei's arrival in China and her meeting with her half sisters occasion textual meanings far more ambiguous and contradictory than one recent critic's stress on generational wholeness, "nurturing sisterhood," and "pure family romance" can encompass.[2] Indeed, as a replacement for her mother, Jing-mei experiences a displacement of self, a profound misrecognition that has the effect of fracturing the female subject in relation to her maternal legacy and her familial heritage. When she arrives in China, Jing-mei begins to "feel different," and she wonders if perhaps this is the moment her mother had assured her would happen, the moment when she would be transformed, like a "werewolf," into someone who thinks and feels Chinese. Yet at the same time, Jing-mei realizes that at thirty-six years of age, she has never known what it means to be Chinese (306–7). When she sees her half sisters for the first time, she does not see her mother's face reflected back to her in an image of wholeness and unity, but sees instead only a "part" of her that is Chinese. And when the three sisters are photographed, together forming a composite replica of Suyuan Woo, the result is less an image of maternal restoration than an image of maternal dispersion across a field of multiplied, divided, yet connected female subjects who now may begin the process of communally (re)membering and reinterpreting the past. Thus, as the passage cited at the outset of this chapter suggests, Jing-mei's relocation within the maternal family romance means, in part, that she can let that romance go.[3]

Certainly, by returning Jing-mei to the motherland, Tan turns the Freudian Oedipal family romance on its head and reroutes the construction of female subjectivity through the image and symbol of the mother. At the same time, however, the narrative reveals that what Jing-mei has discovered in China is *not* her mother, but rather her chance to reinvent with her half sisters a past that they share, yet do not share. "Mother," in this instance, signifies their wish for a common origin, yet at the same time signifies all that they cannot hold in common, their cultural and social differences. In this way, the final photographic image provides a brief but impermanent flash point of mutual recognition as Tan dramatizes the elusive and contradictory nature of maternal origin; she explores the incongruity of all concepts of "origins" and "identity," particularly to the extent that these concepts are thought to cohere within the subject by virtue of her successful passage through the family romance. In this way, Tan's novel challenges the Freudian formulation; however, it also challenges *all* formula prescriptions for family romance, including, although not limited to, the Western feminist family romance. Rather than unify the romance, *The Joy Luck Club* explores its multiple dimensions and nuances. Thus, the novel challenges stereotypes and avoids the difficulties that follow from singularizing or bisecting identity. Nationality, ethnicity, gender, culture, and family are shown in their multivalent and contradictory guises.

When their photograph is taken with her father's Polaroid camera, Jing-mei and her sisters "watch quietly together, eager to see what develops" (331). Similarly, reading Trinh T. Minh-ha's *Woman, Native, Other: Writing Postcoloniality and Feminism* requires that one study the photographs of women's faces that disrupt the continuity of writing on the page. These images are directed at making visible that which feminist theory has rendered largely invisible: the faces of the (female) other. The photographs construct the meanings of Minh-ha's text as an interweaving of image and symbol, a braided inquiry into the relations of Third World women to language and writing. Minh-ha defines the dominant politics of Third World women's discursive positioning as an imposed separation of margin and center, private and public, image and symbol, inarticulation and voice, writer and other. However, when we listen to the voices of these women we hear the "end of a soliloquy confined to the private sphere," and "the start of a possible sharing with the unknown other—the reader, whose collaboration with the writer alone allows the work to come into full being."[4]

Thus, for women of color to speak and write is for them to dissolve Western politics of oppression by initiating "a possible sharing," a displacement of the signifying hierarchies that subordinate the margins to the center, the receiver of the gift to the giver of the gift. "Let her who is sick with sickness pass on the story, a gift unasked for like a huge bag of moonlight."[5] Such gestures, Minh-ha suggests, reveal the potential of language to redefine culture as dynamic, polyphonic, and contradictory.

In Amy Tan's *The Joy Luck Club*, women's stories are similarly imagined as gifts of moonlight. Recounting her childhood in China, Ying-ying St. Clair, one of the Joy Luck mothers, explains how she nearly drowned in Tai Lake after accidently falling off a floating pavilion her family had rented for a picnic in honor of the Moon Festival. Pulled from the water by fishermen, Ying-ying is unable to locate her family and is set on shore, lost, frightened, and alone. Searching the crowds for her relations, she approaches a stage where an announcer has introduced the Moon Lady. Ying-ying is captivated as the Moon Lady performs a shadow play, a soulful lament for a husband whom she has lost because of her deceitful and selfish desire for everlasting life. "For woman is yin," Moon Lady cries, "the darkness within, where untempered passions lie. And man is yang, bright truth lighting our minds" (82). At the end of the performance, the audience is informed that Moon Lady will now grant wishes to anyone who has one . . . for a small fee. The crowd laughs and disperses, but Ying-ying rushes toward the stage to have her wish heard, the Moon

Lady's features coming clearly into focus as she begins to descend the stage. "I walked closer yet," recalls Ying-ying, "until I could see the face of the Moon Lady. . . . A face so tired that she wearily pulled off her hair, her long gown fell from her shoulders. And as the secret wish fell from my lips, the Moon Lady looked at me and became a man" (83).

This passage in Tan's novel, like many of the other stories recounted, presents a powerful meditation on the transformative nature of truth, location, identification, and desire. Ying-ying learns that women must disavow selfish wishes, must cultivate a state of desirelessness. Yet she also sees that she and Moon Lady are similar. They have both transgressed, and as a result they have lost their loved ones forever. However, the Moon Lady reveals to Ying-ying that no condition is permanent. By removing her wig and becoming a "he," Moon Lady presents an embodiment of difference *in* sameness. The opposition of sameness and difference (or femininity and masculinity) is revealed as a highly stylized, and culturally inflected performance, a performance evoked for the specific occasion of storytelling. In truth, however, what Ying-ying learns is that identity is always a displacement, as she explains after being reunited with her family that "even though I was found—later that night after Amah, Baba, Uncle, and the others shouted for me along the waterway—I never believed my family found the same girl. . . . And I remember everything that happened that day because is has happened many times in my life. . . . How I lost myself" (83).

In this way, *The Joy Luck Club* appropriates many of the conventions of Western feminism's matrifocal family romance only to gradually unveil the illusory construction of the false unities and reductive oppositions that underlie these romances. The novel explores the contradictory tonalities of mother-daughter relationships, beginning with a Chinese mother's story of coming to America and her dreams for her daughter. "In America I will have a daughter just like me. But over there . . . nobody will look down on her, because I will make her speak only perfect American English" (3). However, the paradoxical articulation of filial indebtedness through the displacement of the mother-tongue and the perfect mastery of the "other" tongue suggests that the daughter cannot be "just like" the mother, nor can she speak just like the perfect American. The articulations of a Chinese American "self" in relation to such reductive interpretations of maternal attachment and cultural difference form the primary contradiction of the narrative.

Indeed, *The Joy Luck Club* stresses that there is no one way of being Chinese or American. One is neither both nor either/or. Rather, both these adjectives describe multiple, dynamic possibilities. Consequently, Tan does not seek to accommodate the Western family romance to Chinese American femaleness, nor does she seek to accommodate Chinese

American femaleness to the family romance. Rather, her novel demonstrates the various and contradictory modalities of cultural hybridization that define the American family romance as a field of contestatory voices and Chinese American family romance as one kind of contest among voices. The female subjects that are produced through this complex process are contrasted with a mythical American identity that remains, for many of Tan's characters, desirable although elusive. To speak "perfect American English," from the mother's point of view, is to defy a legacy of vocal reticence, to become a unified and centered self.

In *The Joy Luck Club*, the move toward a de-Oedipalization of narrative is encoded as the rejection of this notion, as Tan's mothers and daughters work toward an embrace of multiple constitutions of gender, culture, and family. To wit, Tan's Chinese-born mothers and American-born daughters must learn to engage in the "possible sharing with the unknown other" who exists within as well as outside the self. The novel traces the ebb and flow of a process through which mothers and daughters learn to become adept writers and readers of each other's lives despite cultural and language differences that fragment them.

At the same time, *The Joy Luck Club* participates in the contingent establishment of a matrifocal family romance. This is partly evident in the narrative's emphasis on "the evolution of female identity . . . formed in relation to the mother through the achievement of individuation in the context of connection." [6] However, the maternal focus is further stressed in the almost palpable absence of men from the novel and from the family histories that are recounted throughout the narrative. This absence is particularly striking when one considers the extent to which an all-male bachelor society virtually defined Chinese American culture until the War-Bride Act of 1945 made it possible for Chinese women to emigrate and join their husbands and sons. [7] Earlier popular works such as Louis Chu's *Eat a Bowl of Tea* satirically portray the downfall of old order Chinese patriarchy and the decline of traditional family hierarchies that became increasingly apparent with Chinese women's arrival in the United States.

Chu portrays New York City's Chinatown in the late 1940s as a utopian male-only "family" that functions more like a social club where men complain, compete with one another, gamble, and talk disparagingly of their wives back home who wait patiently for checks from husbands they have not actually seen for as many as twenty years. For the young couple Ben Loy and Mei Oi, Chinese American masculinity and femininity are redefined as women come to terms with the new freedoms afforded them in the West and as men struggle with phallic inadequacies resulting from their inability to integrate Chinese cultural traditions with American economic and social realities. [8] In the face of racism and capitalist competition and in context with a postwar America that champions youthful rebellion and reckless individuality, patriarchal loyalty quickly disintegrates into a mockery of the father's unquestioned authority. The bachelor society's efforts to maintain order and power is inevitably unveiled by the newly arrived woman's rapid integration into new cultural patterns that prohibit male isolation from the "new world."

Placed alongside Chu's novel and feminist-inspired narratives such as Maxine Hong Kingston's *The Woman Warrior*, Tan's *The Joy Luck Club* shows not only the rift between generations of women but the rifts between the sexes that resulted largely from the destabilizations of pre-Communist Chinese gender hierarchies within a postwar American order of male-female gender relations.[9] As Auntie An-mei recalls from her childhood in China, fathers were no more than stern portraits hanging on the walls, portraits that seemed to follow the daughter with their eyes. Thus held within the obliging gaze of absent patriarchs, Chinese women were conditioned as agents of cultural continuity, links in "the chain of guardianship and of transmission."[10] A large portion of the hope held by the Chinese mothers of Joy Luck for their daughters is expressed in terms of the contradictions imposed on them as transmitters of Chinese culture, which includes a cultural imposition of speechlessness on women. Moreover, as each of the four mothers tells the story of her past life in China, what she conveys is not a unified culture but a culture rent by historical crisis and upheaval, the drama of the diaspora.[11] Thus, there is no cohesive Chinese culture for these mothers to pass on to their daughters. All that can be transmitted are pieces. For the Joy Luck daughters as well, American culture seems to offer nothing coherent, but a multitude of nonlinear directions and choices, "and each decision meant a turn in another direction" (214). However, by discovering ties to a fragmented mother tongue—a tongue that does not bilaterally divide silence from speech, Chinese from American, but rather explores the multiple, overlapping dimensions of both—the daughters of Joy Luck challenge the patriarchal imposition of cultural strictures in both Eastern and Western contexts, thus dissolving prescriptive standards for both matrifocal and patrifocal family romance.

However, in addition to the expectant gaze of old order and new order Chinese communities, Chinese American women have been subject to the gaze of American feminists whose reliance on "theory" has tended, in many cases, to universalize the psychosocial dynamics of mother-daughter relationships. Along these lines, Shirley Geok-lin Lim has argued for American feminism's need to examine its own reliance on Asian stereotypes. This reliance, Lim observes, is embodied in terms of maternal metaphor. In this way, the prevalence of filial duty and familial indebtedness in Confucianist society is appropriated by American feminists who find the Eastern notion of piety useful for assuming a debt of gratitude owed by Asian feminists to those feminists (white American) who have invited them to partake in "sisterhood" or theoretical discussion.[12] In contrast to the hierarchical family relationships mandated by Confucianism, American feminism insists on an illusion of its own embrace of difference, although, as Lim argues, there is an inherent hierarchy equally as powerful, albeit less up-front. Consequently, Lim likens her experience with American feminism to her earlier encounters with British colonialists who exact indebtedness and obligation. Once again, she claims, the reification of cultural difference is used to subordinate Eastern culture to Western notions of unity, consensus, and centrality.

Cultural centrality, demonstrated through language or discourse, retains here an association with dominance. If invited to assimilate into the center, ingratitude on the part of a Chinese American would register as a kind of betrayal. In *The Joy Luck Club*, Rose Hsu Jordan perceives that her American husband, Ted, needs her to be grateful to him for marrying her, which means that he needs her to be passive and dependent. However, it is these same qualities that eventually cause Ted to ask for a divorce. He claims that he wants to end the marriage because of her inability make decisions; however, his dissatisfaction mainly stems from the false premises on which he married Rose to begin with. It is suggested that Ted employs marriage as a form of rebellion, a way of denouncing his controlling mother whose racism rears its head early in their courtship. Privately assuring Rose that Ted's profession would never allow for a "mixed" marriage, even though she personally has nothing against minorities, Mrs. Jordan inspires Ted to defend his attachment to Rose. They cling to one another ever more desperately. "I was victim to his hero. I was always in danger and he was always rescuing me. . . . The emotional effect of saving and being saved was addicting to both of us" (125). According to Rose's own mother, her daughter is passive because she is without wood, a condition that refers to Lao-tzu's order of the five elements.[13] However, the power dynamic that is played out in Rose and Ted's courtship and doomed marriage is also the result of the West's romantic idealization of the East as sublimely subservient yet inscrutable, two-faced. Naturally, the mothers and daughters of Joy Luck remain, each in her own way, ambivalent about their assimilation into a culture where such contradictions prevail. As Lim has explained in another context, this ambivalence forms a "a dialectic":

[M]inority writers, especially first-generation immigrant writers . . . contain within themselves this double perspective; as in an optical illusion, their identities encompass more than one figure simultaneously. . . . This double, even triple or multiple perspective exists simultaneously for the same figure, but we cannot see both simultaneously; only through a switch in focus can one envision one or the other figure. Though we know both figures exist in this optical illusion, we can only see one at a time. Human sight cannot hold both contradictory visions in one glance. So too with the identity of alien and American. For while immigrants are both simultaneously alien and American, they are conscious of only one or the other at any time.[14]

In a section of the novel entitled "Double Face," Lindo Jong speaks precisely of this bifurcating dilemma and the American tendency to equate cultural ambivalence with deceit. According to her daughter, Waverly, this perception is fine so long as you get what you want. But her mother worries. "I think about our two faces. I think about my intentions. Which one is American? Which one is Chinese? Which one is better? If you show one, you must always sacrifice the other" (304).

For the Chinese American daughters of *The Joy Luck Club*, the difficult process of "clearing a space" for the sharing of stories—with one another, with mothers, and with (unknown) readers—entangles them within, and yet allows them to realign, these ethnic polarizations that divide the Chinese American against herself. These processes are what constitute a family—a constant reexamination and reinterpretation that must take place within individuals as well as within communities. Like culture, family is dynamized by subtle forms of competing activities that offer alternative, ever-changing, intersubjective possibilities. In this sense, the Joy Luck Club is a family, or a form of "fictive kin," that speaks to the potential of familial reconfiguration within and across cultures. The activities that make up the club are basically eating, mahjongg, and talking. All constitute subtle forms of competition between the mothers, who, in their indirect assertions of who is the best cook, or whose daughter is most dutiful and industrious, discover a "safe" context for rehearsing power relations that become specifically embodied within the club's activities.

The absence of a uniform American cultural life is described when Jing-mei joins the mah-jongg players and confesses that she is out of practice, having played only a few times with Jewish friends in college. "Not the same thing," scoffs Auntie Lin. Jing-mei recalls once asking her mother to explain the difference between Chinese and Jewish mahjongg. "Entirely different kind of playing," Suyuan had responded, first in English. "Jewish mah jong, they watch only for their own tile, play only with their eyes." Then she began speaking Chinese and added, "Chinese mah jong, you must play using your head, very tricky. You must watch what everybody else throws away and keep that in your head as well. And if nobody plays well, then the game becomes like Jewish mah jong. Why play?" (22–23). These "different" ways of playing mah-jongg articulate competing cultural and ideological beliefs, which, presumably, are *all* a part of Jing-mei's "American" cultural situation. The tensions between separation and attachment, individualism and the collective mind, also reiterate one of the central themes of the mother-daughter plot, a theme reinforced by feminism's emphasis on the fluidity of feminine ego boundaries, its greater capacity for individuation and empathy in the context of unsevered maternal connection. These issues are certainly salient for Jing-mei as she hesitates to assume her mother's place at mah-jongg. Yet her memory of Suyuan Woo's distinction between Jewish and Chinese mah-jongg reveals that gender and culture are intricately intertwined, mutually constructive and destabilizing. This is made evident in Suyuan Woo's cultural reclamation and exaltation of the powers of attachment, a move that she enacts specifically through language.

As many of the mother's histories recount, by integrating their thoughts with the thoughts of other Chinese women they were able to harness strengths and powers that made it possible for them to subvert the old Chinese system of gender oppression by participating within it. Lindo Jong describes the process though which she extricated herself from an arranged marriage. At first, she is powerless within her new family, tyrannized by her mother-in-law who regularly abuses Lindo for not becoming pregnant, all the while remaining ignorant of the fact that her son will not sleep with his new wife. Gradually, by learning the family's system of myths, fears, superstitions, Lindo is able to construct a ruse that eventually succeeds in convincing her mother-in-law to install a concubine for her son. Everyone saves face, and in the process Lindo gains an enormous advantage over her husband and mother-in-law. Later in life, she conveys this lesson to her daughter, Waverly. "I was six when my mother taught me the art of invisible strength. . . . 'Strongest wind cannot be seen' " (89). Waverly becomes an unbeatable chess master, a child prodigy. She accomplishes this by learning to integrate her mind with the minds of her opponents. However, Waverly becomes embarrassed by her mother's tendency to boast loudly and randomly of her daughter's triumphs at chess, as if the credit were hers. Waverly withdraws from the next chess tournament in protest. The contest of silent strengths is played out between mother and daughter as Waverly defiantly asserts her separateness. However, this move to individuate ultimately works to her disadvantage. At the next tournament, Waverly finds she has lost the power to win.

The Chinese cultural stress on empowerment through the communal mind or the integration of one's thoughts with the thoughts of others is rehearsed as the Joy Luck members strive for balance so that everyone holds equal claims, equal responsibility, equal ownership. Balance is structurally foregrounded in symmetrical pairings, a reiteration of fours. There are four mothers, four daughters, four directions, and four corners at the mah-jongg table. The Joy Luck families have a common capital account, which they go over at the start of the meeting. Auntie An-mei makes precisely ten wontons per person, no more no less. "We got smart," she claims. "Now we can all win and lose equally. We can have stock market luck. And we can play mah jong for fun, just for a few dollars, winner take all. Losers take home left-overs! So everyone can have some joy" (18). By resisting and assimilating into this balance of the elements, the Joy Luck daughters redescribe their mother's understandings of culture and ethnicity. Furthermore, these gestures toward and away from an idealization of balance convey the daughter's particular dilemma of having to be "like" mother and at the same time "like" other American women of their generation. Mother-daughter relationship is portrayed as lacking an essential or untroubled matrilineal paradigm. Rather, it is dramatized as a relationship dependent on disjunctures, communal discussion, and constructive reinterpretation for its meanings.

In this way, *The Joy Luck Club* adopts some elements of the Western feminist formulation of maternal family romance. For example, the narrative is structured by an intersubjective arrangement of narrative voices that are at once inside and outside the cultural conventions of Joy Luck. This, indeed, is the situation in which we find Jing-mei Woo at the outset of the novel as she expresses her ambivalence about being asked to take her mother's place at mah-jongg. Reading these tentative, conflictive tonalities requires that we read both ethnicity and gender as dynamically interactive, situated both inside and outside the family, and different from those interactions interpreted by those who remain only on the outside, looking in, or only on the inside, looking out. Indeed, *The Joy Luck Club* does not attempt to apprehend Chinese American culture through static discursive positioning, but through the forging of individual discursive spaces that confound categories of West and East, self and other, writing and talking, while affirming a balance of voices whose meanings rest on their shared occupation of a much larger discursive arena, the text itself. Nevertheless, "balancing" retains its power to denote cultural instabilities and conflict. When An-mei Hsu loses her Christian faith as a result of the accidental drowning of her son, Bing, she places her leatherette Bible underneath a table leg that is too short, "to correct the imbalances of life" (122). In this way, the Western Bible is rendered irrelevant to her loss, but is nevertheless employed to uphold, literally, her renewed reliance on Chinese cultural beliefs.

The imbalances that result from Western feminism's tendency to position itself outside the East, as master of the "other" culture, are perniciously apparent in Julia Kristeva's *About Chinese Women*, a controversial piece of theoretical writing that locates in both the tonal speech and pictorial writing of the Chinese language a system of communication that preserves the child's original dependence on the mother's body.[15] By locating the Chinese language within a "pre-Oedipal, pre-syntactic, pre-symbolic . . . register," Kristeva discovers an essential stratum of Chinese life that honors a matrilineal prehistory of the family.[16] The maternal stratum persists, Kristeva argues, not only in the tonal and imagistic qualities of the Chinese language but in what she identifies as "a sort of reticence in metalanguage," a reticence that resists the logic of causes and essences — all the principles of the Western metaphysical tradition — in favor of a "dramatic combinatorium," or the effective maintenance of contradictions that keep alive the order of paradox and the ceaseless instability of any unified essences.[17] Thus, for Kristeva, the Chinese are "two-faced people"; however, this two-facedness again is tied to mother's body and to a kind of language that prevents our separation from her, a rebuff to Freud's theories of female development that oppose a resentful identification with a castrated mother figure to an envious, self-abnegating desire for father.[18]

Based on Kristeva's analysis, it would seem that integration into Western culture constitutes, for Chinese women, an initiation into the Oedipal dilemma, an acquiescence to the mandates of a patriarchal language system that imposes strict binary separations of maternal and paternal spheres, symbolic and semiotic practices. In actuality, however, *About Chinese Women* constitutes the Western theorist's own family romance with the Chinese "other." In this, Western language (conceptualized as the Father) meets Eastern language (conceptualized as the Mother), to produce a dissident offspring, perhaps the theorist herself. Kristeva's seduction by the mother language, or mother culture, is conditioned by her distance from that culture, as well as by her theoretical mastery of that culture — a reconnection to maternal jouissance that at the same time insists on individual authority. Thus, the question "Daughter of the mother, or daughter of the father?" becomes salient precisely at the instant when gender sameness and cultural difference collide.[19]

As I have argued throughout this chapter, *The Joy Luck Club* works in subtle and inconsistent ways to decenter the maternal family romance, thus revealing that it and its romanticized feminist corollary, the "sisterhood" of women, are peculiarly Western constructs. In some contexts, these concepts may serve to dominate and exact indebtedness from "other" female subjects whose cultural marginalization may be "liberated" by their universalist presumptions. Thus, in an interesting reversal, *The Joy Luck Club* seeks, in a sense, to ethnicize the maternal familial romance, while studies such as Kristeva's *About Chinese Women* attempt to maternalize (and familialize) ethnicity.[20] However, the transcultural values that some theorists attribute to sexual difference are challenged by Minh-ha's insistence that sexual difference has "no absolute value," no cross-cultural Oedipal (or anti-Oedipal) hookups, but only meanings that are "interior to the praxis of every subject."[21] That Western writing about Chinese women holds, in Minh-ha's words, to the "prevailing logic of acquisition and separation" is apparent throughout Kristeva's analysis, as her critics have argued.[22] In this regard, Kristeva's familialization of ethnicity appropriates Chinese women for a post-Oedipal family romance that is possibly more relevant to Kristeva's difficulties with Western cultural strictures than to a desire to actually hear the voices of Chinese women. Conflict or a lack of confluence between Western metaphysics and Chinese gender articulations or between Chinese culture and feminism's theoretical dissolution of the speaking subject appears to concern Kristeva less than her determination to see her own reflection in the faces of Chinese women who constitute the object of her critique of phallogocentrism.

In this way, Kristeva's text has often been used to highlight certain problems that may be viewed as emblematic of Asian women's vulnerable status within modes of Western thought—including feminist thought. Consequently, if Minh-ha seems less willing than Kristeva to theoretically undermine the possibility of a productive identity politics, it may be because Western feminists such as Kristeva have performed this work from positions of assumed privilege, as theorists and speakers for the "other." Indeed, a feminist theory of representation that affords no stable positioning to subjects within language, regardless of culture or gender, is possibly less responsive to women "otherized" by Eurocentrism than a feminist practice that grants all subjects the possibility of agency and coherence within diverse systems of representation.

For example, maternal self-sacrifice, which Freudian Oedipal dynamics would cast in terms of castration and daughterly identification, is portrayed in *The Joy Luck Club* as inseparable from the Chinese sense of historical responsibility and filial continuity that *is* the daughter's desire and her access to full participation in culture, family, and language. This desire connects each generation of daughters to their mothers with knowledge of the latter's unrepayable devotion. The Chinese teaching of *xiao*, defined by Rey Chow as "filial piety," perceives the mother-daughter relationship as a "fundamentally unequal transaction," and the gesture of compensation as a blurring of the binary opposition that commonly structures the Western understanding of exchange between subject and object, giver and receiver.[23] Chow thus identifies the representation of Chinese mothers' relentless self-sacrifice and the daughters' desire to reciprocate that sacrifice as productive of a potentially deconstructive understanding of the Oedipal separation of female identification and desire. In other words, sacrifice is transformed into self-sacrifice, "for with understanding comes the most intense feelings of physical interaction with the mother."[24] What in Oedipal terms is seen as castration, or the daughter's acceptance of lack, is reconceptualized as a mutually empowering, intersubjective practice. This practice does not require the sacrifice of one *for* the other, but rather supports a mutual constitution and connection of responsive subjects.

In *The Joy Luck Club*, issues of maternal sacrifice and indebtedness are woven throughout the narrative and gesture toward both the strengthening and the disintegration of historical consciousness. An-mei Hsu remembers that on the occasion of her grandmother's death, her mother (who had been disowned from the family for becoming a rich man's concubine) prepared a traditional soup with herbs. While cooking, she took a sharp knife and cut a piece of flesh out of her own arm to put in the soup.

Tears poured from her face and blood spilled to the floor. . . . This is how a daughter honors her mother. It is *shou* so deep it is in your bones. The pain of the flesh is nothing. The pain you must forget. Because sometimes that is the only way to remember what is in your bones. (41)

Here, in the narrative space between filial indebtedness and the aesthetics of the body, the pain An-mei desires to feel is not her own pain, but her mother's. In this way, she demonstrates that forging a connection to history involves an ironic subversion of Oedipus: the daughter articulates her physical desire for *and* identification with the mother's body, her achievement of subjectivity *and* objectivity through the aestheticization of the mother's pain.

Along with certain forms of self-sacrifice, the Joy Luck mothers envision power in specific nuances of silence. These "articulate silences," to use the phrase King-kok Cheung has coined, challenge both the feminist valorization of speech as the essence of identity *and* the perception of reticence as a unifying cultural trait among Chinese and an authentic marker of cultural difference.[25] At the same time, the mothers hope that in America their daughters will develop strong, independent voices. "Over there nobody will say her worth is measured by the loudness of her husband's belch. Over there nobody will look down on her, because I will make her speak only perfect American English" (3). Furthermore, the mothers imagine that their daughters will one day be grateful for the opportunity to enjoy these freedoms that would have been unavailable to them in China. Yet the frustrations that both mothers and daughters face are produced by these hopes; for if the mother's goal is to sacrifice the motherland (and the mother tongue), with the expectation that filial indebtedness will provide eventual compensation, what form can compensation take in a culture that places obligation beneath the imperatives of individual fulfillment? In this way, mother-daughter psychology is shown to be largely inflected by social and political beliefs that differ dramatically from culture to culture. Lindo Jong affirms the basic incongruity of Chinese "reticence" versus America's celebration of individual "expressiveness" through consumer engagement when she laments, "I wanted my children to have the best combination: American circumstances and Chinese character. How could I know these two things do not mix" (289). That a refusal to speak might constitute a form of revolution is suggested by An-mei Hsu's account of her mother's suicide. By artfully planning her death, An-mei Hsu's mother commits her own voice to eternal silence so that her daughter will inherit voice through her sacrifice. Indeed, this sacrifice teaches An-mei how "to shout," or how to reject miseries that profit others at the expense of one's self-respect. Thus, when An-mei's daughter, Rose, admits that her marriage is failing and that she is seeking help from a psychiatrist, An-mei refers to him as "just another bird drinking from your misery." "A psychiatrist does not want you to wake up," she warns her daughter (272). She then recounts a story that she read in a Chinese newsmagazine of Chinese peasants who had been tormented for thousands of years by flocks of magpies that fed brazenly off the tears and misery of the people.

> But one day, all these tired peasants—from all over China—they gathered in fields everywhere. They watched the birds eating and drinking. And they said, "Enough of this suffering and silence!" They began to clap their hands, and bang sticks on pots and pans and shout, "*Sz! Sz! Sz!*"—Die! Die! Die! (272–73)

The triumph of the peasant farmers in China prompts her to ask, "What would your psychiatrist say if I told him that I shouted for joy when I read that this had happened?" Here, An-mei allegorically links the repressive conditions of precommunist peasant life in China with America's middle-class compliance with mental health "experts." In this way, the passage questions the American tendency to mystify, vilify, or feminize Eastern silences as manifestations of veiled intentions or passive servility. This is achieved by contrasting the peasant revolution to an American self-expressiveness or the popular consumption of therapies designed to transform self-expression into compliant nonresistance.

Furthermore, Tan's novel seeks to show that silence, like speech, is multiple, diverse, and contradictory. *The Joy Luck Club* does not envision silence as the opposite of speech, nor does it envision speech as liberation from the constraints of silence. Rather, the novel explores the destabilizations that certain nuances of speech and silence enact on one another. From her mother, Waverly Jong learns that "a little knowledge withheld is a great advantage one should store for future use. That is the power of chess. It is a game of secrets in which one must show and never tell" (96). However, her mother, Lindo, responds, "she learned these things, but I couldn't teach her about Chinese character. . . . How not to show your own thoughts, to put your feelings behind your face so that you can take advantage of hidden opportunities" (289).

But even within cultures, silence does not convey unified meanings owing to the fact that the contexts in which it occurs are always inflected by gender, class, race, and a host of other differences that determine vocal performance. In the West, silence and reticence have retained strong associations with the feminine, and Chinese American critics have pointed out the American tendency to feminize Chinese culture (and virtually all Asian cultures) in images that reduce vocal reticence to passivity, docility, and the absence of conventional masculine subjectivity. By examining the multiple effects of silence, *The Joy Luck Club* imagines possible forms of connection between gender, ethnicity, language, and silence; furthermore, as the novel seeks to undo the hierarchical ordering of verbal and nonverbal articulation, it simultaneously undermines gender hegemonies.

Early in the narrative, Jing-mei speaks of her mother's tendency to change the ending of her Kweilin story every time she tells it.

Sometimes she said she used that worthless thousand-*yuan* note to buy a half-cup of rice. She turned that rice into a pot of porridge. She traded that gruel for two feet from a pig. Those two feet became six eggs, those eggs six chickens. The story grew and grew. (12)

Jing-mei recalls that as her mother told stories she would simultaneously cut the bottoms of old ski sweaters, gifts from well-meaning relatives in Vancouver, and unravel threads of yarn as she stitched together her past. In this way, Suyuan Woo's life, her relation to her daughters and to language itself, is transformed every time her story is retold. Like the old sweaters, the stories she offers her daughter are "gifts of moonlight," which must be perpetually disassembled and reassembled in order to have future value. Similarly, in *The Joy Luck Club* the mother-daughter family romance never becomes fixed in its form, but remains living and dynamic. The romance represents the mother's history as a field of contestable and variously embodied meanings. Consequently, the mothers and daughters of Joy Luck are positioned so as to facilitate an ongoing, multisubjective interpretation of their relations to one another. Taken one by one, the stories that make up *The Joy Luck Club* retain their own structural integrity while at the same time refer the reader forward and backward to other voices, other readings. As a result, one cannot accurately say that the whole text is more powerful than any one of its parts, because this "whole," as it were, is constantly being reconfigured, like the Joy Luck families themselves.

As the histories of the Joy Luck mothers demonstrate, mothers and daughters in old China could not form strong physical ties because of the daughter's inevitable servitude to her husband's home, ancestors, and living family. In China, when a woman married, she cut all ties to her own mother and became a servant to her new mother-in-law. This contingency of kinship is reiterated by the daughters' narratives in which weddings, marital difficulty, and divorce are recurrent themes. Rose Hsu Jordan, Waverly Jong, and Lena St. Clair all deal with failed marriages. Jing-mei remains single, and there is no evidence that she is eager to marry. While their circumstances contradict the importance of family in Confucianist Chinese society, the theme of familial plasticity rehearses the historical rupture of kinship bonds and the splintering of subjects. Ultimately, this fragmentation is not resolved through the reestablishment of a pre-Oedipal mother-daughter symbiosis, but is productively explored, acknowledged, and finally embraced as a conflictive language that history insists they speak.

With its achingly heartfelt conclusion, *The Joy Luck Club* suggests that *home*—in the sense of motherland—is embodied in an image of maternity that must be perpetually taken apart and reconstructed by subsequent generations who remain internally fragmented, always partial strangers to one another. Although the novel enacts the frequently noted circular rhythms of the feminist text by returning Jing-mei to China, the China she returns to is not her mother's China, but an estranged homeland. Similarly, Suyuan Woo's "long cherished wish," as it turns out, is not the restoration of mother-daughter-sister unity, but the possibility of a shared peace derived through a recognition of the "other" who stands between and within them.

Chapter 8
Reconstructing Kin:
Toni Morrison's *Beloved*

In "Reading Family Matters," Deborah E. McDowell narrates the on-going controversy surrounding a small but outstanding group of black female writers and critics' accusations that these writers are fracturing the image of an already besieged black American nuclear family. The complaint, which has been registered in the news media and academic journals, suggests that these writers—Toni Morrison among them—have betrayed the black family by failing to shoulder responsibility for re-storing to it an image of wholeness and unity. Admittedly, McDowell observes, the "family romance is de-romanticized in writings by the greater majority of black women," whose portraits of domestic life do not simply paint Norman Rockwell in black, but rather seek out the distinct voices of black women, themes appropriate to their experience within the nuclear family, and narrative forms that place black women at the center of stories about family.[1]

To my mind, McDowell's defense shows how the politicization of black women's family narratives serves to highlight interpretive conflicts that are culturally specific, as well as gender specific. For example, if we proceed from Marianne Hirsch's treatment of family romance as "an imaginary interrogation of origins" that "describes the experience of familial structures as discursive," we run the risk of recuperating cul-tural biases implicit in the Freudian paradigm, such as an ethnocentric notion of family structure and a Western notion of origin as an ulti-mately knowable locus of truth.[2] However, the Western grand narrative tradition of family romance has little relevance to a people displaced from their homeland, denied their claims to origin, separated from one another, forbidden their language, and refused participation in the dominant discursive economy to which they are subordinated. Regard-less of where one stands on "family values," experienced readers of

African-American fiction will rightly claim that the "de-romanticization" of the black family romance owes a great deal to the complex forms of economic and psychological oppression that black women and men have experienced both within the nuclear family and within the larger economic structure. In contemporary literature, this matrix of racism, sexism, and classism is registered in recurrent images of family violence, absent fathers, and woman-centered black families that function without the acknowledged presence or support of men.

The cultural significance of these images, however, can be traced to a bigger picture of which African-American family structure is only a part. That picture *is* the historical processes of American social and economic development. Its organizing principle is racial oppression, or more specifically the dynamic of relations of domination perpetuated by the institutional enslavement of Africans who were brought to the American colonies as indentured servants as early as 1619.[3]

Toni Morrison's Pulitzer Prize–winning novel *Beloved* is a critical interrogation of family romance that examines the social deconstruction of African-American history and family life in the years before, during, and after the Civil War when the United States became engaged in the project of "Reconstruction." More importantly, for the purposes of my analysis, it is a novel centrally concerned with the need to rediscover or literally re-member the fractured stories of the past so that these stories might preserve lost culture, restore the familial and community bonds that, although severely weakened by generations of institutional enslavement, still function reciprocally to construct identity. As the novel demonstrates, it is these structures of narrative, these stories, that empower and culturally legitimize the family.

While the reconstruction of family relations remains a central focus of *Beloved*, there is also significant stress placed on the need to dismantle the boundaries that separate family from community, private from public concerns. The novel brings about the gradual merger of those inside and those outside the haunted house at 124 Bluestone Road. Morrison suggests that a family closed off from caring relationships with nonkin is a family doomed to be consumed by the spirits of the unresolved past. As Sethe gives herself over more and more to Beloved's insatiable hungers, a symbiotic union forms between the two that leaves Sethe starved and weak while Beloved grows fatter by the day. The women's withdrawal into 124, and into the reflective eyes of each other, is expressed in a series of interior voice passages that seem to blend together into one familial voice, although Morrison structures each section so that it must be read separately from the others, thus maintaining the integrity of individual consciousness within the triad.[4]

Like Morrison's earlier work, *The Bluest Eye, Beloved* stresses the point that no family matter exists undetermined by public consequence. However, *Beloved* holds the distinction of being a ghost story that challenges white-dominant culture's frame of reference for experiencing family romance. Morrison's artistic narrative style, her blending of the powers of the past and the present, the living and the dead, the private sphere and the public sphere, unsettles the definitional boundaries of the Western European traditions of family romance and novelistic realism. In short, Morrison's critical project, like Hirsch's critical project on mother-daughter family romance, appears to take "as its point of departure the intersection of familial structures and structures of plotting."[5] But what has not been sufficiently addressed, to my mind, is the extent to which *Beloved* explores the pulling apart of narrative and familial systems in order to redefine the structures of African-American kinship and the structures of an African-American storytelling tradition as culturally deconstructive and reconstructive.

Comparing families to minefields, Mary Helen Washington writes: "We walk and dance through them never knowing where or when something or someone is going to explode."[6] Indeed, there has been—and still is—much to say about the explosive mother-daughter relationships depicted in *Beloved*.[7] But what need be acknowledged are the actual shapes that familial representations take within historically specific communities of women, and the forms that make communication—even explosive communication—possible between generations separated by the brutality of a slave-labor economy which places the value of a dollar above the value of human relationship.

The central event of Morrison's intricately woven narrative is a brutal act of infanticide: After sending her three children ahead to safety and while expecting a fourth, Sethe escapes from a Kentucky plantation known as Sweet Home. While in flight, she gives birth to a daughter with the aid of a white girl and arrives with the new infant to 124 Bluestone Road, a house situated near Cincinnati, Ohio. The house belongs to Baby Suggs, the mother of Sethe's husband, Halle. Halle's escape is botched, presumably by his fall into madness, a result of witnessing Sethe's rape at the hands of the master's nephews. Sethe, however, is reunited with her three children, Baby Suggs, and the attentive local community, whereupon she experiences twenty-eight days of freedom before the master of the plantation, schoolteacher, catches up with them. When she sees his wagon approaching the house at Bluestone Road, Sethe takes her children to the shed out back and in a desperate effort to protect her children—to put them someplace where they'll be safe—she tries to kill them, although she only succeeds in cutting the throat of her eldest daughter who bleeds to death in her arms.

Realizing that his "property" is ruined, schoolteacher returns to Kentucky empty-handed. Sethe survives with her remaining children, two sons named Howard and Buglar, and the new infant, Denver, named after the white girl, Amy Denver, who stopped to soothe Sethe's wounds and help her deliver during the escape. After serving a sentence in prison, Sethe returns to 124 where she, Baby Suggs, and Denver withdraw into the house, rejected by the community, which stands in harsh and disbelieving judgment of what they perceive to be an inexcusable crime. Terrified of their mother, Howard and Buglar run away and are never heard from again. The murdered child's tombstone is engraved with only the one word "Beloved," in return for which Sethe barters sex with the stone carver. Baby Suggs, once a great healer and spiritual leader of the local black community, retreats to her bed where she gradually deteriorates to the point of death. And the house at 124 Bluestone Road becomes violently haunted with the angry spirit of the murdered child.

Sethe and Denver continue to live with the spirit, in the house that glows red with confusion and despair, until the day when Paul D, a former slave from Sweet Home, appears on the front porch of 124 after many years of aimless drifting. The narrative opens with his arrival, a moment that marks the beginning of a healing process for both him and Sethe; as they begin to reconstruct their lives and their grief through the sharing of stories, they discover a connection to a past that must be confronted and exorcised if they are to have a future. In relocating one another, they relocate something lost within themselves. Subsequently, the house begins to quake with the thunderous spirit of resistance to the past, Beloved. Paul D manages to rebuke the spirit and restore a momentary calm, yet in the same instant he realizes the dismal conditions under which Sethe and Denver have been living all these years.

Shortly after Paul D's arrival at 124 he coaxes Sethe out of her seclusion to attend a local carnival that has sanctioned a day for "black only" attendance. When he, Sethe, and Denver return to the house, exultant and feeling almost like a family, they find a young woman, fully dressed and wearing a broken-rimmed hat, sitting on a tree stump. When questioned about her circumstances and origins she says only that her name is Beloved. Beyond this she appears to have no memory, no history, and no identity. Gradually, Beloved begins recalling details and moments from the past that only a family member could possibly know about. Beloved demonstrates powerful need; at first, she craves anything with sugar. As her recovery progresses she becomes ravenous for information about Sethe's past. Storytelling thus becomes the treatment Sethe administers in order to nurse Beloved back to strength.

The question Beloved's emergence occasions is twofold: Is this young woman the ghost of the murdered child assuming human form? And, if she *is* the child returned from the dead, *why* has she returned, and what does she want? There is disagreement among critics concerning these questions, as well as the symbolic significance of the mysterious figure. While the majority agree that Beloved *is* a ghost, a visitor from the spirit world who makes visible the potent connection between the living and the dead, others have argued that she is a living being, an escaped slave who has been traumatized senseless, and upon whom Sethe merely projects her wish of reestablishing a bond with the daughter she was driven to murder.[8] However, in their efforts to determine whether Beloved's presence is natural or supernatural, physical or metaphysical, critics may be missing the point. My reading of Beloved is that she represents, above all, the undecidability of signifying relations between family matters and family shadows, public history and personal mythology. In this way *Beloved* is a text that opens up, rather than limits, the possibilities of meaningful connection between history and romance, family-making and storytelling. These processes are necessarily multiple, contradictory, and constitutive of what I have been calling throughout this book post-family romance.

This "connection" that Beloved represents is suggested by the bridge on which Beloved claims she stood before finding her way to 124. In this way, Beloved is perhaps best understood as an embodiment of history held aloft by a foundation we call memory, a foundation that is shown to be partial and fragmentary. And indeed, history and memory, both individual and collective, are precisely the intertwining forces that construct and at the same time threaten to destroy the kinship group. Mary Helen Washington makes a relevant point when she observes that "much of what we call family is constructed through memory—what we remember and pass on."[9] It is my view that Beloved represents the family as well as the familial. She is as much the family Sethe, Denver, and Paul D have lost as she is all the families separated and dismembered under the slavery system. She represents all children taken from their mothers and fathers, all lovers unwillingly separated and lost. And the reason she comes back is precisely the reason why this novel had to be written: in order to multiply the historical perspectives and interpretive options that keep families alive. Beloved will remain the undoing of kinship structure until she reaches this understanding, and the way she reaches it is by demanding that the past be remembered through the gradual stitching together of stories. She *is* this need for stories, stories without which Sethe can never move forward, take hold of her life, her kin, and find the courage to love again.

As a study of the connection between the historical and the familial, *Beloved* is concerned with the healing of the black American family and the "reconstruction" of kinship structures. These structures had been violated by the economic imperative that drove the slavery system: as commodities, enslaved women and men had no right to themselves, to one another, or to their children. Consequently, what Baby Suggs calls "the nastiness of life was the shock she received upon learning that nobody stopped playing checkers just because the pieces included her children" (23).[10] Under the slavery system, permeable and unstable kinship structures were often necessary so that parents could entrust their children to someone else if they were sold away or separated. Often, as a result, children were parented more by a community of caretakers than by their biological parents, and in this sense "family" came to mean a structure of relations capable of transcending blood kin to form an extended family including neighbors and friends. By necessity, "family" had to be structured to include these "fictive kin," a communal network of caring individuals. *Beloved* explores this vital connection between the biological family and fictive kinship relations as necessary for blacks' survival, although contrary to the Freudian triad, which has served as a prominent cultural reference point for conventional understandings of what family means.

In the cultural and economic redefinition of family life that followed the Civil War and the gradual abolishment of the slavery system, many freed blacks were forced again to sacrifice their ties to family and community with their realization that their new "freedom" meant little more than abject poverty. Morrison describes this transitional period after the Civil War when freed blacks sought to reconstruct the pieces and fragments of the family and of themselves:

Odd clusters and strays of Negroes wandered the back roads and cowpaths from Schenectady to Jackson. Dazed but insistent, they searched each other out for word of a cousin, an aunt, a friend. . . . Some of them were running from family that could not support them, some to family; some were running from dead crops, dead kin, life threats and took-over land. Boys younger than Buglar and Howard; configurations and blends of families of women and children.(52)

Karen E. Fields's argument that "the essence of slavery was the creation of free-standing individuals, not families or communities" provides a useful gloss to the above passage. "As units of a commodity to be bought, sold, or put to use, individual slaves stood apart from any authoritative claim to human connection."[11] The economic institution of slavery destroyed black families not only by the forced separation of kin, but by the radical isolation and appropriation of the individual-as-merchandise.

Beloved's relentless need, her demand to be seen and heard, constitutes an outraged cry against this isolation. Her assumption of human form takes place at exactly the moment when Sethe, Denver, and Paul D begin to form some semblance of a communicative triad. "[Beloved] had appeared and been taken in on the very day Sethe and [Paul D] had patched up their quarrel, gone out in public and had a right good time—like a family" (66). Beloved's arrival at this pivotal moment suggests both her desire to be included in this family-like group, and her infantile need to sever Sethe's newfound lifeline lest her memory be reconciled and her name forgotten. It is significant also that the ghost of the murdered child appears just as her mother returns from a carnival, her first "social outing in eighteen years" (46). The family bond that Sethe, Denver, and Paul D reestablish takes place in the context of a life-affirming ritual, a celebration of the continuous cycles of birth, decay, death, and rebirth. As they head toward the carnival they pass a lumberyard fence where "up and down . . . old roses were dying. . . . The closer the roses got to death, the louder their scent, and everybody who attended the carnival associated it with the stench of the rotten roses" (47). The possibility of a new life juxtaposed with the sickly sweet aroma of imminent death anticipates Beloved's image and the confrontation of the living and the dead that her arrival occasions. The bringing together of extreme opposites, the pathos of change and renewal, references the Bakhtinian vision of carnival as a popular impulse that is ultimately "about freedom, the courage needed to establish it, the cunning required to maintain it, and—above all—the horrific ease with which it can be lost."[12] Through her association of the carnival with the fetid roses Morrison evokes the fragile new freedom that Sethe experiences as the restoration of family and community.

However, implicit in this meditation on freedom is the burden of historical consciousness; it seems that the extent to which familial bonds can be mutually reclaimed by Sethe, Denver, and Paul D is the extent to which they mutually confront and multiply interpret the past. The ghost of the murdered child loudly invites this opportunity, for as Rebecca Ferguson notes, "what is commonly called the supernatural is also the manifestation of history."[13] In *Beloved*, the persistence of the supernatural signifies the black community's need to sustain a hold on its history, its identity, and especially its kin. Consequently, it should come as no surprise that Beloved's restless spirit is provoked by all expressions of human attachment and familial intimacy.

The formal composition of Morrison's novel lends truth to the claim that "the narrative of family is as unpredictable as families themselves."[14] *Beloved* makes rigorous structural demands on readers and requires attention as close and exacting as Beloved herself requires from Sethe. The collective process of memory unfolds and is given shape with frequent tense shifts. The "action" of the novel alternates between past and present as fragments of stories, symbols, and codes are gathered and exchanged between characters. Also gathered are the different voices of all those who come into contact with the spirit of the murdered child; individual identities begin to take shape as each character explores her or his relation to Beloved. Narrative point of view alternates through various re-memberings of the past. Imagistically dense stream-of-consciousness passages recall, in Beloved's voice, the experience of crossing the ocean by ship. Her references to what seems to be the "middle passage" merge with references to birth. The conflation of these images suggests a continuous process of being born into the past. The "dark place" Beloved recalls evokes in the same instant the safety of the mother's womb and the dismal bulk of the slave ships. The context of this passage is a series of first-person narratives similarly marked by opening declarations of affiliation to Beloved, the multiple points of view generated by generations of mothers and daughters seem to merge into one consciousness, yet at the same time they remain separate and autonomous voices. As the language and formal appearance of these passages become transformed into poetry, the women's voices blend and mirror each other in their cadences of speech, phrases, and metaphors. Kinship is thus shown to be held together by an economy of symbols, a web of language that—like the family—is dismembered and fractured.

In *Beloved* family and language must be jointly reconstructed. Family is defined as a process of reading, a history of interpretive acts unique to each kinship group although these acts have ties to the larger cultural community. Claiming kin requires that one be able to share in a common language and read the symbols that constitute it. Under the system of slavery these fundamental structures of signification—the essential textuality of family—are suppressed, silenced, and even outlawed. When the signifying economies of enslaved Africans were rendered worthless, so were their cultures and identities. When the freedom to make and exchange meanings is denied, the freedom to form and claim family is denied. However, Morrison suggests that the victims of slavery managed to preserve kinship structures through the study and interpretation of countertextual forms. In this way, *Beloved* is about the painful process of reestablishing familial literacy. This process necessitates the creation of an amalgam formed of diverse cultural symbols. Not unlike the phrase-linkings that pluralize the concept of justice in Anne Tyler's *Searching for Caleb*, in *Beloved* decontextualized units of signification that survive slavery by virtue of courage and/or memory are combined with new symbols adopted from the dominant culture in the piecing together of a language with which to affirm alternative kinship bonds.

Throughout *Beloved* there is emphasis on such countertexts that covertly preserve family unities and values. Trees, for example, are a recurrent image Morrison deploys to symbolize hope for the restoration of familial security. When Paul D escapes from his imprisonment for the attempted murder of his white master, Brandywine, he is instructed by the Cherokee Indians to follow the blossoming tree flowers to the North and to freedom:

"That way," he said, pointing, "Follow the tree flowers," he said. "Only the tree flowers. As they go, you go. You will be where you want to be when they are gone." So he raced from dogwood to blossoming peach. When they thinned out he headed for the cherry blossoms, then magnolia, chinaberry, pecan, walnut, and prickly pear. . . . From February to July he was on the lookout for blossoms. When he lost them, and found himself without so much as a petal to guide him, he paused, climbed a tree on a hillock and scanned the horizon for a flash of pink or white in the leaf world that surrounded him. (112–13)

When Paul D first encounters the scar on Sethe's back, the result of a brutal whipping, she describes it for him as Amy Denver had described it for her eighteen years earlier, as a chokecherry tree. At that moment it occurs to Paul D that what Sethe has on her back is

nothing like any tree he knew because trees were inviting; things you could trust and be near; talk to if you wanted to as he frequently did since way back when he took the midday meal in the fields of Sweet Home. Always in the same place if he could, and choosing the place had been hard because Sweet Home had more pretty trees than any farm around. His choice he called Brother, and sat under it. (21)

Here, Morrison establishes an ironic connection between Paul D's invocation of fraternal intimacy and the brand that Sethe bears on her back as a relentless reminder of the perverse inhumanity that she was forced to endure. The scar on Sethe's back tells its own story which Paul D reads as if he were deciphering braille. "He rubbed his cheek on her back and learned that way her sorrow, the roots of it; its wide trunk and intricate branches. . . . And when the top of her dress was around her hips and he saw the sculpture her back had become, like the decorative work of an ironsmith too passionate for display, he could think but not say, 'Aw, Lord, girl'" (17). Sethe's scar, like Keats's Grecian urn, holds the past frozen in time; her body constitutes the text on which history is written, and her only chance of reclaiming herself, for herself and her family, is to seize the power of interpretation, to suffer the past on her own terms. By reading the scar as a tree—a symbol of human attachment and growth—rather than a symbol of defeat, Amy Denver, Sethe, and Paul D collectively assert themselves as writers rather than as blank pages passively waiting to be written upon.

The same sense of irony is conveyed in the image of Beloved sitting on a tree stump when Sethe first encounters her in human form. Her arrival at 124 threatens the familial structure that Sethe is on the brink of rediscovering. In the context of Morrison's vocabulary of symbols, the tree stump must be seen as the literal cutting down of the family tree that Paul D attempts to nurture when he proposes to Sethe that at last they "can make a life . . . a life" (46).

The inscription on Sethe's back connects her to one of the few memories she has of her own mother. Sethe remembers that as a small child she was taught to recognize her mother by the brand with which she is marked as property.

> Back there she opened up her dress front and lifted her breast and pointed under it. Right on her rib was a circle and a cross burnt right in the skin. She said, "This is your ma'am. This," and she pointed. "I am the only one got this mark now. The rest dead. If something happens to me and you can't tell me by my face, you can know me by this mark." (61)

In this way, Sethe is taught how to read kin, how to ascertain her own identity, and how to interpret the world around her. When Sethe asks her mother to "mark the mark on me too," she is slapped across the face instead. Only years later does she understand why, and by then she has her own mark, a tree on her back. To young Sethe, however, the cross within the circle is her family name, the only one she has ever been taught to recognize. Because she lacks this mark, she feels a lack of connection to her mother. But her mother knows what that brand really means in a system that commodifies, buys, and sells human life. It conveys the information that she is an extension of someone else's identity, one that has been permanently burned onto her body. That she has internalized this mark and lost her claim to any semblance of self-possession is made evident in her instructions to Sethe: "This is your ma'am. This." In other words, the slaveholder's brand does not substitute for her true name, it has become her true name as a result of profound dislocation, both external and internal.

The slap Sethe receives upon asking for the brand is presumably meant to awaken her to the recognition that, in a very literal sense, her people are not her people, and her beloved is not her beloved. My rewording of the novel's biblical epigraph is meant to emphasize the essential point that enslaved blacks were economically, psychologically, and *linguistically* blocked from passing on to future generations their own names and signifying economies. When Sethe asks for the brand, of course, she does not realize that she is asking to be given over to the system and marked as a piece of property. However, her mother's position is such that she can do no more than try to make passionately clear to Sethe the truth that Paul D echoes years later when he tells her, "You your best thing, Sethe. You are" (273). Thus, on an abstract level, Sethe's mother's violent expression of mother-love anticipates the violence that Sethe will eventually be driven to inflict on her own daughter: both women attempt, in other words, to save their children from the mark of slavery, to put them someplace where they'll be safe.

When her mother is hanged Sethe is given neither the reason why nor the chance to locate the brand that would positively identify the body. When she matures and chooses Halle to be her husband, Mrs. Garner, the wife of the self-styled "humanitarian" and master of Sweet Home, assumes the limited role of mother to Sethe. She gives her a pair of crystal earrings and turns a blind eye when Sethe steals some fabric to make herself a wedding dress. It is important to see these small gestures as *both* affirmations of servitude and expressions of genuine caring, especially in light of recent scholarship that historicizes the complex construction of "trust" in slave-slaveholder relations within American slave economies.[15] However, it is equally difficult to ignore the fact that Mrs. Garner has far more to gain from her attachment to Sethe than Sethe does from her. Along these lines, Fields argues that "the mother-daughter relation [they] stitch together is inherently unstable because it cannot be upheld beyond the voluntary complicity of the two, and because nothing sustains it but their separate desires." The relationship that Mrs. Garner permits to exist between them is, in short, "a mutually self-interested exchange" that joins slave owner and slave together in a paradoxical alliance that is exploitative and yet contains rarefied elements of a genuine love and sense of connectedness.[16] Ultimately, Mrs. Garner's ministrations reflect the policy of her husband that his "niggers is men every one of em. Bought em thataway, raised em thataway" (10). By envisioning Sweet Home as one thriving happy family and himself the noble patriarch, Garner promotes his superiority within the slaveholding community and indulges the fantasy that his "progeny" honor his authority not because their lives are at stake but because they are free to form attachments based on mutual interest.

When schoolteacher takes over the plantation after Garner's death he initiates a reign of terror based on his conviction that "definitions belong to the definers—not the defined" (190). In this context, schoolteacher represents an extreme embodiment of the Western logocentric assumption of the written word as constitutive of the domain of knowledge and power. His fanatical abuses of power stress domination through the controlling authority of the logos. He symbolizes the distortions of knowledge that naturalize the "scientific" view that blacks are fundamentally inferior to, perhaps even less human than, whites. In the name of education, he sustains and perpetuates an ideological construction—and here I refer to ideology in the Althusserian sense of its having a definite structural logic—of blacks as beasts of burden, as when Paul D is collared and given the bit. His assumed status as both master of the plantation and master of scientific discourse serve as his license to conduct "experiments" on Sethe, as when he watches and writes it up as one of his nephews holds her down while another nurses at her breast, thus stealing the milk that she had saved for her babies.

Schoolteacher claims the discursive power to construct and withhold identity. He seems to regard himself as a new Adam, the authorized giver of names. In turn, he regards enslaved blacks as the animals of Eden, passive recipients of the name. Here it is useful to reference Morrison's own meditation on the cultural devastation of this systematic hierarchy: "If you come from Africa, your name is gone. It is particularly problematic because it is not just *your* name but your family, your tribe. When you die, how can you connect with your ancestors if you have lost your name? That's a huge psychological scar."[17] Thus, one of the more radical gestures of the enslaved subject is the destabilization of the racist hierarchy through the courageous act of self-appropriation and self-naming. The slave, Joshua, enacts this subversion when he renames himself "Stamp Paid," thus signifying the extent of his sacrifice to the white man and his decision to never owe anything to anybody again. Sethe's name is itself a radical act, and a thread that links her to the past. The story we are told recounts the ship's voyage from Africa, during which Sethe's mother was raped repeatedly by white men. The children conceived of these rapes she throws overboard. However, since Sethe is conceived with a black man whom she truly loved, she gives her life, and more than that, her father's name.

Such signifying links to one's origin provide a basis, albeit fragile, for the construction of identities not dictated by the brands of slaveholders. The power of this connection, however, is experienced not simply in the knowledge of the father's name, but in the exchange of stories that provide a context in which the name functions as an arbiter of history and identity. That Sethe's stories can only be related to her in pieces, rather than in grand narrative fashion, suggests that any strengthening of the boundaries of self or of kinship ties must proceed by self-conscious acts of piecing and stitching. Neither genealogical coherence nor totalizing narratives are intrinsic to her knowledge of origin. The instability occasioned by this fractured sense of self is as easily inherited by subsequent generations as is a complete family tree. This is certainly implied when Denver first attempts to learn the alphabet from Lady Jones. Her efforts are aborted when Nelson Lord confronts her with a question about her mother's crime; significantly, the question comes when she is practicing how to write the letter *i*. Unable to answer his question, Denver quits school just when she would have mastered the mark that denotes *self*. She joins her mother, withdrawing into the haunted interior space of 124, leaving the little *i* and the written word behind.

Denver makes two important sacrifices when she walks out of Lady Jones's classroom. She surrenders her connection to the surrounding community and so relinquishes its support. Also, she abandons her studies of the English alphabet and the written word, which, in the period of Reconstruction, represent freedom whereas at Sweet Home they had meant certain death. The irony of this shift is doubled when we consider that by renouncing absorption into the dominant culture's alphabet Denver also renounces the local community, which both she and her mother desperately need for nurturance and affirmation. Indeed, one of the salient themes of *Beloved* explores the vital correspondence and exchange between the private language of the socially marginal family and the language of the surrounding community as it becomes shaped by the dominant existing social orders. In a sense, Denver's attachment to family matters develops in accord with her embrace of the outside community. It is this mutually empowering exchange that finally makes it possible for Denver to "get a read" on her mother and on the destructive voracity of her dead sister's spirit.

Toward the conclusion of the novel, when Beloved's ghost has been exorcised, Denver once again takes up the study of "book stuff" from Miss Bodwin, another white "schoolteacher." Although Miss Bodwin's will is good and her motivations humanitarian, her interest in Denver alarms Paul D, especially when Denver proudly informs him that Miss Bodwin is "experimenting" on her. Denver's bid for an education and Paul D's concealed impulse to warn her, "Watch out. Watch out. Nothing in the world more dangerous than a white schoolteacher" (266), intersect to form a lethal possibility that Morrison subtly invites readers to consider: a "white" education may represent, for Denver, another form of enslavement to the master's discourse.[18] While the formal institution of slavery may have become obsolete, the systematic structure of racial oppression and its denial of African culture, identity, and history continue in the socially and morally sanctioned institutions of education and language. Indeed, in this context, Paul D's inability to read the newspaper article describing Sethe's act of infanticide may suggest not that he has been deceived by Sethe, nor that he is ill-equipped to make sense of the world around him, but that the "literate" culture's interpretation of her act is, and by necessity should remain, in competition with his own. When he learns of the episode from Stamp Paid, Paul D struggles less with the moral implications of the slaying than he does with the need to comprehend Sethe's decision in the terms appropriate to his own read on the past he and Sethe share and the future they may yet have.

This is what Paul D himself suggests when he tells Sethe that "he wants to put his story next to hers" (273). Given the novel's emphasis on stories as constitutive of familial bonds, these words can be understood as no less than an acknowledgment of the internal interpretative struggles and contradictions that define a new configuration of American family romance. It is here, at last, that Paul D is moved to claim kin, to commit to and honor not one woman, but the multiplicity of stories and readings that they have collected. He thus enlists his participation in a multivoiced process of deciphering and interpreting common experience. In *Beloved*, family is represented by this process. At the novel's conclusion, Paul D recognizes in Sethe both the mother whose love is "too thick" and the child whose life was too short. What led to Beloved's death was not the whim of one momentarily deranged woman, but the fear and demoralization of all the Sweet Home men and women: Baby Suggs, Halle, Sixo, the Pauls, and himself as well. At last, Sethe's "story was bearable because it was his as well—to tell, to refine and tell again" (99).

What must also be embraced here is the paradox that these stories are both life-sustaining and toxic. This idea is made manifest when, in the immediate aftershock of the child's murder, Baby Suggs hands Sethe her living infant, Denver, to nurse. Too late, Baby Suggs notices that Sethe's nipple is covered in blood: "So Denver took her mother's milk right along with the blood of her sister" (152). In an earlier passage, Sethe recalls that while escaping from Sweet Home she was impelled onward by the weight of milk in her breasts and by the urgent need to deliver her milk to the baby waiting for her at 124. In these powerful images, Morrison indicates that the post–Civil War black family was nourished by the combination of these essential elements: mother's milk, the blood of relations lost to the violent reality of slavery, and the stories that are passed down to each subsequent generation, even if they require raising the dead; for to be denied these stories, complete with their painful contradictions, is as potentially debilitating as being denied food or any form of basic nourishment.

Although some critics of the novel have focused attention on the conflict over Morrison's depictions of men as weak, absent, or violent, and her depictions of women as too passively dependent on the men who leave and/or abuse them, it is important to note, I think, that in *Beloved* gender warfare remains subordinate in comparison to the larger issue of discursive warfare between the white-dominant culture's interpretation of black history and the interpretations that blacks have pieced together from their own wealth of family stories and exchanges. This system of exchange is largely structured by Sethe, Denver, and Beloved who briefly form a version of the three-woman family for which Morrison has been alternately criticized and praised. In support of the latter approach, McDowell references the line "They were a family somehow and [Paul D] was not the head of it" (132) to show how Morrison validates the all-female household and undermines the patriarchal structure of the nuclear family. [19] However, while Morrison affirms female strength and autonomy, I think it is equally valuable to consider that the female triad in *Beloved* excludes male participation ultimately to the detriment of its members' physical and emotional health. In this, I do not mean to suggest that Paul D is Sethe's salvation or her rescuer. Rather, I want to stress that his participation in this family—a participation clearly *not* based on a hierarchy of gender-specific roles—is vital insofar as it disrupts the passive consensual character of the private sphere that exists prior to his arrival. By diversifying the field of response to Beloved's spirit, Paul D destabilizes any unitary understanding of the past. However, I would also argue that the life-sustaining power of this destabilization is ultimately recognized by neither Paul D nor Sethe, but by Denver who, in the end, emerges as the unlikely hero of the novel.

My case can be made simply: Denver achieves heroic status in the novel because it is she who finally finds the courage and means to cross the boundary that divides home from the world, or the private family from the public sphere. It is Denver who reaches out to the community for help. In accomplishing this she demonstrates one of the central assumptions of the novel: the family cannot survive in isolation but requires the strength and protection of a much wider network of "kinfolk." By reestablishing this tie with the local community, Denver not only saves her mother's life but also engages the powerful presence of the "thirty women" whose arrival at the climactic conclusion of the novel helps drive Beloved from 124. In this way, Denver represents hope for the future.

However, this hope is contingent on maintaining a link to the past. Indeed, it should be noticed that by saving her mother, Denver reconnects spiritually with her father, Halle. Just as Halle works to buy Baby Suggs's freedom, Denver frees Sethe from enslavement to Beloved's ravenous appetite for the mothering she never had. Thus, while Sethe retains a tie to her father in name only, Denver retains a tie to Halle through heroic action. Both father and daughter make use of what resources they can muster—beating the odds in both instances—in the interests of securing a future, and both pay a dear price for this opportunity. Halle gives up five years of Sundays, ironically a day when families often visit. Denver puts an end to her sister's visitation, sacrificing their camaraderie, in favor of reestablishing the essential reciprocal tie that defines family as a network of "kinfolks." The preservation of family is thus defined in *Beloved* as "a communal effort . . . where the knitting together of the family, like the telling of the stories, is a shared project."[20]

Undeniably, Beloved's presence among the living prefigures their recognition of a communal loss that can only be mended by a communal effort to restore lost ties; however, Beloved also functions as a persistent reminder of the unique loss suffered by each occupant of 124. Ultimately, what defines Beloved in the context of the familial relationships that the novel explores is that she assumes the shape of something slightly different to all who embrace her. She is their worst fear and their most profound need combined. For Denver, who has suffered not only the loss of a sister's companionship but the judgment and neglect of the community as well, Beloved is the "interested, uncritical eyes of the other" (118). To Paul D, Beloved is his "shame," or the utter depth of inhumanity and demoralization he experienced at Sweet Home when he was collared and given the bit. This was the moment that came closest to unmanning him. When Paul D describes his memory of the incident to Sethe, he recalls looking up to see a rooster named Mister staring stupidly at him as he stood staring back, mute and morally transformed by the shaft of metal in his mouth. As Paul D explains, "Mister was allowed to be and stay what he was. But I wasn't allowed to be and stay what I was. . . . Schoolteacher changed me. I was something else and that something was less than a chicken sitting in the sun on a tub" (72). Beloved forces Paul D to reencounter this moment—which he has long since locked away in his heart—when she sexually seduces him with postures that remind Paul D of the days at Sweet Home when he had been guiltily driven to copulate with calves. Beloved thus "fixes" him, like the bit in his mouth and the concealed misery in his heart. The seduction returns him to a former unmanned state, the memory of which Paul D dreads as he struggles to define his potential role as a "free man" in this family and within the larger community. His shame and doubt over the uncertain boundaries between human and animal love is later projected onto Sethe when he suggests that her infanticide was an animalistic response to a situation requiring human forethought. "There could have been a way. Some other way. . . . You got two feet, Sethe, not four" (165). Such boundary confusion leads Paul D to abandon 124 and withdraw to the basement of a local church where, like Ellison's Invisible Man, he goes underground to begin "a covert preparation for a more overt action." [21]

For Sethe, Beloved's return is an opportunity to redefine motherhood in terms of new cultural possibilities, to be a mother who administers to a child's growth rather than chopping it down for fear of having it perverted. But the past can neither be changed nor forgotten, only internally confronted and externally shared through the telling and exchanging of stories. So why then the echoing in the final chapter of the line "This is not a story to pass on"? Perhaps this is a warning that the cycle of separation and loss must not be repeated; paradoxically, however, it seems that the only way to prevent the repetition of such severed familial bonds is to transform death into life through the creation of a post-family romance that is also a ghost-family romance. The romance must be told and retold in order to make peace with what was lost, so that freedom in its fullest sense may be attained. *Beloved* is a novel that defines "freedom" for the post–Civil War black family not as freedom from the Southern plantation, nor as freedom won by means of an emancipation proclamation, but as the freedom "to get to a place where you could love anything you chose" (162).

Indeed, *Beloved* may not be a story to pass on, but it is a story that had to be told in order to counter and multiply the dominant cultural and historical patterns of family romance. In this way, a textual debate might be initiated, one capable of acknowledging the degree to which "real" families (produced by blood and legally sanctioned marriage relationships) and fictive kin mutually redefine one another. Making families, like making romance, may also involve processes of unmaking that are culturally specific and that no two persons will necessarily interpret in the same way. Morrison's novel asks us to consider the possibility that Sethe's impulse to infanticide—based on her own reading of history—is in its own context a valid expression of claiming kin. For Sethe, there is a death richer in interpretive possibility than life, and there is a love powerful enough to bridge the distance.

Chapter 9
"Family" Romance (Or, How to Recognize a Queer Text When You Meet One)

In the summer of 1991, during Denver, Colorado's Gay Pride Celebration, the local PBS television affiliate broadcast "Out in America," a panel discussion of lesbian and gay politics. One of the topics addressed was "family values," or the gay political agenda's lack thereof. The issue prompted Larry Kramer, the founder of ACT UP and one of the featured panelists, to deliver a repudiation of the "maudlin sentimentality" that characterizes right-wing glorifications of the family. "Some of us don't want families," he contended. "Some of us went through hell with family—you're looking at one of them."

"But," interjected Andrew Humm, moderator, "don't you have a family of gay and lesbian associates around you?"

"Yes," replied Kramer, "but that's a different thing. There's all this maudlin sentimentality about the family."

At the time, in the midst of pride parades and gay rodeos, Kramer's remarks seemed more like a personal lament than a political foreshadowing of Amendment 2 and the national explosion of Christian right-wing pro-familial terrorism that would soon become a depressingly familiar cause célèbre among lesbian and gay civil rights activists. And just one year later, in the June 16, 1992, issue of *The Advocate,* journalist Donna Minkowitz sharply criticized gays *and* feminists who, in their resistance to charges of antifamilialism, were responding by "painting Norman Rockwell in lavender" and by "tearfully protesting that we can serve the family gods." "The truth is," she argues, "we shouldn't have to invoke our parents or convince anyone that we're capable of stable monogamous unions with offspring to win the civil rights protection we deserve." This ardent defense against the pro-familial, right-wing rhetoric of the Bush-Quayle campaign ardently aligned feminists and lesbians, as well as "queers and all women," all who share, according to Minkowitz, similar investments in opposing "society's holiest institution."[1]

In the summer of 1993, this common investment was given a whole new meaning by Banana Republic's "Chosen Family" ad campaign, which adorned New York City buses and billboards with decidedly "queer" family images. One of these ads featured three women wearing short hair, tank tops, and lots of faded denim. One of the models, Ingrid Casares, had recently been called an "infamous homewrecker" by the comedienne Sandra Bernhard, allegedly for coming between Bernhard and the pop singer Madonna. In contrast, the family triad depicted in the Banana Republic ad looked to be getting along splendidly, languishing in an open Mustang convertible, their arms loosely draped around one another as Casares tenderly kissed the hand of the woman in the driver's seat.

Notwithstanding the American media's longtime predilection to play with homoerotic images, I suspect that the "Chosen Family" was not the "different thing" that Larry Kramer had referred to in 1991, a difference that permits the erotic to exceed its customary containment within the Oedipus only to be recontained by capitalism's romance with marginality and difference. But are families of choice a "life-style" that all lesbians and gays can afford? And for those who can, are families of choice materially and affectively different from families of origin? Do they offer the possibility of lesbian and gay empowerment, or do they run the risk of engendering the very maudlin sentimentality, the same romanticization of origins that Kramer rejects, that Minkowitz relocates from the personal to the political sphere, and that Banana Republic reconstructs as an elite consumer base, our chosen family?

What does the family romance want with queers, and what does queer culture want with family romance? According to Kramer and Minkowitz, not much. Quite possibly, however, they overstate their resistance in order to ally activist groups resistant to sexist, homophobic organizations like Friends of Families and the American Family Association. In the process, their arguments obscure the fact that "family" and "consensus" are by no means synonymous terms; commitments to the family romance clearly have different ideological resonances for lesbians than for straight women or gay men. The risk of not being attentive to these differences is that queer activists create a new family of antifamilial liberationists whose political claims are seemingly authenticated by appeals to the category of individual experience, such as Kramer's, or by appeals to a consensual adversary monolith that exists outside patriarchy, as Minkowitz suggests.

Accordingly, theory affirms what the new rhetoric of "Queer Chic" has packaged in three words: "Out Is In," or more specifically, coming out of the closet always constitutes a kind of co-option by the powers-that-be, powers that appropriate queerness in order to reaffirm dominant values and preserve class, race, and gender hierarchies.[2] Queer theorists have become increasingly alert to the possibility that being out in such a fashion is not enough. For example, Diana Fuss observes that gay and lesbian studies have begun the process of recognizing, via Lacan, "that any outside is formulated as a consequence of a lack *internal* to the system it supplements. The greater the lack on the inside, the greater the need for an outside to contain and to diffuse it, for without that outside, the lack on the inside would become all too visible."[3] Similarly, Judith Butler suggests that "a Foucaultian perspective might argue that the affirmation of 'homosexuality' is itself an extension of a homophobic discourse," because it promotes an oppressive hetero/homo dichotomy.[4] And in Eve Kosofsky Sedgwick's call for a more complex understanding of the production and distribution of "ignorance" in regard to same-sex desire, she appeals to a deconstructive interpretation of the public/private binarism used to structure rhetorical relations of sex and knowledge within modern Western culture.[5] Practical evidence of these warnings against the construction of in/out, hetero/homo, straight-family/queer-family dichotomies for the purpose of promoting political or cultural unity may be discerned in Bill Clinton's open campaign courtship with the gay vote, a romance that led to the heartbreak of "Don't Ask, Don't Tell." Out is in, indeed.

While not all participants within lesbian and gay culture(s) agree on the proper uses and abuses of "outing," or "closeting," my sense is that a large part of the widespread cultural remappings that have produced post-family romance is the "queering" of the American family. Queer family romances such as Dorothy Allison's *Bastard out of Carolina*, Robert Ferro's *The Family of Max Desir*, Fannie Flagg's *Fried Green Tomatoes at the Whistle Stop Cafe*, and David Leavitt's *The Lost Language of Cranes* and *Equal Affections* contribute to this remapping process by dissolving a heterocentrist model of queer-free domestic space and its corollary, a properly sexed male or female subject free of homosexual desires. The question I want to take up in this chapter concerns how these "queer" family romances critique Oedipal imperatives and cultural norms even as they assert their formal legacy.

The recurrent focus of lesbian and gay writers on deconstructing and reconstructing the family romance shows that the symbolic currency of the family plot retains its value even as it continues to undergo redescription. For example, how might we understand lesbian/gay culture's adoption of the word "family" as the signifier of one's participation within a queer community? The word "family" here suggests an alliance with mainstream values and practices that homosexuality is often defined in opposition to. The queering of the term disrupts the idealization of biological origins and reasserts the fundamental yet often invisible sense of unity that nonheterosexuals and nongender legibles have increasingly come to claim as a source of political empowerment. However, the appropriation of the term also disrupts appearances of coherence and consensus within cultural life, suggesting a plural and contestatory model of signification itself. Such appropriations recommend the need for "deviant" or noncentric subjects to claim participation in the consensual symbolic order for their own assertions of public and private legitimacy. To come out by identifying oneself or someone else as "family" is to trouble deeply the boundaries between culture and biology, the personal and the political, the familial and the social. To be "out," in this regard, is to persistently dislocate and resituate the family, thus foregrounding the contradictions of the romance that constitutes it.

Dorothy Allison's novel *Bastard out of Carolina* provides a useful point of departure for exploring these strategies in contemporary lesbian fiction that self-consciously redescribes the traditional genre of family romance. The novel begins with an epigraph from James Baldwin. "People pay for what they do, and still more, for what they have allowed themselves to become. And they pay for it simply: by the lives they lead."[6] These words provide an appropriate frame for the novel, which concerns the choices and material limitations that collectively define and defy working-class family life in a rural South Carolina community in the morally restrictive 1950s. The epigraph reflects the main character Ruth Anne Boatwright's angry wish for revenge against the forces and agents that would condemn her name and spirit to oblivion because she is poor, female, and illegitimate. Ruth Anne, or "Bone" as she is called by her extended family of aunts, uncles, and cousins, encounters these forces both within her family, as her stepfather's favorite target of physical and sexual abuse, and in the surrounding community, as a bastard, a piece of poor, white trash whose biological father has disappeared and whose mother is unconscious at the moment of her daughter's birth, a birth prematurely brought on by a car crash that renders Anney incapable of naming her child or signing any of the official papers documenting her paternity.

While Allison's novel has been much praised for its thoughtful, unsentimental treatment of the subject of domestic violence and sexual abuse, less discussed is the novel's complex meditation on its own formal transgressions in relation to family romance, the narrative blueprint it rehearses and redefines. Abandoned and effectively bereft of parentage from the start of life, Bone still retains a powerful, albeit ambivalent sense of belonging to the notorious Boatwright family, a white-trash clan known for their hard-drinking, shiftless men and proud, angry, hard-hearted women. Bone's mother, Anney Boatwright, is a case in point, although she is distinguished in her youth by good looks and a fierce determination to make a better life for herself and her children. It is this determination that leads her to marry Glen Waddel, or Daddy Glen, who begins beating and sexually abusing Bone almost immediately after the wedding. As the beatings continue and increase in their frequency and intensity, Anney and Bone remain silent about the abuse, even when relatives gingerly question Daddy Glen's relationship to the children, and again when a doctor challenges Anney's false explanations for Bone's various bruises and fractures. To protect Bone, Anney begins sending her to the homes of various aunts and relations, and it is here—in the community of women—that Bone begins to understand the complex social nature of her mother's loves, desires, and needs. Anney loves Bone, but she cannot leave Daddy Glen because she needs the additional income that he sporadically provides and because she herself is afraid of emotional abandonment. In addition, she fears the social stigma that the community attaches to any woman who lives husbandless and whose children are bastards.

The novel ends with Bone's being brutally raped by Daddy Glen in a scene so graphic and disturbing that several of my students have refused to read it all the way through. What, they ask, might Allison's motivation be for presenting such a horribly violent scene? I suggest that their questions be considered in light of the fact that Anney walks in on the final moments of the rape, thus mimicking, in part, the reader's role as sole witness to Daddy Glen's crime. Subsequently, Anney chooses to leave Greenville County indefinitely with Glen in pursuit of a new life, a life without her daughter. Bone remains in Greenville, in the surrogate care of her Aunt Raylene, a confirmed loner and fringe-dweller of the community who we learn in the final pages of the novel, is also a lesbian.

As Bone grapples with the paradox that loving a child isn't necessarily enough to choose her over a husband or to fend off the cultural imperatives that construct relations of consensus against relations of illegitimate "difference," Raylene confesses that she was once deeply in love with a woman to whom she "did a terrible thing" by forcing her to choose between their relationship and the woman's child. Her lover chose the child and sent Raylene home alone, for good. "It should never have come to that. It never should. It just about killed her. It just about killed me" (300).

How does this confession of a thwarted lesbian love affair provide closure to the narrative as it's developed up to this point? Certainly, it complicates the text's running discourse on choice by suggesting that while there is a socially perceived difference between families of origin and families we choose, biology doesn't necessarily legitimate origin, and choice doesn't necessarily eclipse the power of cultural convention. In short, Raylene's confession specifically addresses the formal expectation of novelistic closure by suspending it in favor of multiplying the ways that Bone (and readers) might interpret her situation: Anney's departure is *both* a choice and a patriarchal imperative. Bone's abandonment, like Raylene's, is *both* a form of rejection and an expression of love. In this way, *Bastard out of Carolina* posits family romance as a cultural field of competing and contestatory discourses. In so doing, Allison effectively "outs" the family romance, identifying it as a transpositional genre defined by its own internal contradictions and by its formal reevaluation of the metaphors—for example, houses—and historical documents with which families unify and legitimate accounts of their origins.

Ultimately, *Bastard out of Carolina* offers a queer perspective on the family romance not from the outside looking in, but from the inside coming out. Raylene's revelation of lesbian desire works to "recapture and reassert a militant sense of difference" (in Alexander Doty's words) that finally unveils family romance as a "consciously chosen" field of competing desires and open-ended possibilities for identification.[7] In this sense, the novel functions in much the same way that lesbian and gay uses of the word "family" do. Allison, an openly lesbian author, does not reject the family romance but exposes the contradictions that motivate the form. *Bastard out of Carolina*, like the redescribed birth certificate that Anney deposits with Bone before departing with Glen, is a blank page yet to be written upon. However, its very openness is nevertheless produced by family traditions and legacies that invite upon themselves the dynamic gesture of redescription.

Still, if to "out" the family means in some sense to affirm an "oppressive dichotomy" of public/private and hetero/homo, where does this leave or lead the dichotomy of gender, of masculinity/femininity, which rests upon the strict separation of sexual identity and desire? Does queerness in the family romance transcend or retain standard gender oppositions and hierarchies? And ultimately, if transcendence is not possible, how is gender recontained, or restabilized, even as the queer family romance otherwise exceeds the confines of the closet and the limits of heterocentrist sexual expression? To answer this, I will refer back to Minkowitz for a moment, who, in her entreaty to "queers and all women," seems to assume that the cultural politics of gender and sexual orientation are roughly interchangeable. Such conflations make it easier to align the feminist movement with the lesbian and gay civil rights movement; however, this is a risky business insofar as it invites a parallel conflation of a traditionally gender-directed critique and a newly developing sex-directed critique. Feminism would thus seem to authenticate political claims made on behalf of gay men, lesbians, bisexuals, and queers, whose inscription within the Oedipal family—whether it be tragic or joyous—is effectively denaturalized by feminism's problematic tendency to construct heterosexuality as an oppressive universal norm. Feminism has tended to view masculinity as cultural license to female sexual domination, a privilege consolidated by the familial order. Femininity, in contrast, has been generally understood as the cultural effacement of female desire, the reproduction of women as silent and passive objects of male sexual desire. Such gender-specific distinctions that subordinate sex to relations of power/powerlessness have come sharply under fire of late by queer critics, many of whom suggest that a nongendered critique of subjectivity is not only possible but necessary for a productive reading of the multiple subject-crossings and contradictions that shape nonheterosexual identities. Still, as critics of popular culture have been especially quick to point out, gender remains crucial to mass cultural practices of production and reception, and queer practices are no less influenced by cultural conceptions of "femininity" and "masculinity," even when they strive to subvert them.[8]

As queer formulations of the connection, or nonconnection, between sex and gender emerge, one should consider the possibility that gay male writers, as well as lesbian writers, may have far more to gain by challenging feminism's antisex biases than by challenging oppressive patriarchal familial ideology.[9] David Leavitt's novel *The Lost Language of Cranes* provides a popular narrative context for exploring the limits of alliance between gays and feminists in redescribing the family romance. Leavitt, of course, remains one of the more noted literary voices of the post-Stonewall era. At twenty-four years of age, he published a short story in the *New Yorker* and became widely hailed as the first "out" gay writer to be published in the prestigious magazine noted for its stylized fiction. Leavitt's subsequent portrayals of contemporary urban gay culture, although severely criticized by the gay press for neglecting to deal with the impact of AIDS, have received much attention and praise from the mainstream press. This is especially true of the *New York Times* wherein, during the 1980s, Leavitt was routinely featured as the foremost cultural spokesperson for "guppies," young, gay, upwardly mobile, urban professionals who (with the possible exception of an occasional march on Washington) are more committed to IRAs and Ikea home furnishings than to their parents' 1960s-styled grass-roots activism. In Leavitt's second novel, *Equal Affections*, his protagonist Danny Cooper reflects on this historical irony, claiming "it was generational, the children of the divorced or unhappy households of the seventies seeking to recreate in adulthood the stable family home they never had, but hoped for, all through their growing up. They do not run away; they do not go to ashrams or to visit the Great Wall. They stay home. They open Insured Market Rate Accounts."[10]

Leavitt's frank portraits of gay relationships and his thoughtful treatment of the processes families engage when one or more of their members reveal themselves to be gay perform complex cultural work that emphasizes the extent to which homosexuality and heterosexuality are always interdynamic, always mapped across one another in the family plot. Of course, the unconditional acceptance and support that most of Leavitt's gay characters receive from their white, well-to-do families strike some readers as idealistic didacticism, just as Joanne Woodward's claim in *Philadelphia* that she didn't raise her kids "to sit on the back of the bus" prompted some reviewers in the gay press to roll their eyes in disbelief. Still, and with all classist presumptions aside, *Philadelphia*, like *The Lost Language of Cranes*, works effectively to de-vilify gay men by "middle-classifying" the referent.[11] In addition, both *Philadelphia* and *The Lost Language of Cranes* direct themselves to queer viewers/readers by legitimating them as cultural creators and users and by making queerness visible within the context of America's "holiest institution," the family. Furthermore, both *Philadelphia* and *The Lost Language of Cranes* are accessible to audiences who identify as heterosexual because by employing popular narrative conventions and forms, such as the legal drama, the hospital drama, and the family romance, they contain the code within the comfort range while directing readings to the familiar.

In the 1970s, toward the conclusion of PBS's groundbreaking cinéma vérité documentary *An American Family*, viewers watched in amazement as—right on camera—Pat Loud told her husband, Bill Loud, that she wanted a divorce. In a subsequent episode, the Loud's eldest son, Lance, came home from New York City to announce before his family—on camera—what attentive viewers already knew, that Lance is homosexual. The sequencing of these scenes is worth considering, insofar as it multiplies the possibilities for reading the text. One of these possible readings demonstrates the extent to which women's liberation leads to gay revelation. Feminism and Stonewall, in this sense, might be read as mutually joined in a conspiracy against the patriarchal family, mutually responsible for the radical collapse of gender and sexual hierarchies. And by "radical," I mean literally at the perceived root of these hierarchies, the family.

However, while the stability of the patriarchal family would appear to be jeopardized by the disclosure of male homosexuality, Leavitt's male characters repeatedly demonstrate that, to the contrary, it is gender difference, and *not* homo/hetero sexual difference that threatens the sanctity of the "new" American family.[12] Leavitt's frequent characterizations of unhappy, unfulfilled, and/or disease-stricken women and their young, stability-starved gay sons who equate class status with emotional security suggest a prominent force behind those unhappy families of the seventies: the feminist movement, with its critique of male sexual dominance and its insistence that women would be better off exploring themselves and one another rather than catering to their husbands and children. The question that I find puzzling is why—in a cultural setting where it remains difficult, if not dangerous, for gay couples to live openly, for them to adopt children, for them to keep their jobs—Leavitt has been hailed as "*the* poet of the New American Family" (emphasis mine).[13] Why, in a society in which homosexuality is largely perceived to be the antithesis of family life, has Leavitt been raised like a lightning rod for popular American fiction's recuperation of the family romance?

In this chapter, I want to consider the possibility that in its overturning of male sexual hierarchy—a move that isolates sex to leave traditional hierarchies of gender, race, and class intact—*The Lost Language of Cranes* recuperates mythical notions about the primacy of paternal privilege in its consolidation of male social and sexual authority. Unquestionably, for some readers *The Lost Language of Cranes* effectively legitimates the cultural struggles of white, upper-middle-class gay males for whom "family" remains the dominant signifier of a unified identity and an affirmative gay sexuality. Male homosexuality, in this frame, is not the antithesis to family romance, but rather the consolidation of its ultimate potential. However, the realization of this potential seems inappropriately compensated for by a reamplification of gender difference that assumes a too-direct link to a naturalized male/female sexual predisposition. Thus, the text seems only able to legitimate gay men when it unites them by positing women as gay men's "other." For Leavitt, outing the family romance does not mean multiplying the possible strategies for representing and connecting sexual desires and gender identifications, but rather it means unifying these strategies in ways that serve to trivialize or demonize women. The problem is that by trivializing women, Leavitt trivializes all gender and severely limits what it might mean to identify as a "gay man" within the family.

Although Tania Modleski's concerns about the postfeminist silencing of women within certain articulations of gay studies have been rightly criticized as overstatements, especially given the recent expansion of feminist methods, her suggestion that "constructions of homosexuality intersect with misogynist constructions of femininity" seems virtually overdetermined in Leavitt's romance.[14] Of course, any politically identified family romance—be it feminist, gay, lesbian, Republican, Fundamentalist Christian, and so on—may have a great deal to gain by conflating sex with gender, a possibility "deeply embedded in the American cultural tradition."[15] Although Modleski argues that this is a privilege reserved for men, her argument is worth considering for its applicability to a multitude of possible social relations and cultural agents:

A man may hold femininity in contempt at the same time that he appropriates it. Insofar as such attitudes assume the character of the fetish, and operate according to a strategy of disavowal, they form part of the larger "postmodern" culture as this culture has been theorized by various critics. The disavowal often involves the illusion that one can not only have it all, but also *be* it all—male and female, father and mother, adult and child—without altering the power structure in which men rule over women and adults over children. (90)

That this essentialist formulation might work to the effacement of *both* women's and men's mobility across sex/gender continuums is evidenced by a critique of family romance as it is redescribed in *The Lost Language of Cranes*. The novel portrays a young man's coming out and his father's simultaneous recognition that he, too, is gay and has been denying it all his married life. Philip, the son, and Owen, the father, have experienced their desire for men in very different ways. Owen's anonymous sexual encounters take place during furtive Sunday afternoon trips to downtown porn theaters. Philip, the product of a post-Stonewall sensibility, has assumed a socially legible gay identity and a place within a young, educated, monied gay male community; his parents are the only ones who do not know about his sexuality or about his new relationship. Philip's most recent lover, Eliot, is the adopted son of a gay couple, one of whom is Derek Moulthorpe, a famous writer of children's books that Philip loved as a child. Eliot and his family are the fulfillment of Philip's longing for a gay family romance, a fairy tale come true. Derek and his lover, Geoffrey, are a stable, longtime couple who bring to life all of Philip's childhood wishes, erotic fantasies, and longings. Philip, who (interestingly enough) works for a publisher of romance fiction, believes that his own quest for romantic love has found its object in Eliot.

As the American family undergoes redescription, Leavitt suggests a new figurative blueprint for its romanticization, a consensual gay male culture, or a "queer sphere," into which women are occasionally permitted entrance (mainly when accompanied by a fellow of the sphere) but are generally left standing outside the door, like Virginia Woolf outside the "Oxbridge" library, without access to the realm where "true" power and knowledge of sex are stored. In this way, male homosexuality poses no threat to male homosociality, or the shoring up of privilege based on social bonds between men.[16] A character named Celia, from a Leavitt short story entitled "Dedicated," sums it up succinctly:

"When all the men you love can only love each other," Celia would later tell people—a lot of people—"you can't help but begin to wonder if there's something wrong with being a woman. . . ." That night she stood before those closed steel doors and shut her eyes and wished, the way a small child wishes, that she could be freed from her loose skirts, her make-up and jewels, her interfering breasts and buttocks. If she could only be stripped and pared, made sleek and svelte like Nathan and Andrew, then she might slip between those doors as easily as the men who hurried past her that night . . . she might be freed of the rank and untrustworthy baggage of femininity.[17]

Carol Iannone, whose insightful essay "Post-Countercultural Tristesse" refers to this passage, points out that a recurring character in Leavitt's fiction "is the rejected or superfluous female, sometimes unmarried, more typically divorced, abandoned, or neglected, a victim, in a sense, of changing cultural patterns."[18] Here, Iannone draws upon a pervasive theme in Leavitt's fiction—masculine independence (from women) and feminine dependence (on men). While maleness allows the typical Leavitt character entrée, mobility, and participation in the "changing cultural patterns" of sexual expression, femaleness means being denied participation as cultural producer, as user, or as interpreter of these patterns. To be female is to be illiterate, nonproductive, and trapped in the abject body and mind of the "other." Sexless and undesirable, femaleness for Leavitt is the irreducible affirmation of a superior gay sexuality and sociality that remains uncritically reliant on women's passivity for its assertions of exclusivity. While men move freely across spaces both domestic and public, both inside and outside of the closet, the condition of femaleness remains spacelessness, self-loathing, and lack. However, it is precisely these qualities in women that Leavitt's gay characters often define themselves in opposition to as they seek out freer, less suffocating expressions of male-to-male communion. This makes women rather important to defining the gayness of Leavitt's world. Consequently, no element of male homosexuality or homosociality in Leavitt's romance can be understood outside of its connection to women and to traditional gender stereotypes associated with patriarchal political and economic structures. Thus, the novel serves as a case in point that queer family romances defined in opposition to feminism's critique of gender run the risk of reproducing the same codes that in recent historical contexts have worked to equate the oppression of women with the oppression of homosexuals.

In its driving concern with reclaiming a lost language of male-to-male desire within the family, *The Lost Language of Cranes* exhibits a need to contain abject femaleness in the figure of Rose, Philip's mother and Owen's wife. Rose is a book editor described as a person who notices details above all else, so it seems strange that her son's and husband's homosexuality has eluded her. However, the details that Rose notices are presumably textual, not sexual. In the arena of personal relationships she is a stiff, emotionally withholding woman who seems to expect little more than that others contain themselves as well. Consequently, she dismisses Philip's announcement that he is gay. "I don't believe that just because something's a secret it therefore by definition has to be revealed. . . . Keeping certain secrets secret is important to—the general balance of life, the common utility."[19] In fact, much of the narrative is organized around the secrets that family members withhold in order to keep the illusion of unity in place. Owen hides out in porn theaters. Philip remembers his adolescence as a long kept secret: masturbating in locked bathrooms; hiding all his books with the word "homosexual" on the cover; concealing his relationships with lovers. Rose admits that she also holds secrets she would never dream of sharing with anyone. Here, she refers to two affairs, one with the husband of an old friend, the other with a former coworker. These affairs represent the sum total of Rose's concession to doubts about whether other men find her attractive; however, Rose is unable to read these doubts as possible responses to the lack of romance and sexual dynamic within her marriage. These affairs offer displaced evidence that Owen feels for her "what men should feel for women" (306). To be wanted in this way, for Rose, is to indulge a guilty pleasure, quickly consumed and suppressed, like the Burger King Whoppers she lusts after and occasionally succumbs to "with great guilt, wolfing down the criminal burger in a corner . . . always afraid of being seen" (17). In the novel, junk food does for Rose what gay sex, at first anyway, does for Owen. It marks her as an outlaw, but at the same time provides her with an anonymous space where she can fulfill desires unimaginable within a culture where femininity implies a selfless concern for the hungers of others. In these terms, Rose's secret binges of eating and sex take on a punitive quality as she seeks revenge for Owen's failure to meet her erotic needs. Toward the conclusion of the novel, when Owen finally admits to Rose that he cannot keep his attraction to men a secret, he is quick to add that neither one of them has been faithful, and that he has known all along about her affairs. "I figured I was getting what I deserved—as punishment," he explains (306). He goes on to say that he still loves her and wants to uphold the conditions of their marriage contract, to continue living with her. Rose recognizes at this point that her "life is like the punch line to a stupid joke" (305), and she senses that now *she* is being punished for her failure to recognize that the "contract," which Owen wants to perpetuate, has always cast her in the role of victim, an isolated obstacle within the family romance that her husband and son have secretly conspired to colonize and reconstruct while she's been out sneaking burgers.

But why should Owen's and Philip's journeys toward negotiating queer father/son identities hinge on Rose's victimized self-perception? The repeated emphasis on Rose's sense of herself as a failure and a martyr underwrites her status as a figure of fetishistic disavowal that both Philip and Owen feel they must appease in order to escape. In this regard, Leavitt perpetuates an American cultural mythology of dread feminine power, a mythology that has recently been reexamined by critics such as Joseph A. Boone who locates in the sexual politics of the classic American quest romance a radical critique of nineteenth-century gender hierarchies.[20] In these terms, Huckleberry Finn's flight from Aunt Sally suggests not a rejection of the feminine, but a hidden wish to subvert the ideological subordination of gender to culturally restrictive narrative forms such as the marriage plot. Indeed, the formal absence of women from many of the plots Boone looks at does suggest a destabilization of the narrative conventions, conflicts, and resolutions that traditional gender dichotomy orchestrates. However, Leavitt's insistence on women's abject *presence* in a text that has no difficulty affirming homoerotic openness seems to indicate that no gay male character need assume a role analogous to woman's subordinate social role so long as "real" biological women remain formally positioned to absorb the fear, rage, victimization, loneliness, and rejection that homosexual men are, of course, also vulnerable to in homophobic culture. Leavitt's sweet, shy, sensitive gay men who fear a loss of the social privileges that male homosociality affords remain boundaried by this fearful closeting of the feminine. "In my day," Rose lectures, "people cared about more than just self-gratification. There were more important things. You did without for the larger good" (173). Finally, we have to wonder why Rose is handed these lines that even Aunt Sally knew better than to spout. Such rhetorical imprisonments make it difficult, if not impossible, for Leavitt's gay men to acknowledge the feminine and maternal elements within their own expanding self-definitions.

Philip, for example, wants to be mothered, as is demonstrated by his awkward attempts to elicit affection and warmth from Rose. Yet, when Owen is on the brink of tears after leaving Rose, Philip finds that he is unable to embrace him, and can only offer platitudes of assurance that "tomorrow will be different" and "you *will* feel good again" (318). Philip reads *Mademoiselle* magazine, scanning the pages for advice on relationships. He gets lost in sultry romance novels with titles like *Tides of Flame*, and sees himself in the plights of fictional lovers like Sylvia and Steve. Yet, right before he and Eliot make love, Philip is unable to recognize himself when he spontaneously erupts, in "a voice that belonged to Greta Garbo . . . 'I am yours'" (27). Gradually, this creeping connection with the feminine leads Philip to the conclusion that his passion for Eliot, his desire to be sexually submissive makes him "less than he had been before he met Eliot. A void now ached in him to be filled. . . . And there lay the difference between them; for when it ended, Eliot would have things to return to, 'projects,' whereas Philip would have less than he'd started with, would have a gaping hole in him" (107–8).

This dread of "the gaping hole" (commonly associated with the sex that lacks the phallus) produces within Owen an increasing awareness of the dangers that lurk at home, in the domestic space that he and Rose share. Owen's furtive Sunday afternoon excursions to the porn theaters, where he seeks safety within "the collective, heaving horniness of thousands of men, initiates and veterans, swallowing and gulping and gripping in tandem with the presences on the giant screen" (22), allows him to explore a new territory of male desire, but at the same time reinforces the sense of spatial barriers used to keep women and gay men in their place. Owen's wish to remain married to Rose even after telling her that he's gay indicates that while he sees possibilities for expanding the boundaries of male identity, he remains equally attached to the plurality of spatial possibility that marriage affords men.

In *The Lost Language of Cranes*, Leavitt's gay fathers and sons "light out" for a new nonphallic masculinity not unlike Deleuze and Guattari's "schizo-subjects" who challenge the family's institutional "territorialization" of desire and unscramble the repressive social codes that normalize physical and semiotic exchanges. However, on closer examination, Owen and Philip simply exchange one limited version of male subjectivity for another, a unified, territorialized body without women. Rather than radically releasing desire from the Oedipal closet, the text narrativizes a recontainment of desire that maintains binary separations of gender and identification by simplistically inverting the Freudian formula to the exclusion of women rather than the inclusion of flux. Deleuze and Guattari's distinction between schizophrenia as a process of productive decoding and the schizophrenic as a reified identity is thus usefully compared to the distinction made by some lesbian and gay theorists between feminization as a means of renegotiating gender hierarchy and the feminist as a figure responsible for the essentializing and universalizing tendencies of political criticism. While schizophrenia and feminization are privileged theoretical processes open to appropriation, they become appropriated principally at the expense of schizophrenics and feminists, dysfunctional entities and obstacles in the way of masculine mobility. The marginalization and mutual disavowal of these historically contingent figures work to universalize the trope of the deviant/woman and recuperate the very exclusions that schizo-analysis and feminization would seem to be attempting to overturn. In *The Lost Language of Cranes*, in the struggle between disavowing gay sexual desire and disavowing femininity, the latter must ultimately lose as femininity comes to constitute the "outside" to the privileged world of gay male insiders. Thus, the more women are moved out of the romance, the less men are required to sneak, lie, cheat, and construct themselves as figures of abjection in the family nexus.

The Lost Language of Cranes wants above all else to assure its readers that gay is *not* the antithesis of family life, as Rose suggests when she warns, "It's one thing to do what you want when you're young. But later. To be alone. No family" (174). To this, Philip argues that gay people can have families too, can adopt children, can form lasting unions. Accordingly, the novel contrasts different family structures as its affirmation of a pro-gay familialism, a familialism we choose.

Philip's joyless nuclear family with its embittered mother is redeemed when the child comes out and, in a sense, fathers the man, restoring to Owen the vocabulary of desire that he has repressed all his married life. The final passages of the novel depict Owen and Philip together in an egalitarian father-son communion, their exchanges no longer governed by the power hierarchies that structure relations with women. After Rose asks Owen to leave, he shows up at Philip's apartment in need of a place to sleep. Philip prepares a makeshift bed for his father, as Owen helps himself to a carton from the refrigerator—orange juice, too old to be drinkable.[21] Philip offers him some fresh juice, which Owen refuses as he describes Rose's reaction to their conversation: "One minute she's so angry, the next so—sad, so weak" (315). Closure is thus inscribed with the elimination of the "weak" mother whose punitive withholding of maternal comfort to guilt-ridden men renders her unable to love or be loved.

Eliot's gay male triad is the favored kinship structure of the novel, the queer-family ideal. Like Philip, Eliot enjoys affluence and cultural privileges; however, unlike Philip, Eliot has no female mother to appease or seek favor from; his only commitments are to himself and to a number of mysterious free-lance "art" projects that occupy his seemingly structureless days. At one point Eliot boasts that he never had to endure the difficult process of coming out to his parents, as Philip is undergoing. He supposes that he only would have had to come out if he'd been straight. Clearly, these are the only two sexual possibilities that Leavitt admits, gay or straight. Any other positions along the continuum—bisexuality, transsexuality, asexuality—are removed. Similar to Freud's family romance, the family is established as a structure of consensus and containment, the difference here being that identifications and desires are collapsed onto the figure of masculinity. In this way, familialism remains fully coextensive with the assurance that men will both have and be the phallus, with all the privileges it carries, and with no need to negotiate the differences that exist outside masculinity or the differences that inhere *within* masculine configurations. The inversion is laudable to the extent that it presents a parody of the family, a send-up of the holy triad as a hypermasculine institution that validates homosexuality as the "normal" sexual orientation. However, such facile reversals also make it possible to retain binary oppositions that polarize femininity and masculinity and keep patriarchal gender hierarchies in place.

Jerene, Eliot's black lesbian feminist Marxist roommate, amplifies and embodies those "differences" left otherwise unexplored in the novel, differences of race, female desire, and politics. Jerene also serves as a footnote to histories otherwise bypassed in the narrative, an embodiment of the collective struggles of the feminist and civil rights movements. Jerene, like Eliot, is adopted, and when she comes out to her adopted family they unconditionally disown her, thus providing the antithesis to tolerant, restrained, and reflective families such as Philip's and Eliot's. Although Jerene's family abandons her, she continues to love them and attempt contact with them in the hope that they'll come around.

Beyond the reality of rejection that many gays and lesbians experience after coming out to their families, Jerene's formal service to the narrative is as a trope of social difference: that much established, lesbian feminist politics is represented as primarily a matter of what clothes women wear and whether or not they deem it appropriate to shave their legs. As she grows tired of her flannel shirts and mannish attire, the lackluster dress code of the politically correct lesbian feminist, Jerene—on a sudden whim—goes shopping at the Laura Ashley store for something frilly and forbidden. Finding more than she bargained for, Jerene gets a date with the salesgirl—oddly enough, also named Laura—and begins undergoing the stereotypical transformation into a femme lesbian, the lipstick dyke she was apparently meant to be. Regrettably, Leavitt's account of this transformation lacks the elements of parody and masquerade that were so crucial to the "do me," pro-sex lesbian presentations of the 1980s. Instead, like the lyric so pointedly parodied by the butch lesbian performer Phranc, Jerene simply discovers that she "enjoys being a girl." But in actuality, what she likes is precisely what Banana Republic offers in its "Chosen Family" ad, an elite consumer base, a commodified lesbian "life-style." Laura Ashley's association with a market predominantly white and middle class is apparently deconstructed by Jerene's participation; at the very least, her conversion suggests certain contradictions of race and class that one might expect a black lesbian Marxist feminist to be vaguely aware of. However, Jerene is content simply to "buy in," her customer satisfaction ostensibly indicating a shift in the lesbian-feminist styling of gender politics.

All the same, Jerene, like her unfinished dissertation, seven years in progress, remains uncertain and adrift. Leavitt explains, "She needed work that would completely occupy her, which would leave no space for rumination on her own life or condition" (52). Like the unfinished business with her family, Jerene is emotionally and intellectually stuck in gear, paralyzed and frustrated. It isn't until Laura comes into her life that Jerene is able to mobilize: she gives up on her dissertation, locates her grandmother in a nursing home, and begins making peace with her past. Laura, the daughter of a wealthy Park Avenue family, is pale, needy, frightened by "supermarkets, large dogs, men" (261). Laura clings to Jerene for strength and maternal protection; in exchange, she initiates Jerene into the joys of refined bourgeois femininity.

While Leavitt's vision of lesbian romance smacks of classically racist themes, it is Jerene who, in her dissertation research, discovers the crane-child story from which the novel's title is drawn. Jerene's dissertation on lost languages—"children babbling in their bedrooms"—leads to the case study of an abandoned baby boy named Michael, the unwanted child of a mentally retarded woman who had been raped. Alerted by neighbors, police and social workers arrive at a tenement to rescue Michael only to find him healthy, reasonably content, and engaged in a bizarre form of infantile play. The child is fixated on a construction site visible from a window by his crib. Michael's love object, it turns out, is a crane whose noises he imitates and whose motions he mimics. When he is removed from the apartment, Michael throws a hysterical tantrum. Years later—an institutionalized adolescent—he continues to move and speak like the mechanical crane. For Jerene, the significance of the crane-child story is that "each, in his own way . . . finds what it is he must love, and loves it; the window becomes a mirror; whatever it is that we love, that is who we are" (183).

The crane-child story itself becomes an allegory of the intractability of identity categories and the impossibility of cultural transformation. For Leavitt, the story serves as the main thread that links together the variously hermetic and deterministic familial relations and identity structures depicted in the novel. Sexuality, it would appear, is formed mimetically, within a closed system. Once formed, identity and desire are fixed and immune to external influences. Eliot's sexuality is openly and unilaterally formed by his upbringing around openly gay men, just as Philip's sexuality is secretly and unilaterally formed by his upbringing by a closeted gay father. Such determinations may mark one of the political objectives of the text, to demonstrate that homosexuality is *not* a choice, not a life-style one might pick up at Pier 1 Imports, but an essence formed by social interactions that, once inscribed within the psyche, overturn any notion of a biologically determined, natural heterosexuality. Leavitt's gay and lesbian characters seem happiest when they desire what they are. However, for Philip desire and identification are based in sexual desire. For Jerene, they are based in the contingencies of gender, as easy to replace as your wardrobe. This difference seems crude in its determination to negate the possibility that sex might intersect with gender, or cross over gender, in instances that might involve women with women, men with men, or men with women, or that the contingencies of gender and sex might complicate masculine homosociality.

A consensual gay male culture: this is the romance of *The Lost Language of Cranes* which recuperates the spatial defenses of the closet in its redescription of family romance as a process of "coming out" to a world of sexually alive men and "shutting out" the world of sexless, angry, lost women. However, because desires and identifications always *are* conflictual, contradictory, and transgressive, *The Lost Language of Cranes* only succeeds in staging a spectacle of gender, sex, race, and class exclusions viewed through lavender-tinted lenses. In Leavitt's fictional world, all the men are white, all the daddies are rich, all their sex is vanilla, and none of them don prom dresses. In short, homosexuality is to David Leavitt what Manhattan is to Woody Allen: a fantasy of racial and class hegemony in romance drag. In Leavitt's case, the fantasy has been imbued with ideological power through his pursuit of realist narrative tones and through the media's packaging of him as a delegate of liberal pluralism. However, in its insistence on aligning gay male culture with sexual, cultural, and economic consensus Leavitt's novel has the effect of recuperating—and, indeed, celebrating—the very familial and social regimes that produce homophobia as being, to sex, what sexism is to gender. Yet the boundaries dividing these practices are never so clear as Leavitt would have us think.

As I indicated in the introduction to this book, the contemporary "crisis" of the American family, a crisis reflected in the campaign to reinstall "family values," is largely an indication that the boundaries of private and public have been undergoing an intense period of redefinition. Indeed, part of the troubling of these boundaries has been the post-Stonewall call to come out, to ask, to tell, and to make public what was once only imaginable—when imaginable at all—as private. However, this process of cultural coming out has produced a politically charged intensification of the discursive oppositions between sex and gender, with gay/male linked to the former and feminist/women linked to the latter. And while I remain skeptical about the usefulness of oppositions that oppose gender and sex, or families of origin and families we choose, I do think that queer writers and readers may be in a particularly privileged position from which to apprehend the family romance's potential as a nomadic means of cultural reevaluation. Still, it is sometimes difficult to recognize a queer family romance when you meet one, unless you are attuned to the subtle codes by which these romances "come out" to produce, as Sandra Bernhard has detected, "portraits Norman Rockwell forgot to paint."

David Leavitt has demonstrated that outing the family does not preclude the possibility of getting "in" on the profitability of its representation. Ironically, Pat and Lance Loud's recent efforts to sue the producers of *An American Family* over royalty entitlements suggests on some level that they too have come to recognize not merely the performative function of those daily narratives that constitute the family, but their exploitation by the very technology of their liberation from the family. And as we begin to theorize the family romance more as a performance-producing genre than an identity-producing genre, we may want to understand it in relation to a camp aesthetic, which, when applied, may reveal the extent to which all sexed identity is essentially marked and reaffirmed by performativity.[22] If, as Butler argues, identity is a site of necessary trouble in this redefinition process, then family may be understood in some sense as the original troublemaker. Similarly, *Paris Is Burning*, Jennie Livingston's documentary on drag balls and houses and their impact on members of New York City's gay underclass, shows the potential of drag to subvert the conflation of sex and gender while multiplying the possible meanings of family and motherhood. The documentary is an example, I think, of what the queering of the American family is capable of achieving at its best—an exploration of the ways in which gender and sex are always denaturalized and the family romance is always at odds with itself, serving as an open assertion and displacement of cultural hegemonies.

Chapter 10
The Lesbian Dick: Policing the Family in *Internal Affairs*

A primary feature of lesbian studies' dislocation from feminist studies has been a rejection of the latter's perceived overreliance on binary gender categories, and with that a rejection of a static, discrete analysis of "woman's representation" in popular culture genres. Indeed, to the degree that lesbian theorists have appropriated and expanded on postmodernism's critique of unified identity assertions, the "lesbian turn" in feminist studies presages a transgression of social and symbolic boundaries in its production of counterhegemonic models of feminine bodies, spaces, and aesthetics. And arguably it is here that "the lesbian" and "the family romance" meet to constitute a version of what I have been calling post-family romance. In other words, it is perhaps at this point—the point where the structural oppositions of private and public, masculine and feminine, romance and realism collide—that even the marginal presence of a lesbian agent within a heterosexual narrative framework suggests that sexually perverse female subjects "work" as signifying performers, have access to the public sphere of discourse, and may be viewed as agents of the post-family romance's radicalizing, if not democratizing, potential.

This potential is partly what is at stake in recent discussions of the lesbian phallus. While physically, the lesbian phallus represents, in Marcia Ian's words, an "instrument or agent" of sexual penetration between women, "discursively, the lesbian phallus signifies lesbian subjectivity with full access to the so-called symbolic realm of language, family, sexuality, and culture."[1] Ian's passing reference conveys skepticism toward such gender-neutral idealizations. She reminds us that the phallus, as symbol, nevertheless retains a long history of denotative and connotative associations with the male penis. However, Judith Butler's formulation of the lesbian phallus resists definitions based on a stable history of signification. The phallus itself, she argues, has no existence outside the context or "occasions for its symbolization." Thus, the lesbian phallus has always already exceeded its identification with a preexisting male body, offering "the occasion (a set of occasions) for the phallus to signify differently, and in so signifying, to resignify, unwittingly, its own masculinist and heterosexist privilege."[2]

In this chapter, I want to contextualize the alluring promise of the lesbian phallus with the specific occasion of a lesbian dick, or "that most contradictory and controversial of figures—the lesbian cop."[3] And I want to explore, without necessarily simplifying, the figurative policing of hegemonic complexities that the lesbian dick performs, to her own dissatisfaction, in popular culture. Such a project may seem to run counter to the kinds of reading strategies that I have been at pains to develop elsewhere throughout this book. Indeed, I have stressed the multiple and contradictory discourses that condition the post-family romance across the field of popular genres and modes of representation. However, by interrogating the lesbian dick, I hope to address the means by which such complexities are (albeit partially and insufficiently) dissolved. In these terms, the lesbian dick provides an occasion for the law to signify "sexual difference" differently, which may mean no difference at all. Rather, an overdetermined absence of difference—or, in this case, lesbian difference—may be produced and enforced through the Oedipalization of the lesbian signifier. This process is quite prominent in the realm of Hollywood film, where the possibility of Oedipal subversion is an ever-present mechanism of seduction. Indeed, what Hollywood cinema and the family romance share is a mutual complicity in the maintenance and simultaneous subversion of the technology of gender, the revelation of identity as configuration of "excess and contradiction," a remembered coherence.[4] Still, I want to question the forcible policing of such disturbances, specifically with regard to the lesbian presence in Hollywood film. While Hollywood's acknowledgment of lesbians in certain contexts would seem to affirm their need for mainstream representational space, the industry's co-determining efforts to unify multiple viewing pleasures undermine the de-Oedipalization of desire presaged by these occasional appearances.

Of course, a prominent concern of much gay and lesbian criticism has been to identify in various cultural operations a kind of disaffected punitive supervision allegedly at work in the production and recognition of sexual diversity. In order to illustrate such a supervisory role, Teresa de Lauretis has borrowed the phrase "sexual indifference" from Luce Irigaray to stress the absence of any conceptual frame for lesbian representation. Assuming the axiomatic position that there is but *one* practice and representation of the sexual, de Lauretis differentiates between Irigaray's designation of "hommo-sexuality," which is the term of masculine heterosexuality (and a pun on the French word for man), and its sound-alike term "homosexuality," which is the discursive mark of gay or lesbian sexual desire.[5] In conventional Hollywood narrative, she argues, the practice and representation of the sexual is understood to be determined by masculine desire, and by masculine desire *only*.[6] Where they occur, homosexuality and its representation are always irretrievably bound to dominant social codes by the contract of heterosexual relations. Thus, as Irigaray has claimed, there is but one sex capable of representation—the hommo-sexual, or masculine heterosexuality. Images of gay or lesbian subjectivity, when and where they appear at all, remain contained within this paradox of "hommo-sexuality," the term of sexual/social indifference and a signifier that works as a kind of smug heterosexual police force.

While recent work in cultural studies has usefully challenged this presentation of the text (and the critic) as the main agents in the production and circulation of meanings, de Lauretis's argument is important for the critique I'm about to offer because of the thematic shifts in sexual politics it identifies and the deconstructive work it both reveals and invites. As a case in point, I want to discuss Mike Figgis's *Internal Affairs* (1990), a film about the Internal Affairs Division of the Los Angeles Police Department.[7] Of particular interest is a lesbian character, Sergeant Amy Wallace, played by Laurie Metcalf, the actress who plays Roseanne's sister on the television sitcom *Roseanne*.[8] The deployment of Metcalf's character in a police drama incorporating many of the narrative principles of traditional family romance illustrates how the trope of lesbianism itself may be evoked and recontained—or revealed only to be self-monitored. The conflict intersects tellingly with the role of the Hollywood film industry, which often functions as a mediating institution between capitalism's romance with spectacularized "difference" and the cultural preservation of Oedipal law and order.

In the gap that opens up between these two structuring forces, multiple audiences equipped with diverse viewing strategies admittedly do exceed and confound the "institutional" ordering of cinematic identifications, desires, and pleasures. Yet, I am interested in the bigger picture that seems to be developing, by which I mean, in the most provisional sense, that there seems to be a pattern of lesbian or bisexual lawyers, police, detectives, or civic figures in popular culture texts who represent the legal institution or who serve in the interest of restoring a romanticized vision of the American justice system as one big happy family. *Internal Affairs* is part of what can only be described as an emergent motif in popular culture whereby lesbian or bisexual female characters are framed within otherwise conventional narratives involving detection, legal process, and the police.[9] Unquestionably, these codings suggest the possibility of resignification within the matrix of the judiciary; however, by inscribing these images within the terms of the Oedipus, or paternal-heterosexual privilege, the lesbian subject miraculously transcends lesbianism to enforce a sort of "Don't Ask, Don't Tell" policy. In other words, she is mobilized to represent the very erasure of lesbianism that her appearance in the text ostensibly resists. And while co-opted lesbian images nevertheless reveal ideological contradictions and injustices in the legal and political system, to perceive of these contradictions affirmatively is possibly to generalize the nature of conflict in police drama and to miss the constantly changing hierarchies of social significance within the field of the popular. We may overlook a history that has that made "the law" a problematic site for lesbian intervention. In the eighties and nineties that intervention is specifically defused by the guise of liberal tolerance beneath which the psychosocial oppression of lesbianism is continually reinforced.

Admittedly, the judiciary domain has long been a favored forum for Hollywood's exposures of corruption and injustice within the law enforcement system. Police drama, both novelistic and cinematic, has long provided forums for decentered critiques of a given society's civic apparatuses, thus affirming "an alternative sense of justice, an alternative vision of law."[10] The post-1960s introduction of feminist themes into the police film has resulted in some of the more significant genre redescriptions and self-reflections on social identities, domestic practices, and civic agency. As David Glover and Cora Kaplan point out,

In this revision the categories of "masculine" and "feminine" are not quite left in place. . . . Women in urban public spaces are no longer simply matter out of place, to be disciplined and punished. The forms, conditions, and limits of female agency are now among the most troubling of all the working assumptions a crime narrative has to make, and can no longer be kept quietly under surveillance.[11]

Consequently, new contradictions occur that may be discerned in the police drama's critique of *both* feminine passivity and masculine sadism. Take Kathleen Turner's *V. I. Warshawski*, and the promotional copy's solicitation, "Killer Smile, Killer Legs, Killer Instincts." The self-conscious reification of the instinctual and the peculiar conflation of sexual desire with a public license to kill typically define the conflictive position of the new female investigator or law enforcer in Hollywood crime drama. Lorraine Gamman analyzes the signifying work of such popular narratives in television and the textual paradoxes that result when blurrings of sexual identity occur: "As an entertainment genre, TV cop shows function ideologically to reproduce notions of male social authority and to legitimate contradictory aspects of police work by securing consent for the most brutal components of the repressive state apparatus."[12] Consequently, police drama featuring female law officers encode them with attributes generally repressed in pre-1960s police dramas—action, movement, psychic if not physical strength, and knowledge. "Such scenarios permit focus on female *activity* rather than on female *sexuality*," Gamman argues in support of the genre's contributions to a revised social order.[13] However, she also relies on a categorical separation of activity and sexuality, an incongruence of female desire and male law, an incongruence that corresponds to a social division of internal (domestic) and external (judiciary) spheres. According to this formulation, when women are represented as the agents of the law the result may be an inversion of spatial metaphors. But it's an inversion that holds structural oppositions firmly in place, thus securing resolution while still allowing for a politically fashionable overhaul and the exploration of new cultural themes.

However, what happens when the agent of the law is a lesbian "dick," a judiciary agent who stands conspicuously outside the definition of woman as a property of Oedipal law? The result is not simply a co-option of feminist politics nor a deconstruction of a patriarchal legal system, but a radical reconceptualization of gender/sex possibility that undermines strategies of simplistic inversion by evoking conditions of strategic perversion. By "outing," so to speak, the full range of sexual possibility, by revealing woman-to-woman desire as a public as well as private issue, the representation of lesbianism within traditional police/crime narrative forms holds the potential to enact powerful narrative disturbances that have equally powerful social implications.

In *Internal Affairs* this potential is nervously held in check, although the contradictory premise of a lesbian police officer whose job it is to protect and defend the patriarchal family retains its subversive potential. This potential is restrained by the Internal Affairs Division, whose operations *effect* the appearance of order and unity. Newly employed by the IAD staff is Detective Raymond Avilla, the main character, played by Andy Garcia. His partner, Amy Wallace, is a highly competent, good-humored career officer whose supposed lesbianism is a thinly veiled secret among the IAD staff. It is significant, in this regard, that at no point in the film does Wallace ever call herself a lesbian or admit to being one. Only the male characters refer to her sexual orientation, and when they do so she is randomly dismissed as "the dyke." The epithet is thrown about as an instrument of containment and desexualization; it renders Wallace useless, harmless, an object of ridicule who holds little currency in the economy of fraternal competitions and devotions that hold the police force together. After his first day of work, Avilla's wife, Kathy, asks if his female partner is pretty. "She's pretty smart. She's a good cop," he answers, ostensibly indicating his indifference to Wallace's private life, but also suggesting that Wallace's sexual availability or unavailability is information far more threatening to his marriage than an assessment of her professional qualifications. Later, when Kathy rationalizes her husband's lack of sexual interest by accusing him of having an affair with Wallace, he shouts, "I'm not fucking my partner, my partner's a dyke!" Suddenly, Wallace's private life is given public voice, but only because her lesbianism serves as a defense when masculine virility is called into question.

This defense function notwithstanding, Wallace's reputation as "a good cop" indicates that she has earned a certain amount of respect from her colleagues. She is grudgingly acknowledged as a member of the tribe. However, Wallace cannot be read exactly like "family," nor can she be read exactly like a woman. Her blue uniform marks her as an arbiter of difference in the world of women. Her sex marks her as an arbiter of difference in the world of cops, much like Avilla's ethnicity marks him as an arbiter of cultural difference, a Latino, whose name is mispronounced by his "racist boss." However, his ethnicity increases his heroic potential by making it possible for him to speak the language of the "mean streets" in East Los Angeles and translate it into the language of the police precinct. Wallace's lesbianism in no way enables her to mediate between social terrains or discourses. If anything, in fact, she is everyone's obnoxious kid sister, a figure who evokes benign tolerance rather than an agent of interpolation.[14] So why, then, is it necessary that Amy Wallace be portrayed as a lesbian?

According to Judith Butler, if we are to understand the reproduction of heterosexual desire through the compulsory function of Oedipal law, we need to see how "the law might be understood to produce or generate the desire it is said to repress. . . . In other words, desire and its repression are an occasion for the consolidation of juridical structures; desire is manufactured and forbidden as a ritual symbolic gesture whereby the juridical model exercises and consolidates its own power."[15] Consequently, when lesbian subjectivity is manufactured within this framework, agonizing conflicts result. In many contemporary images of lesbians, the structural contradictions of what Gayle Rubin termed the "sex/gender system" become mapped against a discourse of liberal tolerance.[16] And it is at this juncture that we discover a deceptive "liberal ideology of pluralism, where social difference is also, at the same time, social indifference."[17] The representation of lesbian subjectivity thus works systematically to assure the erasure of lesbian subjectivity, the rendering of her desire as benign. From this perspective, I would argue that Amy Wallace does not, as appearances might otherwise suggest, successfully represent an alternative justice among the deteriorating heterosexual relations depicted in *Internal Affairs*. Nor is she a valid exception to the Hollywood film industry's relentless reproduction of Oedipal family images. Rather, she is co-opted in the name of a fashionably "sensitive" feminist and liberal gay discourse to reinstate the power of a repressive social agenda whose inconsistencies, we are led to believe, are the inevitable outgrowths of democratic pluralism.

Wallace's place within the IAD system—a system specifically organized to penetrate the private lives of police officers—appears to challenge the authority of the sex/gender system with every move she makes "in the name of the law." As IAD staff, Wallace represents a kind of meta-authority. She is the cop of the cops; it is her job to keep the force clean, and this proves to be no easy assignment. However, the performative effects of this reversal and of the gay/female, straight/male collision works to condense categories of sexual identity rather than to disseminate them across the wide discursive range of social and political possibilities. Wallace's inscription serves basically to stabilize a floundering Oedipal regime by making possible the proper transfer of authority from gruff but tolerant older police brass to an honest, racially diverse younger staff who will maintain a strict separation of male homosociality and male homosexuality. By establishing supposedly symmetrical oppositions of meaning within the boundaries of the department, *Internal Affairs* keeps "female" subordinate to "male" and "gay" subordinate to "straight." In other words, Wallace is positioned to show that transgressive sexuality is nonthreatening, easily containable, so long as it is conflated with the feminine. Her main job is not to critique the force but to reinforce a compulsory devaluation of femininity and homosexuality. In this way, viewer's identifications with Oedipal norms may truly be what is policed in *Internal Affairs*. The film suggests that female social deviance is enfeebled when placed within the boundaries, devices, and rituals of the law enforcement nexus. In this way, we may see Wallace as a fly in the ointment, but she remains a latent fly throughout.

Another way of examining the paradox that Wallace presents is to posit her character within what Eve Kosofsky Sedgwick calls an "open-secret structure."[18] Lesbianism is constructed in the film as a site of self-silencing and obedient patterning on heterosexual (male) expressions of desire. Thus, arguably, *Internal Affairs* participates in the construction of an "epistemology of the closet" that, according to Sedgwick, requires "the deconstructive understanding that particular insights generate, are lined with, and at the same time are themselves structured by particular opacities."[19] As a woman, a lesbian, and a cop, Wallace doesn't so much defy typical representation as much as she helps define a new category of identity, a reification of silences that constitutes lesbian identity by forcing it to conform with the heterosexist opinion that homosexuality is purely a private, "internal" matter. Granted, Wallace is presented neither in a voyeuristic manner "as spectacle," nor is she set up for heterosexual conversion. It is clear that we, as viewers, are being asked to sympathize with her, and most viewers I have questioned *do* sympathize with her. However, our sympathies are carefully filtered through our primary identification with Avilla and his indifference to what makes Wallace "different" from the other cops and the other women portrayed in the film.

How does *Internal Affairs* command the effects of indifference to enforce the recloseting of lesbian desire at the very site of its exposure? In the film, Wallace's dedication to her investigative function, her honest belief in the system, is set against the corrupt, violent, and dishonest organization of the street cops, the worst of whom are arrogant, abusive, racist, sexist, drug-addicted, and willing to turn a blind eye to acts of blatant injustice and exploitation of the judiciary system. Richard Gere plays the leader of this pack, Officer Dennis Peck, a raging and malicious psychopath who becomes the object of IAD investigation when Wallace and Avilla begin to suspect that Peck has supplementary business interests outside the force. They're right. He controls 40 percent of the force by providing second incomes to naive rookie cops struggling to support their young families on a junior police officer's salary. In return, Peck exacts their submission to his command over the affairs of street business and his command over the domestic and sexual lives of the officers.

Peck is an exemplary cop, one of the most productive on the staff. His productivity extends outside the force as well: he is the father of eight children, a ninth is on the way. As it turns out, he is also a hit man for a local crime boss. He launders cash through his numerous ex-wives to cover up his income. By the time the narrative reveals that Peck has connections with local organized crime, we have seen that he is utterly ruthless, sexually menacing, and erotically ubiquitous. Interestingly enough, part of Peck's power over the rookie officers is that he is also a father figure to them, manipulating their emotions in his quest for complete punitive power. Dennis Peck, whose very name connotes crude phallic authority, embodies an excess of "hommo-sexuality," here perceived as reproductive heterosexuality. The inscription of abusive sexual excess is rendered more frightening by images of homoerotic intimacy between Peck and his partner, Van Stretch. The sexual tension in their partnership problematizes homosociality almost to the point of collapsing it into homosexuality. Peck's secret sexual relationship with Stretch's wife, Penny, enacts and at the same time perverts the exchange of women whereby men consolidate bonds of trust and community. Peck's excessive hommo-sexuality reveals the most brutal contradictions of Oedipal masculinity and its historical inscription within the police genre. Very carefully, however, male homosexual possibility is kept anchored to images of extreme psychological dysfunction and sadistic exploitation, as the dynamic between Peck and Stretch crudely suggests in both the pairing of their names and their actions.

Far more than the literal prick of the force, Dennis Peck is an embodiment of a vicious sexual economy in which only those subjectivities rendered marginal by the paradigm of the positive Oedipus complex are explained in terms of excesses or lacks. In *Internal Affairs*, "too much" paternal authority indicates transcendent possibilities. In a society where gay sexual practice is socially and legally contained in terms of secrets, absence, and deviance, the masculine homosocial contract, in excess of its own laws, inverts its own internal value system and becomes an affair of the closets that are integral elements of the corrupt public sphere. A sexual extremist, Peck is the incarnation of an intensely homophobic vision of uncontainable polymorphous masculinity, a nonphallic masculinity fully invested with the authority of the law. "You can trust me," says Peck when a man who has contracted his parents' murder warns him to keep quiet about it, "I'm a cop." Peck *is* the law, and he redefines justice to signify an excess of paternal-heterosexual privilege that ultimately results in self-parody, the policeman's ball as camp. Thus, Peck persistently reveals himself to the force as peckerless. The police department itself becomes a repository for the secret of masculine lack, a state-sanctioned closet where hypermasculine sexuality "tells us more about the fantasies that a fearful heterosexual culture produces to defend against its own homosexual possibilities" than about gay or "lesbian experience itself."[20] Wallace's lesbianism, in this context, is reduced to an asexual reification of benign difference, which is consequently regarded with total and justifiable indifference.

In part this indifference—and the dismissal of lesbianism as a legitimate category of identity—comes about as a result of the presumed incongruence of lesbianism and the heterosexual marriage contract, which remain, in the *mise-en-scène* of the film, the foundation of a just society. Kinship and the potential dissolution of the patriarchal kinship system constitute the organizing tensions of the film, and these tensions erupt on a number of interrelated levels. Almost all of the male characters in film are convinced that their wives are betraying them, whether they are or not. In Van Stretch's abusive relationship with Penny Stretch we see the dark side of a marriage torn apart by drugs, greed, male violence, and female deceit. In Dennis Peck's extended family of ex-wives and children from various marriages we see not so much the possibilities for redefining kinship structures, but a vision of the post-nuclear family as harem over which Peck dominates. It is here, too, that he dictates his extremist view of the essential function of heterosexual marriage: reproduce, reproduce, reproduce. His current wife finally betrays him by going to Wallace and Avilla with information concerning her husband's illegal activities. One of these activities involves a truly harrowing family affair, a floor covering entrepreneur whose immigrant parents control all the stock of the family business. He contracts Peck to kill them because, as he explains, "They don't get it. They won't borrow. They won't diversify. . . . They have no idea how to conduct business today." Peck murders the parents, off-screen presumably, and then proceeds to seduce the floor covering son's wife. When the son catches them together in the bedroom, Peck hands the puzzled man a gun and says, "She paid me to kill you. . . . go ahead, kill her. She's a tramp." Apparently, the son responds by shooting Peck in the foot. The wife is murdered, although it is uncertain which of the men shoots her. The son is also killed, presumably by Peck, or so it appears when Avilla arrives on the scene and finds both bodies.

At such moments, the film's preference for nebulous off-screen murder blurs the boundaries of evil and the law by sustaining a level of uncertainty as to who, exactly, is pulling the trigger. Is it someone outside or inside the family? Is Dennis Peck really any different from any other "family man"? As an antidote to intrafamilial greed, violence, and corruption, the film seems to rally support for the maintenance of separate spheres, the necessary division of intimacy and business. This lesson is dramatized in the subplot depicting Raymond's troubled relationship with Kathy, who, although immersed in her own professional obligations as manager of an upscale art gallery, argues that her husband's obsessive commitment to work has drained their relationship of its intimacy and passion. Here the film sustains a running autocritique of its own generic durability as it equates Raymond and Kathy's marital conflict with the cultural conflict between the masculine sphere of police drama and feminized sphere of the fine arts. While he dismisses the gallery society as trendy and pretentious, Raymond is threatened when he overhears his wife and a coworker talking about the latter's new lover, an attractive artist. The women discuss his "brush stroke." A subtle convergence of sexual politics and cultural politics occurs here as the police officer's sense of displacement and sexual insufficiency among the artistic elite refers us back to Amy Wallace's marginalization and sexual displacement within the hard-boiled police precinct. Both Avilla and Wallace are thus faced with the task of creating discursive spaces for themselves within these gendered spheres where they are clearly outsiders, in spite of their connections.

Alongside the conflicts of the private family there are conflicts within the masculine society of the police force, a family concerned with the reproduction of its own social authority, an order bound by the rights of exchange and by the intensity of the dangers its members face together. Ironically, it is Van Stretch's reported use of "excessive force" on the job that initially alerts Wallace and Avilla to the illegal activities being conducted by Peck. When Stretch begins to break under IAD questioning, Peck arranges an "accidental" shooting during a routine assignment. When Stretch doesn't die right away from the shot fired into his chest, Peck crouches down besides him, cradles his partner's head in his arms in a loving and protective embrace, and then strangles him to death.

As the white male hierarchy begins to self-destruct under the intense scrutiny of Avilla and Wallace—a Latino and a lesbian—a utopian vision of social pluralism, a global family, so to speak, is superficially suggested by the implied need for greater unity among the different individuals who make up the world inside and outside the police force. As Internal Affairs investigators, Detectives Avilla and Wallace share the task of negotiating and monitoring these levels of social relationships. But still they remain marginalized, presumably not because they are ethnically and sexually "different" but because of the fact that they are IAD scum, distrusted and resented by the street cops who see them as promotion-greedy informers and traitors to the familial structure of the department. Consequently, Avilla and Wallace come to rely powerfully on one another for their physical and emotional well-being.

In this sense, the film overlooks its reinstatement of separate spheres and becomes conflictually engaged in a sentimental portrait of cross-gender professional bonding between two agents freed from the burden of heterosexual sexual tension. Consequently, Avilla and Wallace make a great team. However, the more they succeed in getting information about the private affairs of Dennis Peck, the more they threaten to expose him, the more viciously Peck retaliates by infiltrating into the private affairs of Avilla. He threatens to seduce Kathy and produces a pair of her panties, which he tosses in Avilla's face. Yet it is not so clear whom Peck is more interested in seducing, as he exploits his knowledge of Avilla's sexual insufficiency and giggles when Avilla punches him in the nose. Delusional with rage, Avilla tyrannizes and interrogates Kathy until she is demoralized. She has no idea how Peck got her underwear, although she admits having lunch with Peck only because he claimed to be an IAD detective tasked with an investigation of her husband.

In this way, again, *Internal Affairs* points to masculinity's ruination by the cross-mappings of domestic and work space; the film begins to sound like a corporate policy manual disavowing incestuous entanglements between coworkers, then falling back on the conventional romanticization of the asexual attachment of police partners. Again, because

Wallace is a lesbian, this attachment can be safely formed; however, the film ultimately rejects the spatial anarchy of desire in favor of what D. A. Miller has called, in another context, an "undeclared defense of the status quo."[21] Taking issue with Miller's suspicion of the novel as police, or more specifically with his argument that "privacy and domesticity, supposed to be a refuge from power's oppressions, mime their opponent, and make the 'outside' of power the twin of power," Robert Caserio has argued that while indeed some gay narratives collaborate in the construction of a homophobic discourse by cultivating an ideal of the private family, there is no real reason to "see family structure as necessarily—and in every possible form—the ally of supervisory and disciplinary constraint."[22]

True enough, but what's ultimately compelling about the film *Internal Affairs* is precisely that it argues the Miller-Caserio debate from both sides *within* the same text, on one hand positioning a lesbian character as a defender of patriarchy, while on the other hand implying that she is a free agent in this otherwise hostile environment. Ultimately, however, the film unravels its own liberal intentions in much the same way that Miller would unsettle Charles Dickens's efforts to shelter the private family from the police. Perhaps in spite of itself, *Internal Affairs* offers the assurance that no lesbian agent, no matter how good a cop she may be, can disrupt or deter the enforcement of compulsory heterosexuality and the survival of the heterosexual marriage contract, the foundation of the Oedipal family. Indeed, there is no downplaying the recognition that while Avilla's life outside the force has public consequences, Wallace's does not. Or, in other words, her inclusion within the film requires that she be excluded from playing any meaningful part in the self-reflexive critique that makes her role within the all-male, all-straight police force so crucial.

Wallace's lesbian difference becomes social indifference at the point where the film appears to construct an interesting diacritical pattern that could potentially decenter the notions of public authority and private freedom. Intervention, that is interaction between the private and public, between the inside and the outside of the law, is shown to be a fundamental concern of the state apparatus even while the ideology of "family" assures a safe haven beyond the control of the external world. While *Internal Affairs* focuses on the dialectic dimensions of such structural oppositions as private/public, male/female, homosexual/heterosexual, Wallace is given no identity outside the force whatsoever. She appears to have no home, no private life, no lover, not even a friend, and this absence becomes more and more glaring as the narrative progresses.

Why is it that Wallace is the *only* character to be placed in this familial void? Indeed, the film shows all the significant characters in a domestic context. Does Wallace's credibility as a reliable servant of the law depend on her having no attachments in her life other than to her work? "Go home to your wife," she advises Avilla as they work late into the night. Grudgingly, he goes. But if there's anyone waiting for Wallace at home, we'll never know about her. Wallace is relieved of a place in the world beyond the precinct, and Avilla is relieved of having to ask about it. More than anything else, Wallace's complete lack of a life outside the force reveals the narrative's own homophobic pitfalls. The portrayal of Wallace suggests that lesbianism will be tolerated as long as its kept under cover. To represent a woman whom others call a dyke is acceptable, but a woman who "tells" that she is a dyke (or demonstrates a propensity to engage in lesbian acts) is simply not one of the family. By denying her an internal affair of her own, *Internal Affairs* exposes its own "undeclared defense of the status quo." And although I don't want to imply that the credibility of female characters — lesbian or otherwise — depends on their depiction within a romantic or domestic setting, I do think that hegemonic complexity is ultimately what is policed by police dramas that grant visibility to lesbians only to dramatize the powers of their containment strategies.

Interestingly, the assertion of patriarchal authority through surveillance and its replication through the metaphor of the gaze is briefly examined during one of the more provocative scenes of *Internal Affairs*. Avilla and Wallace sit side by side in the front seat of the patrol car. They are following Van Stretch's wife, who they suspect is involved with Peck's money-laundering scheme, and they pass the time eating fast food. Suddenly, without exchanging a word, they are both alerted to the approach of a tall, tan, long-legged woman in a tight, white dress. Both officers gawk at her, then turn to follow her as she passes. Avilla loses interest and turns around in time to see that Wallace has been staring too, just as intently, and is continuing to stare as the woman recedes into the background. In the next beat, Wallace turns around to see Avilla looking at her. She meets his inquisitive expression head-on, grins, and takes a suck from the straw of her soda. Avilla is nonplussed as new knowledge about his partner registers with him. In the following instant the "serious" action of the film resumes as Penny Stretch finally appears.

In this sequence Wallace wordlessly names her desire through the action of visual cruising, and she becomes the sexually transgressive agent whom, perhaps, we have been waiting for throughout the film. Indeed, Wallace's "look" is a highly erotized moment in the film, a risky co-option of masculine authority that allows her to take pleasure in the spectacle of female commodification. The look functions in excess of the police-sanctioned task of tracking Penny Stretch, underscoring the erotic possibilities of Wallace's voyeuristic involvement with the law. What the audience sees is the replication of a nonheterosexual construct within a heterosexual setting. Furthermore, Wallace's casual girl-watching appears to parody heterosexual naturalness, and the imperative of heterosexual production that obsesses Dennis Peck. For sure, Wallace's gaze is anything but a (re)productive gaze.

However, in the same instance, her gaze is co-opted by Avilla, and a brief moment of competition occurs in which we may wonder who's really looking at whom. While acknowledging Wallace's visual agency, the text promotes Avilla's "look" at Wallace's looking and draws viewers' identification in a way that is meant to resolve and contain the moment. Ultimately, the look provides him with inside knowledge concerning the "rumor" about Wallace. Lesbian desire thus becomes constituted in a countergaze that invites a surrender to the law, or to a masculine desire to "know" what the woman wants. What she wants, apparently, is what men want. Accordingly, the camera interprets the Chandleresque object of desire as a projection of hard-boiled masculine fantasy, the conventional femme fatale of police dramas of the past. The steamy Latin rhythms in the background, the stylishly aloof articulations of the woman's hips as she walks, and her packaging as an embodiment of the L.A. "look" declare that there may be more than one desire capable of representation; however, no sooner does this possibility erupt than it is monopolized by the markings of sexual (in)difference. No meanings are exchanged between the two women—presumably the female passerby is not aware that she is being watched. Rather, there is an attempt to define Wallace's look as an imitation of the male look, a move that tries, however unsuccessfully, to recontain desire in the sphere of male authority. In this way, "the conventions of seeing, and the relations of desire and meaning . . . remained partially anchored or contained by a frame of visibility that is still heterosexual."[23] Through the hegemonically policed production of visual pleasure, lesbian sexuality, or the possibility of its representation, is appropriated by the paternal function.

Consequently, Wallace's gaze works to constitute both her and Avilla's authority over the erotic, a democratized erotic, rather than to constitute a lesbian space in conflict with masculine space. Although, undoubtedly, some viewers will take pleasure in looking at a woman looking at a woman, still the reverberations of pleasure are carefully contained within a double cross; the possibility of lesbian representation remains caught in the tropism of heterosexuality. Immersed in the world of macho cops, Detective Wallace may flirtatiously arrest the masculine gaze, but no one is looking back at her except the police. Lesbian desire is thus carefully contained in a glance that reconstitutes the police as author and lesbian as imitator. Wallace's position as a cop allows her recreational access to the men's locker room, which functions in this case as a kind of structural alternative to the closet.

Internal Affairs boasts of challenging the boundaries of private and public, gender, and erotic possibility through the inclusion of a character whom everyone knows to be a "dyke." But this is mainly paying political lip service to the notion of liberal gay discourse. In every way, the film's strategies of representing sexual difference are shot through with caution and resolution. Toward the conclusion of the narrative, internal affairs, both public and private, are set straight, so to speak. Dennis Peck seriously wounds Wallace in the final manhunt scene, and we witness the ambulance ride to the hospital as Avilla stout-heartedly spurs her on to "hang in there." We never find out whether or not she survives; all we are left with is Avilla's assurance that she is "a fighter." Once again, as John Leo argues, the gay presence has served its main purpose, providing an opportunity for straight characters to become liberalized. The "dramatic problem" is not to resolve the dilemma of the lesbian character, but to reaffirm the conventional hierarchy by representing "a properly liberal reaction within the 'normality' of social pluralism and consensus."[24]

From this point on, Detective Wallace remains outside the narrative focus. Avilla finally "gets his man," shooting Peck dead in his own bedroom where he finds him holding Kathy hostage. The destruction of megalomaniacal sexual desire within the police department's kin-based social organization reestablishes the primacy of an egalitarian heterosexual contract. Raymond and Kathy are presumably reconciled; the maintenance of the heterosexual marriage contract is demonstrated to be a matter of public importance. The law is proven to be powerful enough to contain subversive sexual identities, so long as those identities remain detached from sexual practice. Corrupt sexual activity is shown to exist along a continuum of exteriorized kinship systems that become chaotic and dangerous when they dare to move beyond the limits of Oedipal law.

Kate Adams has demonstrated how in post–World War II literature the discourse of psychoanalysis once acted as the lesbian's chaperon "whenever she came out into the mainstream of popular culture."[25] What I have attempted to show here is how the combined social forces of second-wave feminism and the gay/lesbian liberation movement have impacted on the police drama, which has begun to construct itself as a chaperon for lesbians. In the case of *Internal Affairs* we see how this text-appointed role of chaperon is affirmed through an alliance of police drama with family romance. Indeed, perhaps we are no longer culturally concerned with the psychic origins of a "disorder" but rather with the legislative effects of sexual politics that threaten to dissolve Oedipal masculinity and those popular genres called up by them. If so, the representation of lesbian subjects will require representation, containment, and framing within self-reflexive crime narratives that police the referent but at the same time perpetuate the myth of a democratized patriarchy. For example, Wallace finally has a chance to introduce herself to Avilla's wife when they are at an officer's funeral and Wallace is dressed in full uniform. Here, the convention of dress constitutes a legally "produced and approved identity."[26] Again, lesbian identity is co-opted to dramatize the anonymous agency of heroes who transform the law and represent our most valued constructs of truth and knowledge. However, the text cannot repress the lesbian's potential to reveal that the *law* as an origin for social order is nothing more than a parody of the desire for order and absolute authority.

In conclusion, the formulation of an "authentic" lesbian image in Hollywood film, whatever that might mean, "depends on separating out the two contrary undertows that constitute the paradox of sexual (in)difference."[27] It will also require a willingness to explore the injustices and corruptions of Oedipus. However, in its defense of the Oedipal status quo, *Internal Affairs* is an example of one contemporary film that registers social anxiety at the postmodern prospect of isolating but maintaining the sexual and the political, the private and the public, the police and the policed, the internal and external affairs of the body. For even when she is constituted for the purpose of consolidating the power of the patriarchal family, the lesbian character in Hollywood cinema assists postmodern critique by revealing the extent to which no lesbian phallus exists undetermined by Oedipal history, just as no family affair exists undetermined by a lesbian dick.

Chapter 11
Home Viewing— *Terminator 2: Judgment Day*

These days, family romance is as close as your VCR. Without question, home video has evolved into a distinctive narrative form with its own conventions, codes, and framing devices. The logic of these devices seems to be grounded in the presumption of a domestic audience fascinated with home technologies that might allow for the limitless consumption of familial images that unify and naturalize gender relations and norms.

I formulated these conclusions recently, while preparing remarks for a presentation on the film *Terminator 2: Judgment Day*, Arnold Schwarzenegger's massively produced, top-grossing sequel to the equally spectacular *The Terminator*. Unexpectedly, my home viewing encounter with *Terminator 2* became defined by a sequence of trailer footage, preliminary messages that are central to a reading of *Terminator 2* as a post-family romance.[1] The video begins with a public service announcement sponsored by "The Partnership for a Drug Free America." Appearing at the presidential desk, framed beneath the presidential shield, is George Bush. As the camera zooms in, we are invited to share an intimate moment with the former president whose report on the war against drugs concludes with the consoling assurance that "America is turning off drugs because Americans are making it happen."

This announcement is followed by a sales pitch for previously viewed home videos that can be purchased at reduced cost from your local video store. With these videos and with the right home technology, it becomes possible for your family to watch favorite moments from your favorite films— *Terminator 2*, for instance—over and over again. The voice-over begins, "All around the world people are asking . . ." as a white, well-groomed family—mother, father, and teenage son—in casual sports attire are seen gathered together on the living room sofa marveling at

T2's special effects. "Whoa, how did they do that?" the father exclaims. "I gotta see that again." He takes charge of the remote control as the nuclear family appears remotely bound in their mutual awe of the mystery of cinematic illusion, a dreamscape more familiar than the family itself. Their partnership is underwritten by the addictive pleasures of repetition. And before our eyes the son thrills to the occasion of the father's compulsion, thus, we may suppose, becoming initiated into a reproductive function proscribed by a domestic romance with marketable technologies.

Contradictory principles of postmodern Oedipal pleasure continue with the following trailers for *Basic Instinct* and *Defenseless*, two films depicting gruesome murders, graphic sex, and, in *Basic Instinct*, a tantalizing lesbian psycho-killer whose now-infamous genital flash scene is featured, then sharply cut at the instant she uncrosses her legs before the eyes of the law. Both films, we are told, are soon to be available on videocassette for home viewing; yet the editorial mandate that disavows the Medusa spectacle of Sharon Stone's private parts suggests a level of indeterminate unavailability where nonreproductive female sexuality is policed. Or, in other words, the laws of technology defer the moment when viewers, faced with Medusa, will turn to stone at the horrific sight of the family's betrayal.

In a final recuperative gesture, however, the sequence concludes with another public service announcement for children's physical fitness that features none other than the star of *Pumping Iron* himself, Arnold Schwarzenegger. Taking a break from overseeing a field of athletic youths geared up for competitive play, he faces the camera and elicits parents to join him in yet another partnership, a shared commitment to keeping kids in good shape, physically conditioned, disciplined. Clearly, children's protean, presexual bodies are our salvation, the raw material of uniform spectacle, a lean, mean capital. However, Schwarzenegger doubts the sincerity of our pledge; he closes with a familiar warning to those who might not be taking his endorsement seriously: "I'll be back." And, indeed, as the performative embodiment of a peculiar paternal hybrid—Mr. Universe, Mr. Rogers, and the Terminator all in one—Schwarzenegger becomes both the effect *and* excess of a discursive crisis centered on the lack of a father, a lack that is compensated for and disguised by the indirect suggestion that it is, in fact, the adult viewer who may be in need of a little discipline.

Sitting there in my own living room, thirty-five years old, middle-class, lesbian, contentedly childless, gripping the rewind on the remote control in order to play the trailer footage over again, I considered Andrew Ross's observation that "while the ideology of familialism is everywhere, the families themselves are increasingly thin on the ground."[2] And granting the allusive limits of textual margins, I began to think that perhaps I had already seen the true feature presentation, a family romance in which the Oedipal triangle is offered the chance to repeatedly fall in love with its own image, an image sanctified by another holy trinity of sorts: Bush, Schwarzenegger, and the American patriarchal nuclear family for whom intimacy and consumption are mutually enhancing exchanges and for whom advanced technology means both a refuge from the market imperatives of the public sphere *and* a distraction from the emotional demands of the private sphere.

Which brings me at last to the main event, *Terminator 2: Judgment Day.* Undeniably, this *is* entertainment. However, it is entertainment rife with social and aesthetic contradictions owing to the fact that beneath the ostensibly antinuclear, antiwar premise and in spite of the narrative's seeming willingness to explore the boundaries of feminine subjectivity and conventional gender definition, *Terminator 2* is an undeclared defense of the ideology of familialism, a high-tech, spectacle-intensive, action-packed endorsement of the right-wing "family values" agenda that attempts to align government with an increasingly militant religious right in order to more deeply align American nationalism with, among other things, control of the body, and particularly women's reproductive functions. In its terrifying depiction of mother-child relations severed by nuclear Armageddon, *T2*'s subtextual message is brought to dramatic light: the crisis of the family, a "crisis" perpetuated by unlawful pleasures, feminism, and a flabby liberal democratic body that have undermined the "natural" family, may, if left unchecked, threaten our national security as well. The cultural response that *Terminator 2* loudly affirms is "the restoration of the father in Hollywood cinema" and the legitimation of guerrilla familialism.[3]

Moreover, the restoration of American economic and military supremacy is at issue here. The alleviation of our national anxiety is equated with the disciplining of the American family and the valorization of the Oedipal triad, a configuration that the film fetishizes as an antidote to the feminization of the public sphere and the potential dissolution of masculine authority. The film's romantic obsession with the innate naturalness of the mother-child bond registers cultural nervousness regarding reproductive technology and the disappearance of biological motherhood. However, his role within the film as both a father figure and a cybernetic organism ("living tissue over a metal endoskeleton," we are told) vitally links technology with the family. The more specific link, however, is with paternal power, the masculine terrain of American myth where outlaw boys become heroes and naive prepubescent games revert into capitalist and militarist spectacle. *Terminator 2*, in this sense, is a distinctly American family romance that is also a narrative of empire, the empire of the family whose intimate relations with machines can be ultimately rewarding, as the commercial for previously viewed home videos suggests, so long as fathers are responsible for the external remote controls and mothers relinquish control of their internal biology.

This nostalgic parable for the recuperation of threatened paternal authority is presented as a revisionary myth that questions public indifference to the perception of a general collapse of the traditional family romance. And, indeed, *Terminator 2 does* challenge the proliferation of nuclear arms, the valuing of machines over human life, the interference of social institutions with the private life of the family, and even the traditional representation of women as passive. However, these positions ultimately serve as platforms from which to launch contradictory arguments for the remasculinization of America through weapons technology, the sanctity of the heterosexual nuclear family, and woman's natural incompatibility with science and technology, or the dominant forms of cultural discourse. What I hope to do in the following pages therefore is tease out some of these oppositional codes or double crosses that play throughout the video text, double crosses as potentially threatening to the de-Oedipalization of American culture as Sharon Stone's crossed legs. By engaging this critique, my hope is that we begin to see how the home video constructs its own mechanisms of erasure, or, to use a term that I will explain later, its own "deniability" factor. And in this sense, perhaps, the narrative provides an alternative framework for understanding the ways in which genre—specifically family romance—is being redescribed in the postmodern moment. For it seems as though *Terminator 2* is self-consciously propelled by a network of structural dysfunctions not unlike the "dysfunctions" that allegedly afflict the contemporary family and that propel a thriving self-help publishing industry as well. Paradoxically, the family becomes defined within this industrial dynamic as both "the problem and the cure," both the source of our national malaise and the key to moving beyond it.[4] In *Terminator 2*, similarly, we are told that the family must change, but the text can only convey this message by insisting that we leave it alone.

In Freud's own fetishization of the Oedipal triad, he defines "family romance" as a specific result of individual imaginative activity, a subjective fantasy that serves "as the fulfillment of wishes and as a correction of actual life."[5] In this regard (and as I argue in detail in Chapter 2), family romance is a narrative paradox, a bid for cohesive identity that defines family relations precisely by denying them, thereby making possible "the later stage in the development of the neurotic's estrangement from his parents" or the achievement of mature familial ties.[6] This anxious process of negotiating conflict between myth and reality, actual and imagined national identity, is extravagantly portrayed in *Termina-*

tor 2, a family romance that simultaneously maintains and subverts the late-capitalist sensibility that has gradually instituted the family as the ultimate domestic commodity, not so much a means to an end but an end in itself.

At heart *Terminator 2* registers profound nostalgia. However, the past it constructs as the object of nostalgia is the now. Fredric Jameson's discussion of contemporary film identifies this complex engagement of historicity as a particular aesthetic effect, "an experience of our present as past and as history," an underhanded reminder that the moments we occupy will one day be processed and nostalgically recreated just as we have done to history.[7] By examining film's complex situation of itself within history we see how it provides an allegorical confrontation with the present. This constitution of the "present as the past of a specific future" produces "the estrangement and renewal as history of our own reading present."[8] Indeed, *Terminator 2* is not about altering the course of the future; it is about rewriting the present moment as we have rewritten and will continue to rewrite the past.[9]

The communication of this theme is achieved not so much through defamiliarization, as is typical in the science fiction genre, but through "refamiliarization" with the present as history. The text's appropriation of Christian mythology through the reinscription of the immaculate conception and the birth of Christ ennobles the West and its crusading logic of colonization and domination by divine right. In the original *The Terminator*, Arnold Schwarzenegger plays a cybernetic system sent back in time from the future to Los Angeles in 1984 where his mission is to kill Sarah Connor, the woman destined to give birth to a son named John who will become the great military leader of the human resistance in the post-nuclear-apocalyptic "war against the machines."[10] Sarah conceives this son with Kyle Reese, a soldier from this future world and a comrade of John Connor the adult. On a voluntary mission, Reese travels back in time to rescue Sarah from the Terminator and to meet the woman who in his own time will be "the legend . . . the mother of the future." If Sarah dies, a savior will never be born to deliver the remains of the human race from evil.

Sarah and Kyle's union lasts only one night in a cosmic gap between present and future, a place out of time. Although not technically an immaculate conception, as the lovemaking scene between Sarah and Kyle visually demonstrates, John Connor's conception is a *scientific* impossibility. Sarah's pregnancy is thus neither a purely spiritual symbol nor a biological precept, but a national imperative. Her body is sacrificed not for God, but for country; yet the reiteration of Christian symbolism establishes a clear relation between the two, a relation that forms the central theme of the narrative and suggests that woman's body is a consolidating agent of state and religious law. This theme is reinforced throughout *Terminator 2*. The sequel opens with a reminder that full-scale nuclear war and the loss of three billion human lives is set to occur on August 29, 1997, as a result of a takeover by Skynet, the computer defense system developed by the Cyberdyne corporation. John Connor, an angry and delinquent ten-year-old, is in the care of surrogate parents. Sarah Connor, "the mother of the future," is being held at a maximum security hospital for the criminally insane where her entreaties for help to save the world from pending nuclear devastation are treated as massive paranoiac delusions. Sarah Connor sees the big picture, and her reading of it is: "You're already dead . . . dead!" Her "psychosis" is manifest in her relentless attempts to represent, for herself and for anyone else who'll listen to her, this historical totality, which Jameson argues has become increasingly unimaginable within the postmodern turn and which is thematically figured as conspiracy.

Sarah's only hope is to get to her son, whose life she knows is threatened and whom she must protect so that he may lead the human resistance in a future that may still be redescribed. The psychiatric correctional institution, which interferes with the essential relations of mother and child by refusing to let Sarah be visited by her son, is depicted as unequivocally evil. The private family is controlled by the state, placed under constant surveillance by health and correctional "services," mediated by the master narrative of psychoanalysis. In the maximum security facility where Sarah is incarcerated, prisoners/patients are abused physically and sexually by uniformed attendants who, by implication, seem far sicker than those put in their charge. A smug team of medical professionals led by the incompetent Dr. Silberman, a figure of modern medicine at its most exploitative and dishonest, strolls the corridors chuckling over the peculiar hallucinations of the patients.[11]

As horrifying as this depiction of the state-sanctioned policing of the family seems, *Terminator 2* presents an even more ghastly vision of the future, metonymically represented by Sarah's vision of a children's playground ablaze in post-nuclear-catastrophe. Her recurring nightmare depicts a scene of attentive mothers and happy children, all of whom are radiated and instantly turned to ash with the explosion of the nuclear firebomb. The repetition of this image, its emphatic situation behind the text's opening credits, indicates an overriding preoccupation with a jeopardized private sphere. "Children look like burnt paper," Sarah describes. "Then the blast wave hits them and they fly apart like leaves." Gradually, we suspect that Sarah's vision of looming catastrophe is not meant to frighten us in terms of global destruction and mass extermination, but in terms of the irreparable loss of the nuclear family, the core of which is the mother-child bond. Sarah's waking nightmare is thus a powerful register of the contrary emotions evoked within a culture that is becoming increasingly dependent on technology, yet at the same becoming increasingly reactionary and mistrustful with regard to any possible connections between these technological advances and changes in the nuclear family, the roles of women, and the breakdown in the traditional separation of market and domestic spheres.

For the last decade or so, critics of contemporary culture have become increasingly aware of the extent to which images of cybernetic organisms pervade popular culture and the negotiations of consumer capitalism in an "age obsessed with replication."[12] Like Sarah's dreadful premonition, the cyborg, in Mary Ann Doane's words, "holds in tension two different perspectives on technology."[13] Accordingly, Doane argues that cyborgs represent "the dismantling of binary oppositions, the collapse of boundaries, and the failure of a stable identity previously safeguarded by the oppositions animal/human, organism/machine, physical/nonphysical."[14] However, in *Terminator 2*, the structural dualisms that support the narrative—nature/culture, feminine/masculine, private/public— are dialectically sustained by *two* cybernetic organisms sent from the future, one programmed to destroy John Connor, the other programmed to protect him. Ultimately, they are on a collision course for a showdown that will determine the fate of children everywhere: nuclear war or nuclear family. Schwarzenegger returns as the model T-101, although in his new role he undergoes a transformation from cybernetic killer to cybernetic father, the ultimate parental system. Schwarzenegger's fatherly cybernetic system exists as a symbol of the bond between humans and machines; however, he also represents "an invidious network of invisible power relationships made possible through high technology."[15] The killer cyborg, a T-1000, is a more advanced prototype made of liquid alloy, which can form solid metal shapes, knives and various other sharp instruments and assume the form of any person or object it has physical contact with. In this way, the video experience resembles a sort of cybernetic *My Two Dads*, which, by splitting the father into binary opposites, makes the distinction between good and evil seem unambiguously clear. At the same time, however, the text enacts an interesting reversal: The model T-101, in need of clothing, weaponry, and transportation after his arrival in the present, confronts a vicious motorcycle gang in a honky-tonk bar and emerges dressed in black leather, wielding a sawed-off shotgun, and riding a Harley-Davidson. The T-1000 steals a gun and clothing from a Los Angeles police officer, the camera steadily framing the patrol car door, which reads, "To protect and serve."

In spite of such simplistic cross-codings, it is not difficult to see the gender-inflected contrast between these two cybernetic systems. While

Schwarzenegger's brawny, wide-jawed, hunk of a Terminator is supremely masculine, the T-1000 has delicately defined features and a petite, lithe frame. His ability to transform his body parts into razor-sharp knives and shears almost literally suggests a castrating bitch. On separate occasions, the T-1000 assumes the form of John's mothers, both surrogate and biological, in order to trap him. His fluid form intensifies this association with feminine embodiment. Indeed, there is something profoundly sinister in the T-1000's figuring of the female, a figure that insidiously links danger, death, technology, and woman.

The assumed incompatibility of femininity with technology is emphatically underscored within current popular culture genres, yet at the same time the theme of mechanical reproduction is identified by many social, cultural, and feminist theorists as one of the more salient features of postmodernism. The theme is made manifest in autoreferentiality, or autocritique, which often takes the form of a play with reproductive technology within the work of art. Thus, mechanical reproduction subsumes the place of "natural" reproduction so that, as Jean Baudrillard describes, the referent slips away and we are left with the simulacrum as our only graspable reality.[16] However, does this suggest that woman slips away, insofar as she represents the nonessential agent of biological reproduction? Feminist theorists are as divided on this question as they are on the social, political, and aesthetic implications of a yes or no answer. Although Luce Irigaray, according to Doane, indicts technology as "always the tool of a phallocentrically designed project aimed at conquering and controlling nature as maternal origin," feminists such as Donna Haraway see within cyborg mythology the potential for empowering social relations among feminism, science, and technology, especially since too much contemporary feminist critique assumes and relies on the very binary categories that oppress women.[17]

In her groundbreaking essay "A Manifesto for Cyborgs," Haraway argues that within the broad historical framework of capitalism's three dominant stages—commercial/early industrial, monopoly, and multinational—there is a dialectical correspondence to "specific forms of families," forms also related to Jameson's three major aesthetic periods of realism, modernism, and postmodernism. Thus, Haraway links the historical structures of capital, kinship, and aesthetics, admitting that while

lived problematically and unequally, ideal forms of these families might be schematized as (1) the patriarchal nuclear family, structured by the dichotomy between public and private and accompanied by the white bourgeois ideology of separate spheres and nineteenth-century Anglo-American bourgeois feminism; (2) the modern family mediated (or enforced) by the welfare state and institutions like the family wage . . . and (3) the "family" of the homework economy with its oxymoronic structure of women-headed households and its explosion of feminisms and the paradoxical intensification and erosion of gender itself.[18]

As the site of binary implosion, the cyborg becomes the perfect emblem for the family of Haraway's "homework economy," the reality of which Dan Quayle denied in his notorious rebuke of television's Murphy Brown and her decision to have a child out of wedlock. Indeed, both the patriarchal and modern nuclear families, as conceptual sites of economic and gender theorization, are hopelessly overcome with the kind of oppressive binary logic that the Bush-Quayle campaign promised to restore in its ideological emphasis on "family values." Cyborg imagery, as Haraway celebrates it, suggests a breakdown in such traditional family systems, in addition to the spatial relations of public and private, and enlightenment notions of centered subjectivity. As a "kind of disassembled and reassembled, post-modern collective and personal self,"[19] the image of the cyborg suggests possibilities for an envisioning of new family systems, systems in which contradiction is accepted and understood as part of the system.

By referring to the instability of John Connor's surrogate parents, both of whom are gruesomely murdered without any show of remorse on John's part, *Terminator 2* becomes a parable of gender instability and the endangered "natural" American family. Janelle and Todd live in a middle-class suburban neighborhood. Todd, a lax disciplinarian who would rather sit in front of the television than provide a strong father figure for a rebellious ten-year-old, is a passive and indifferent family man at best. Janelle, who seems eternally harried and frustrated, nags her son to clean up his room and then nags her husband to talk to the boy when he won't respond.

In contrast, Schwarzenegger's cyborg dad is the ultimate domestic appliance no mother should be without. He is a perfectly functional father who neither smokes nor drinks nor cheats on his wife. In an age when sex has taken on dangerous new meanings, the cyborg is, furthermore, a guarantee against virus and infection. And while divorce and the increased demands of the workplace have resulted in the phenomenon of absentee fathers who see their children only on weekends, *Terminator 2* puts Dad to work at a job that requires that he be constantly at his son's side to guide and defend him.

Thus, *Terminator 2* replaces the idealized American family image of the 1950s and 1960s, and the fragmented family of the 1970s and 1980s, with an image of the new American family as a hybrid of human and machine, a fugitive legion of go-for-broke revolutionaries, well-trained in military tactics and state-of-the-art weaponry. Lest we forget who they are and what they stand for, the station wagon that serves as their getaway vehicle is a reminder. Sarah, John, and the T-101 represent the nuclear family under siege, in flight from psychiatrists, social workers, and the law. In this sense, John's T-shirt, which bears the name of the controversial rap group Public Enemy, speaks for them all; nevertheless, they are heroic in their determination to save parents and children everywhere from certain destruction. And although a far cry from Donna Reed, Sarah Connor still keeps a well-stocked pantry; however, in this case it's an underground vault filled with firearms. When she strikes out on her own in search of the scientist destined to invent the treacherous computer system, she arrives at his home and opens fire, only to collapse in tears when she sees his wife and son, the boy begging for his father's life. Arriving just in time, John Connor consoles his nervous wreck of a mother as the T-101 sits down to reason with the scientist and ultimately wins his allegiance. The scene becomes a parable for the problems that occur when mother leaves home and goes out to work.

The family is in many ways a two-faced referent, and, if nothing else, *Terminator 2* underscores Patricia Mellencamp's observation that "the ideology of familialism is . . . a pivotal social contradiction, the source of our mental health *and* national economic growth (with economic trends tied to bodily images of health and sickness)." [20] The spectacular deployment of Linda Hamilton's ultra-toned, sinewy body can be read as an attempt to restore faith in America's economic supremacy. However, the body is also symbolic as a source of knowledge and humanistic enlightenment. While cyborg bodies challenge both unitary and binary notions of identity and systems of knowledge, Arthur and Marilouise Kroker have argued that "*Epistemologically*, the body is at the center of a grisly and false sense of subjectivity, as knowledge of the body is made a basic condition of possibility for the operation of postmodern power." [21] Sarah Connor's revelation of the future thus assumes an association with the heightened awareness of her body, which she has presumably attained during her detainment in the isolation wing of the psychiatric hospital. Indeed, it seems more than a little odd that Sarah should escape from this sordid experience looking as if she had just stepped out of a Holiday Fitness Spa.

However, throughout *Terminator 2* contradictory inscriptions of the female body enhance the text's denial of its appeal to traditional gender roles and at the same time construct an advertisement for the new ideal of female beauty. Laurie Schulze has usefully defined this ideal in her critique of the "fitness phenomena" as constitutive of a standard of beauty for women determined by "flex appeal." [22] When we first see Sarah Connor, the camera focuses on her glistening biceps as she completes a set of chin-ups. The first information we're given about her conveys unequivocally that she is cut, disciplined, worthy of our admiration, and probably willing to make sacrifices for the achievement of a goal. Of course, muscles are also sexy, and women who display them suggest not only that they are simultaneously aware of and in control of their sexuality, but that they are also in possession of the time and money to exercise it, in which case fitness—which Schwarzenegger solicits in the videotape's preliminary PSA—should be read as a class marker. In her formless trench coat, tank top, and designer eyewear, Sarah Connor looks more like an ad for Banana Republic than an escapee from Bedlam. In this way, her body signifies upward mobility, wealth, power. Hers is a body inscribed with the ideology of consumerism, a petri dish for the reconfiguration of woman as a site of postmodern excess, desire, and contradiction. Sarah Connor may be the new Virgin, but she is also the new Dynamo, an automaton whose muscles appear to have been assembled in accordance with Fordist principles.

As a construct of consumer culture, Sarah Connor exists to be looked at; however, within the patriarchal ideology of familialism that the narrative concurrently affirms and belies, she matters in a maudlin nineteenth-century way as, first and foremost, the "angel in the house," a moral superior, a symbol of the organic. Women in *Terminator 2* thus become the agents for humanistic reform, a liberalizing influence on power-greedy men who are moving the world unwittingly toward nuclear holocaust. Men in *Terminator 2* come to knowledge only through science; women know by virtue of intuition, emotion, and compassion. This is Sarah Connor's contribution to the "new" cybernetic mythology. She provides the natural feminine complement to the masculine drive for scientific and technological mastery. Certainly, men will discover positive uses for mechanical reproduction—as the T-101 suggests—but *not* at the expense of women's organic reproductive role, which it is the state's paradoxical responsibility to protect and privatize. And although the video's ostensible message is a warning against abuses of communication systems, it tends to represent *some* high-tech systems—like, for example, home video technology—as toys appropriate for boyish fun. The video game John Connor plays at the Galleria, a trendy L.A. shopping mall, bears an unmistakable resemblance to the January 1991 video images of the first wave of bombings of Iraq. Such self-reflexive contradictions, which caution against machinery while aligning video-simulated warfare, consumerism, and prepubescent masculine play, are swept aside in the breathtaking bombardment of *Terminator 2*'s cinematic special effects, which equate militaristic aggression with spectacular lights, Dolby stereo sound, and fallen buildings rather than fallen bodies.

Boys will be boys, indeed, and they will inevitably resist women's admonishments to place civilization before exploration, just as Huckleberry Finn resists the Widow Douglas. Like Huck, John Connor *is* the future of American naysaying: courageous, morally intelligent, loyal to the core, and male. *Terminator 2* is a blaring celebration of masculine privilege, a boy's fantasy come true. John Connor is not simply blessed with the perfect cybernetic father, *he* programmed that father *himself* in a future world so that consequently the cyborg adult has to obey the male child. John must control technology, and in return technology will save rather than destroy lives. When John informs the T-101 that he is no longer a Terminator because he "just can't go around killing people," the cyborg asks flatly, "Why?" Schwarzenegger's T-101 is the voice of machinery: dumb, amoral, unquestioning. And although the T-101 comes to learn something about human nature, in the end he must abandon the boy, admitting "I know now why you cry, but it is something that I can never do." Oedipal logic triumphs as the father hands over the reigns of power and privilege to the son who must now make his own way into the future.

The questions that need to be asked, however, are why does this future seem to hinge on the curtailment of women's reproductive freedoms, and how does *Terminator 2* disguise itself so as to appear profeminist to some viewers? One possibility, which I alluded to earlier, is suggested by recent disclosures of George Bush's grand jury deposition, which allegedly indicates that he possessed full knowledge of the Reagan administration's contra arms negotiations but was confident that the matter could be kept secret from the American public owing to the deal's quality of "deniability." In conclusion, I would propose a provisional appropriation of this term for the purposes of deconstructive analysis. If, as an instrument of Republican policy-making, "deniability" served as a response to a public hunger for illusion, to what degree might the deployment of this instrument have identifications with the same Hollywood entertainment industry that gave us, in another associative context, "Star Wars"? Granted, Schwarzenegger's high visibility as a Republican supporter is not in itself justification of the claim that he is in the business of producing party propaganda. Cyborgs may indeed suggest that power is never locatable and always diffuse; however, Schwarzenegger—one of Hollywood's most successful entrepreneurs and power brokers—knows something about our cultural longing to have our illusions unified and our oppositions pure. Cybernetic contradiction may be useful, not only as a means of foregrounding social ambiguities, but as a means of displacing authority so that its source becomes easier to defer, and therefore easier to conceal.

In many ways, *Terminator 2: Judgment Day* epitomized the conservative mythology of the Reagan-Bush years in the same way that "deniability" described its governing logic. While it's certainly possible to read the movie as a precautionary tale about the dangers of communication systems' proliferation, a reading of the home video release suggests that a dangerous proliferation of alternative family systems is actually the nightmare here. In the new cybernetic family romances of the future-present, "deniability" may be portrayed as a threatening feature of the technology in which we invest our trust and our futures; however, denial is a "human thing," to rephrase a popular identity slogan. Machines wouldn't understand. Insofar as cyborgs offer appropriate emblems of fragmented identities, they may also serve as fitting tropes for fragmented families, a kind of genealogical systems breakdown. Indeed, given the current therapeutic emphasis on treating denial within "dysfunctional" family systems, it wouldn't be surprising if—as technology replaces faith in psychiatry—we were to see the cyborg symbol appropriated by family theorists, as well as semioticians and film theorists, as suggestive of possibilities for a new treatment of familial exhaustion and recuperation.

Notes

Preface

1. See, for example, Gilles Deleuze and Felix Guattari, *Anti-Oedipus: Capitalism and Schizophrenia*, trans. Robert Hurley, Mark Seem, and Helen R. Lane (Minneapolis: University of Minnesota Press, 1983).

2. According to the *Standard Edition*, vol. 9, ed. James Strachey (London: The Hogarth Press and the Institute of Psychoanalysis, 1959, 1962, 1964), 1908 is the probable date of composition.

3. Marianne Hirsch, *The Mother/Daughter Plot: Narrative, Psychoanalysis, Feminism* (Bloomington: Indiana University Press, 1989), 9.

4. Richard Chase, *The American Novel and Its Tradition* (Baltimore: Johns Hopkins University Press, 1957); Janice A. Radway, *Reading the Romance: Women, Patriarchy, and Popular Literature* (Chapel Hill: University of North Carolina Press, 1984); Diane Elam, *Romancing the Postmodern* (London: Routledge, 1992).

5. Christine van Boheemen, *The Novel as Family Romance: Language, Gender, and Authority from Fielding to Joyce* (Ithaca, N.Y.: Cornell University Press, 1987).

6. Richard Rorty, *Contingency, Irony, and Solidarity* (Cambridge: Cambridge University Press, 1989), 17.

7. Rorty, *Contingency, Irony, and Solidarity*, 73.

8. Clifford Geertz, *The Interpretation of Cultures* (New York: Basic Books, 1973), 22.

9. George Yudice, "Marginality and the Ethics of Survival," in *Universal Abandon: The Politics of Postmodernism*, ed. Andrew Ross (Minneapolis: University of Minnesota Press, 1988), 217.

10. This line from Bernhard's one-woman show, *Without You I'm Nothing*, refers to the "dark" side of family life in the midwestern community where she grew up.

Chapter 1: Introduction

1. Gilles Deleuze and Felix Guattari, *Anti-Oedipus: Capitalism and Schizophrenia*, trans. Robert Hurley, Mark Seem, and Helen R. Lane (Minneapolis: University of Minnesota Press, 1983), 62.

2. Jane Gallop, *Around 1981: Academic Feminist Literary Theory* (New York: Routledge, 1992), 239.

3. *The Mary Tyler Moore Show*, episode 168, "The Last Show" (airdate March 9, 1977).

4. Alice McDermott, "Dark Domestic Visions? So What Else Is New?" *New York Times* Sunday, October 13, 1991, H32.

5. McDermott, "Dark Domestic Visions? So What Else Is New?" H32.

6. A commentator on National Public Radio proclaimed the 1994 Winter Olympic Games in Lillehammer, Norway, the "Ozzie and Harriet Olympics." His reference was to the news media's extensive focus on the families (or lack thereof in Oksana Baiul's case) of athletes. His remark further evoked the image of Dan Jansen's victory spin around the rink with his daughter, Jane, named for Jansen's sister who died shortly before his losing race at Calgary in 1988.

7. *Granta* 37 (1991), an issue titled "The Family," featured on its front cover the line, "They fuck you up," from the Philip Larkin poem, "This Be the Verse." The line appears alongside a miniscule reprint of a boyhood photograph of executed murderer Gary Gilmore, posed with mother, father, and two brothers. One of these brothers, Mikal Gilmore, is a contributor to the issue. His autobiographical essay, which records his memories of growing up with Gary, is described on the back jacket copy: "Growing up with a murderer in a family in love with the romance of violence."

8. Mark Poster, *Critical Theory and Poststructuralism: In Search of a Context* (Ithaca, N.Y.: Cornell University Press, 1989), 159.

9. The "Grand Hotel" metaphor is a borrowing from Jim Collins, *Uncommon Cultures: Popular Culture and Post-Modernism* (New York: Routledge, 1989), 7. See also, Hayden White, *Tropics of Discourse: Essays in Cultural Criticism* (Baltimore: Johns Hopkins University Press, 1978).

10. Jane Flax, *Thinking Fragments: Psychoanalysis, Feminism, and Postmodernism in the Contemporary West* (Berkeley: University of California Press, 1990).

11. Fredric Jameson, "Cognitive Mapping," in *Marxism and the Interpretation of Culture*, ed. Cary Nelson and Lawrence Grossberg (London: Macmillan, 1988), 351.

12. Fredric Jameson, *Postmodernism, or The Cultural Logic of Late Capitalism* (Durham, N.C.: Duke University Press, 1992).

13. Not to single out Marxists, I should note that feminist critics also express concern that postmodernism's emphasis on a politics of location precludes the possibility of an effective feminist coalition, thus reducing the notion of a unified feminist movement to a utopian fantasy based in principles of exclusion. Of course, other feminists applaud this commitment to the partial, the plural, and the local as a movement away from essentialist identity politics. See Linda J. Nicholson's critical anthology *Feminism/Postmodernism* (New York: Routledge, 1990) for essays that argue from both sides of the issue.

14. Linda Hutcheon, *The Politics of Postmodernism* (London: Routledge, 1989), 17–18.

15. Hutcheon, *Politics of Postmodernism*, 3.

16. George Yudice, "Marginality and the Ethics of Survival," in *Universal Abandon: The Politics of Postmodernism*, ed. Andrew Ross (Minneapolis: University of Minnesota Press, 1988), 216–17. Here, Yudice refers to Michel de Certeau's affirmative example of a subversive practice, *perruque*, or an employee's own work performed under the auspices of work for an employer.

17. For a collection that examines, from a variety of perspectives, the politics of popular romance see *The Progress of Romance: The Politics of Popular Fiction*, ed. Jean Radford (London: Routledge and Kegan Paul, 1986).

18. See Edward Shorter, *The Making of the Modern Family* (New York: Basic Books, 1977), particularly the final chapter, "Towards the Postmodern Family." See also, Donna Haraway, "A Manifesto For Cyborgs: Science, Technology, and Socialist Feminism in the 1980s," in *Coming to Terms: Feminism, Theory, Politics*, ed. Elizabeth Weed (New York: Routledge, 1989), 191; and Judith Stacey, *Brave New Families: Stories of Domestic Upheaval in Late Twentieth Century America* (New York: Basic Books, 1990).

19. Jürgen Habermas, *The Structural Transformation of the Public Sphere: An Inquiry into a Category of Bourgeois Society*, trans. Thomas Burger with Frederick Lawrence (Cambridge, Mass.: MIT Press, 1989).

20. See *Habermas and the Public Sphere*, ed. Craig Calhoun (Cambridge, Mass.: MIT Press, 1993) for a range of illuminating essays that encompass these debates. See also *The Phantom Public Sphere*, ed. Bruce Robbins (Minneapolis: University of Minnesota Press, 1993), especially essays by Nancy Fraser, Dana Polan, and George Yudice.

21. See in particular Selya Benhabib, Nancy Fraser, and Mary P. Ryan's essays in Calhoun, *Habermas and the Public Sphere*.

22. Perhaps, as has been suggested, the Marxism that shaped Habermas's early thought prevents him from taking fully into account the gender specificity of changes that affect participation in both the public and the private spheres. See Nancy Fraser, "What's Critical about Critical Theory? The Case of Habermas and Gender," in her *Unruly Practices: Power, Discourse and Gender in Contemporary Social Theory* (Minneapolis: University of Minnesota Press, 1989), 113–43.

23. Calhoun, *Habermas and the Public Sphere*, 10.

24. Michèle Barrett and Mary McIntosh, *The Anti-Social Family*, 2d ed. (London: Verso/NLB, 1982, 1991), 31.

25. Linda J. Nicholson, *Gender and History: The Limits of Social Theory in the Age of the Family* (New York: Columbia University Press, 1986), 11.

26. For example, in *Gendered Spaces* (Chapel Hill: University of North Carolina, 1992), Daphne Spain offers a critical account of architectural imperatives and their relation to gender norms. In the process she demonstrates that in spite of their disparate historicizations, efforts to reify public and private spheres have proved surprisingly fluid throughout modern history.

27. For an argument that challenges this assumption, see Nancy F. Cott, *The Bonds of Womanhood: "Woman's Sphere" in New England, 1780–1835* (New Haven, Conn.: Yale University Press, 1977).

28. For a useful collection of essays on this subject, consult Jean Bethke Elshtain, *Public Man, Private Woman: Woman in Social and Political Thought* (Princeton, N.J.: Princeton University Press, 1981).

29. Nicholson, *Gender and History*, 4.

30. David Cooper, *The Death of The Family* (New York: Pantheon Books, 1970), 20.

31. Teresa de Lauretis, *Technologies of Gender: Essays on Theory, Film, and Fiction* (Bloomington: Indiana University Press, 1987), 3.

32. Rochelle Gatlin, *American Women Since 1945* (Jackson: University of Mississippi Press, 1987), 126.

33. Toril Moi, *Sexual/Textual Politics: Feminist Literary Theory* (London: Methuen, 1985), 42–49.

34. Josephine Donovan, *Feminist Theory: Intellectual Traditions of American Feminism* (New York: Continuum, 1985).

35. Gallop, *Around 1981*, 22.

36. Jane Rule, *Lesbian Images* (Trumansburg, N.Y.: Crossing Press, 1975).

37. Shorter, *The Making of the Modern Family*, 242.

38. Shorter, *The Making of the Modern Family*, 242.

39. For an unsurpassed rendering of the history of this tradition, see Tony Tanner, *Adultery in the Novel: Contract and Transgression* (Baltimore: Johns Hopkins University Press, 1979).

40. See Eric J. Sundquist, *Faulkner: The House Divided* (Baltimore: Johns Hopkins University Press, 1983), 28–43.

41. Donald Barthelme, *The Dead Father* (New York: Penguin, 1975), 3.

42. See John Barth, "The Literature of Exhaustion" and its companion piece, "The Literature of Replenishment" in his *The Friday Book: Essays and Other Nonfiction* (New York: Putnam's, 1984).

43. Barthelme briefly satirizes the mother function in late capitalism when the Mother appears as the mysterious figure on horseback who has been following far behind the traveling party from the outset of the journey. When at last she catches up with the procession, the Dead Father does not remember her name. Everyone else, however, promptly begins listing grocery items for her to pick up. She vanishes and does not appear in the novel again.

44. Teresa L. Ebert, "Postmodern Politics, Patriarchy, and Donald Barthelme," *The Review of Contemporary Fiction* 11.2 (Summer 1991): 75–82.

45. William Dean Howells, Mary E. Wilkins Freeman, et al., *The Whole Family: A Novel by Twelve Authors*, introduction by Alfred Bendixen (New York: Ungar Co., 1986).

46. See Bendixen's introduction, xiv.

47. Mary E. Wilkins Freeman, "The Old-Maid Aunt," in *The Whole Family* (New York: Ungar Co., 1986), 30.

48. See Dale M. Bauer, "The Politics of Collaboration in *The Whole Family*," in *Old Maids to Radical Spinsters: Unmarried Women in the Twentieth-Century Novel*, ed. Laura L. Doan (Urbana: University of Illinois, 1991), 107–22.

49. Andreas Huyssen, "Mass Culture as Woman: Modernism's Other," in *After the Great Divide: Modernism, Mass Culture, Postmodernism* (Bloomington: Indiana University Press, 1986).

50. Susan Trausch, a columnist for the *Boston Globe*, criticizes Madonna's $60-million deal with Time-Warner, Inc., observing that there is something very wrong "in our world when so much money gets plunked down for so little" ("Proof We All Live in a Material World," *Virginian-Pilot/Ledger-Star*, May 3, 1992, C6). Thanks to Amy Parker for bringing this piece to my attention.

51. For a study of romance that considers the connection between gender and genre in the English literary tradition, see Laurie Langbauer, *Women and Romance: The Consolations of Gender in the English Novel* (Ithaca, N.Y.: Cornell University Press, 1990); for a study of American literature, see Dana A. Heller, *The Feminization of Quest-Romance: Radical Departures* (Austin: University of Texas Press, 1990).

52. In some cases, this "say" extends so far as actually reconstructing popular texts. See Henry Jenkins, *Textual Poachers: Television Fans and Participatory Culture* (New York: Routledge, 1992) for a fascinating account of this process.

53. Janice A. Radway, *Reading the Romance: Women, Patriarchy, and Popular Literature* (Chapel Hill: University of North Carolina Press, 1984).

54. Radway, *Reading the Romance*, 7.

55. Radway, *Reading the Romance*, 222.

56. Radway, *Reading the Romance*, 92.

57. Diane Elam, *Romancing the Postmodern* (London: Routledge, 1992), 12–13.

58. Feminist object-relations theorists such as Jessica Benjamin and Nancy Chodorow have attempted to overturn the Oedipal hierarchy in which maternity signifies a lack of origin, positing instead a feminist romance in which female subjectivity is derived through a primary identification with the female parent. See Benjamin, "A Desire of One's Own: Psychoanalytic Feminism and Intersubjective Space," in *Feminist Studies/Critical Studies*, ed. Teresa de Lauretis (Bloomington: Indiana University Press, 1986), 78–101; and Chodorow, *The Reproduction of Mothering: Psychoanalysis and the Sociology of Gender* (Berkeley: University of California Press, 1978).

59. In *The Anti-Social Family*, materialist feminists Barrett and McIntosh see the family as the foundation of all social inequality, a sexist, classist, racist, and (as the preface to the second edition adds) heterosexist institution that exclusively privileges white, affluent, heterosexual males.

60. In *Haven in a Heartless World: The Family Besieged* (New York: Basic Books, 1977), Christopher Lasch denounces the weak fathers and castrating mothers whose unchecked narcissism has resulted in the child's failure to internalize respect for paternal authority. In one sense, the text constitutes a nostalgic lament for the "classic" family romance, a farewell letter to the Freudian paradigm.

61. In *Brave New Families*, Judith Stacey, through extensive field research and interviews, finds that the modern nuclear family has become—in postfeminist America—a cultural dinosaur. Her work traces the diverse remaking of American family life and concludes that there is no longer any one model or type of family arrangement, but rather diversity, fluidity, and open-endedness typify a new "postmodern family" (16–17). Jacques Donzelot's deconstructive analysis of familialism in *The Policing of Families*, trans. Robert Hurley (New York: Pantheon Books, 1979), although markedly derivative of Foucault's microhistorical method, succeeds in significantly shifting the locus of origin from the family patriarch to the patriarchal state, which he argues has seduced the mother into a complex alliance with professional bureaucracies monitoring health, hygiene, and morals. With similar field techniques guiding her, anthropologist Kath Weston reconceives of kinship structure in terms of lesbian and gay politics, positing "families we choose" as a paradigm for a new revolutionary form of social relations. See *Families We Choose: Lesbians, Gays, Kinship* (New York: Columbia University Press, 1991).

62. Stephen Heath, *Questions of Cinema* (Bloomington: Indiana University Press, 1981), 125.

63. In *Gender and History*, Nicholson indirectly alludes to this new kind of transient subjectivity when she usefully distinguishes nineteenth-century feminism from twentieth-century "second-wave" feminism by citing "a concept which was central to the latter: the concept of a 'role.' This concept implies a solitary being who can *move* among different activities, taking on different norms appropriate to the activity in question" [emphasis mine] (55). Still, the most extensive work on performativity and gender is Judith Butler's. See *Gender Trouble: Feminism and the Subversion of Identity* (New York: Routledge, 1990) and *Bodies That Matter: On the Discursive Limits of "Sex"* (New York: Routledge, 1993).

Chapter 2: Housebreaking Freud

1. Roland Barthes, *The Pleasure of the Text*, trans. Richard Miller (New York: Farrar, Straus and Giroux, 1975), 47.
2. Sigmund Freud, "Family Romances," *Standard Edition*, vol. 9, ed. James Strachey (London: Hogarth Press and the Institute of Psychoanalysis, 1959, 1962, 1964), 238. According to the *Standard Edition*, from which all subsequent references are taken, this is the probable date of composition.
3. Stephen Heath, *Questions of Cinema* (Bloomington: Indiana University Press, 1981), 125.
4. Barthes, *The Pleasure of the Text*, 47.
5. Christine van Boheemen, *The Novel as Family Romance: Language, Gender, and Authority from Fielding to Joyce* (Ithaca, N.Y.: Cornell University Press, 1987), 23.
6. Kaja Silverman, *Male Subjectivity at the Margins* (New York: Routledge, 1992), 15–16.
7. Silverman, *Male Subjectivity at the Margins*, 17–19.
8. Peter Stallybrass and Allon White, *The Politics and Poetics of Transgression* (Ithaca, N.Y.: Cornell University Press, 1986), 153.
9. Michèle Barrett and Mary McIntosh, *The Anti-Social Family* 2d. ed. (London: Verso/NLB, 1982, 1991), 125–26.
10. Rosalind Coward, *Patriarchal Precedents: Sexuality and Social Relations* (London: Routledge and Kegan Paul, 1983), 212.
11. Diane Elam, *Romancing the Postmodern* (London: Routledge, 1992), 12.
12. I am referring here to Robin Wood's definition of the horror genre as "surplus repression," or desires that exceed the cultural standards of representation. Wood's theory is demonstrated in "An Introduction to the American Horror Film," in *Movies and Methods, II*, ed. Bill Nichols (Berkeley: University of California Press, 1985).
13. *Monster in a Box*, dir. Nick Broomfield, New Line Cinema, 1992.
14. The inclination of the film horror genre toward excess has been instructively examined by Robin Wood in "An Introduction to the American Horror Film," in *Movies and Methods II*. Wood's Marcusean approach to Freudian interpretation takes the monster of classical horror as a figure of surplus sexual repression—specifically bisexuality, homosexuality, and female desire.
15. See Carol Clover, "Her Body, Himself: Gender in the Slasher Film," in *Fantasy and the Cinema*, ed. James Donald (London: BFI, 1989).
16. See Julia Kristeva's analysis of the powerful cultural link between maternity and monstrosity in *Powers of Horror: An Essay on Abjection* (New York: Columbia University, 1982).
17. Donna Haraway, "The Promise of Monsters," in *Cultural Studies*, ed. Lawrence Grossberg, Cary Nelson, and Paula Treichler (New York: Routledge, 1992), 295–366.
18. Nancy Chodorow bases much of her work in feminist object-relations theory on the opinion that Freud's instinctual determinism partially blinded him to the sociocultural reproduction of mothering. Juliet Mitchell, whose work in some respects resembles Chodorow's, produced one of the most influential revisionist treatments of Freudian psychoanalysis, *Psychoanalysis and Feminism* (New York: Pantheon Books, 1974), a work that suggests that Freud's account of the family romance has its origin not in biology but in patriarchal relations of domination. In other words, there is nothing essential in Freud's view about the family or relations between men and women. More recently, Silverman corroborates

this point via Jean Laplanche's radicalizations of Freudian texts, citing numerous instances of Freud's separation of sexual drives and their ideological aims.

19. Jane Flax, *Thinking Fragments: Psychoanalysis, Feminism, and Postmodernism in the Contemporary West* (Berkeley: University of California Press, 1990), 16.

20. Sigmund Freud, "'A Child Is Being Beaten': A Contribution to the Study of the Origin of Sexual Perversion," in *Standard Edition*, vol. 17, ed. James Strachey (London: Hogarth Press and the Institute of Psychoanalysis, 1955, 1957, 1962, 1964), 179–204.

21. Coward, *Patriarchal Precedents*, 206.

22. Sigmund Freud, "The Dissolution of the Oedipus Complex," in *Standard Edition*, vol. 19, ed. James Strachey (London: Hogarth Press and the Institute of Psychoanalysis, 1961, 1962, 1964), 178.

23. Feminist critics have been particularly alert to the gender politics of Oedipal destabilizations in narrative. See Teresa de Lauretis's chapter on the Oedipus in *Alice Doesn't: Feminism, Semiotics, Cinema* (Bloomington: Indiana University Press, 1984), 70–83; Laura Mulvey points out the formal connections between popular narrative and the Oedipus myth in "The Oedipus Myth: Beyond the Riddles of the Sphinx," in her *Visual and Other Pleasures* (Bloomington: Indiana University Press, 1989).

24. Coward, *Patriarchal Precedents*, 113.

25. David Cooper, *The Death of the Family* (New York: Random House, 1970), 21; see also, R. D. Laing, *The Politics of the Family* (New York: Vintage Books, 1969, 1977).

26. Flax, *Thinking Fragments*, 99.

27. See, for example, Shoshana Felman, "Beyond Oedipus: The Specimen Story of Psychoanalysis," *MLN Comparative Literature* 98.5 (Baltimore: Johns Hopkins University Press, 1983), 1021–53.

28. See Kaja Silverman, *Male Subjectivity at the Margins* (New York: Routledge, 1992) and Tania Modleski, *Feminism Without Women: Culture and Criticism in a "Postfeminist" Age* (New York: Routledge, 1991).

29. Claude Lévi-Strauss, *The Elementary Structures of Kinship*, rev. ed, trans. James Harle Bell and John Richard von Sturmer, ed. Rodney Needham (Boston: Beacon Press, 1969).

30. In *The Elementary Structures of Kinship*, a structuralist account of kinship relations in primitive societies, Lévi-Strauss conceives of family not as an essential origin, but as a piece in a much larger and more powerful system of mutual exchange based on signification, difference, and reciprocity *between* families. Working from Ferdinand de Saussure's model for structural linguistics, Lévi-Strauss understands and describes kinship and language as composed of similar elements that guarantee the integration of inside and outside, self and other. He conceives of the incest taboo as the most basic and essential assurance of these exchanges and communications. While Lévi-Strauss's analysis of private/public traffic seemed, in some ways, to address the feminist preoccupation with locating a transcultural, transhistorical source of women's oppression, his work did not sufficiently account for the gender politics of this exchange.

31. Gayle Rubin, "The Traffic in Women: Notes on the 'Political Economy' of Sex," in *Toward an Anthropology of Women*, ed. Rayna R. Reiter (New York: Monthly Review Press, 1975), 157–210.

32. Gilles Deleuze and Felix Guattari, *Anti-Oedipus: Capitalism and Schizophrenia*, trans. Robert Hurley, Mark Seem, and Helen R. Lane (Minneapolis: University of Minnesota Press, 1983). Given the considerable demands of this text,

first-time readers might want to consult Brian Massumi's *A User's Guide to Capitalism and Schizophrenia: Deviations From Deleuze and Guattari* (Cambridge and London: MIT Press, 1992).

33. George Yudice, "Marginality and the Ethics of Survival," in *Universal Abandon: The Politics of Postmodernism*, ed. Andrew Ross (Minneapolis: University of Minnesota Press, 1988), 217.

Chapter 3: The Third Sphere

1. From George Nelson and Henry Wright, *Tomorrow's House: A Complete Guide for the Home-Builder* (New York: Simon and Schuster, 1946). Quoted in Lynn Spigel, *Make Room for TV: Television and the Family Ideal in Postwar America* (Chicago: University of Chicago Press, 1992), 39.

2. Betty Friedan, *The Feminine Mystique* (New York: W. W. Norton, 1963), 32.

3. The Oedipal mother has traditionally been constructed as a contestatory field, embodying *both* the forces of stability and destabilization within the family romance. She is anchor and aporia, an all-powerful agent in the child's early moral development and a figure of powerlessness and resentment in the child's later Oedipal entanglements. An interesting essay on the mother dilemma is Coppelia Kahn's "Mother," in *Changing Subjects: The Making of Feminist Literary Criticism*, ed. Gayle Greene and Coppelia Kahn (London: Routledge, 1993), 157–67. See also Marianne Hirsch, *The Mother/Daughter Plot: Narrative, Psychoanalysis, Feminism* (Bloomington: Indiana University Press, 1989); Julia Kristeva, *The Powers of Horror: An Essay on Abjection* (New York: Columbia University Press, 1982); Marcia Ian, *Remembering the Phallic Mother: Psychoanalysis, Modernism, and the Fetish* (Ithaca, N.Y.: Cornell University Press, 1993). For a material analysis of the contradictory role of the homemaker, see Juliet Mitchell, *Women: The Longest Revolution* (London: Virago, 1984). As has been exhaustively documented, the rise of the feminist movement in the United States met with an image of motherhood discursively policed (although not without conflict) by the nineteenth-century "cult of domesticity," held aloft as an idealized point of balance, or ideological resolution. See Nancy F. Cott, *The Bonds of Womanhood: "Woman's Sphere" in New England, 1780–1835* (New Haven, Conn.: Yale University Press, 1977). However, by the mid-twentieth century, with the advent of what Carl N. Degler has called "The Second Transformation" of women's labor patterns, "motherhood" has come to signify the culmination of more than a century of conflict and debate. See *At Odds: Women and the Family in America from the Revolution to the Present* (New York: Oxford University Press, 1980), 418–35.

4. Spigel, *Make Room for TV*, 40.

5. See, for example, Marynia Farnham and Ferdinand Lundberg's *The Modern Woman: The Lost Sex* (New York: Harper and Bros., 1947); see also, on rising birth rates, Rochelle Gatlin, *American Women Since 1945* (Jackson: University of Mississippi, 1987), 51, 55, 61.

6. Spigel, *Make Room For TV*, 1. Spigel covers the industrial and domestic development of television during the years 1948 to 1955, when television assumed a dominant role in American cultural life.

7. Minow's speech, delivered on May 9, 1961, set many of the critical terms for the historicization of television's economic and aesthetic practices during this period. These terms have, over the course of the last fifteen years, been

challenged by an increasing emphasis on television viewers' roles as productive agents in the construction and promotion of "quality television." See Sue Brower, "Fans as Tastemakers: Viewers for Quality Television," in *The Adoring Audience: Fan Culture and Popular Media*, ed. Lisa A. Lewis (New York: Routledge, 1992); Henry Jenkins, *Textual Poachers: Television Fans and Participatory Culture* (New York: Routledge, 1992).

8. In light of this mediating function, Linda J. Nicholson's argument that the twentieth century has witnessed the displacement of the family sphere as the locus of private concerns and its replacement with the sphere of the individual becomes particularly useful insofar as it establishes television as a culminating mark of this development while partially accounting for the ongoing controversy over television's impact on the family. See *Gender and History: The Limits of Social Theory in the Age of the Family* (New York: Columbia University Press, 1986).

9. Ella Taylor, *Prime-Time Families: Television Culture in Postwar America* (Berkeley: University of California Press, 1989), 4.

10. The advent of queer theory has helped bring this multiaccentual tradition to light. See Alexander Doty's *Making Things Perfectly Queer: Interpreting Mass Culture* (Minneapolis: University of Minnesota Press, 1993) for an expert reading of the queer contours of popular television sitcoms.

11. See Margaret Marsh, *Suburban Lives* (New Brunswick, N.J.: Rutgers University Press, 1990).

12. In Thomas Pynchon's *Vineland* (Boston: Little, Brown, 1990), a novel that in many ways explores the cultural parameters of television narrative, a character named Justin recalls the smartest boy he met in kindergarten who explained how to mitigate the effects of his parents by pretending they are just characters in a television sitcom. " 'Pretend there's a frame around 'em like the Tube, pretend they're a show you're watching. You can go into it if you want, or you can just watch, and *not* go into it' " (351).

13. Elayne Rapping, *The Movie of the Week: Private Stories/Public Events* (Minneapolis: University of Minnesota, 1992), 26.

14. See Stuart Ewen's *Captains of Consciousness: Advertising and the Social Roots of the Consumer Culture* (New York: McGraw Hill, 1976). Although more recent critics, such as Spigel, take issue with Ewan's overly generalized construction of mass desire, his study remains a fascinating account of the kinds of relationships advertisers forge with imagined audiences.

15. Lynn Spigel, *Make Room For TV*, 37.

16. Spigel, "Television in the Family Circle," 77.

17. George Lipsitz examines the popularity of ethnic programs in early network television in "The Meaning of Memory: Family, Class, and Ethnicity in Early Network Television Programs," in *Private Screenings: Television and the Female Consumer*, ed. Lynn Spigel and Denise Mann (Minneapolis: University of Minnesota Press, 1992), 71–110.

18. See Aniko Bodroghkozy, " 'Is This What You Mean by Color TV?': Race, Gender, and Contested Meanings in NBC's *Julia*," in *Private Screenings: Television and the Female Consumer*, ed. Lynn Spigel and Denise Mann (Minneapolis: University of Minnesota Press, 1992), 143–68.

19. Andrea L. Press, *Women Watching Television: Gender, Class, and Generation in the American Television Experience* (Philadelphia: University of Pennsylvania Press, 1991), 33.

20. Press, *Women Watching Television*, 28.

21. For an excellent study of American suburbanization, see Kenneth T. Jackson, *Crabgrass Frontier: The Suburbanization of the United States* (New York: Oxford University Press, 1985).

22. William H. Whyte, *The Organization Man* (Garden City, N.Y.: Doubleday, 1956, 1957) 314–15.

23. Rochelle Gatlin, *American Women Since 1945* (Jackson: University of Mississippi Press, 1987), 54.

24. Gatlin, *American Women*, 53; see also, Michèle Barrett and Mary McIntosh, *The Anti-Social Family* 2d. ed. (London: Verso/NLB, 1982, 1991); and Elaine Tyler May, *Homeward Bound: American Families in the Cold War Era* (New York: Basic Books, 1988).

25. R. D. Laing, *The Politics of the Family* (New York: Vintage Books, 1969, 1977), 29.

26. Sigmund Freud, "Family Romances," in *Standard Edition*, vol. 9, ed. James Strachey (London: Hogarth Press, 1959), 237.

27. This episode, for which I have no title, was aired as part of Nickelodeon's "Donna Reed Marathon" (March 25, 1994), subsequent to which the program was pulled from the Nick at Nite lineup.

28. David Marc, *Demographic Vistas: Television in American Culture* (Philadelphia: University of Pennsylvania Press, 1984), 13.

29. Marc, *Demographic Vistas*, 15.

30. Ellen Seiter, "Semiotics and Television," in *Channels of Discourse: Television and Contemporary Criticism*, ed. Robert C. Allen (Chapel Hill: University of North Carolina Press, 1987), 37.

31. Spigel examines the theatrical nature of television's domestic spaces in the chapter, "The People in the Theater Next Door," in *Make Room for TV*, 136–180.

32. Press, *Women Watching Television*, 29.

33. Taylor, *Prime-Time Families*, 26.

34. Jacques Donzelot, *The Policing of Families*, trans. Robert Hurley (New York: Pantheon, 1979).

35. For example, Nina Liebman, in "Leave Mother Out: The Fifties Family in American Film and Television," *Wide Angle: A Film Quarterly* 10:4 (1988): 24–41, makes the wonderful observation that June Cleaver, in a scene from *Leave It to Beaver*, is shown seated at the kitchen table wiping dust off ketchup bottles as she remarks to Beaver that women today can have exciting professional careers and are just as ambitious as their male counterparts (32–33).

36. In "Sit-coms and Suburbs: Positioning the 1950s Homemaker," Mary Beth Haralovich considers the connection between consumer product design and television's idealized image of the female homemaker (in *Private Screenings: Television and the Female Consumer*, ed. Lynn Spigel and Denise Mann [Minneapolis: University of Minnesota Press, 1992], 111–42).

37. Taylor, *Prime-Time Families*, 4.

38. Laing, *The Politics of the Family*, 87.

39. However, his remarks do recall Joan Riviere's "Womanliness as Masquerade" (1929), in which she posits femininity as a performative defense strategy used by working women who feel that they will be perceived as less womanly because of their role in the public sphere. Certainly, it seems possible that Riviere's study might be usefully applied to women's "performance" in the domestic sphere as well, particularly at historical instances when a blurring of private and public is intensified. In *Formations of Fantasy*, ed., Victor Burgin, James Donald, and Cora Kaplan (London: Methuen, 1986), 35–44.

40. See Lynn Spigel, "From Domestic Space to Outer Space: The 1960s Fantastic Family Sitcom," in *Close Encounters: Film, Feminism, and Science Fiction*, ed. Constance Penley, Elisabeth Lyon, Lynn Spigel, and Janet Bergstrom (Minneapolis: University of Minnesota Press, 1991), 205–35.

41. Taylor, *Prime-Time Families*, 39.

42. See "Introduction: Axiomatic," in Eve Kosofsky Sedgwick, *Epistemology of the Closet* (Berkeley: University of California Press, 1990).

43. Commentators have recently remarked on the construction of distinct lesbian and gay positions available within popular sitcoms such as *Bewitched*. See Doty, *Making Things Perfectly Queer*, 47.

44. Taylor, *Prime-Time Families*, 14.

45. For a valuable collection of essays that examine the various nuances of social meaning produced by *The Mary Tyler Moore Show* and other productions of MTM Enterprises, Inc., see *MTM: "Quality Television,"* ed. Jane Feuer, Paul Kerr, and Tise Vahimagi (London: BFI, 1984); see also, Doty, *Making Things Perfectly Queer*, 47–51, for lesbian readings of female character relationships.

46. Craig Gilbert reflects on these questions and describes the conception, production, and reception of *An American Family*, in "Reflections on *An American Family, I*" and "Reflections on *An American Family, II*" in *New Challenges for Documentary*, ed. Alan Rosenthal (Berkeley: University of California Press, 1988), 191–209, 288–307.

47. Simon Frith, "Hearing Secret Melodies," in *High Theory/Low Culture: Analysing Popular Television and Film*, ed. Colin MacCabe (New York: St. Martin's Press, 1986), 69.

Chapter 4: The Culture of "Momism"

1. All quotations are taken from Evan S. Connell, *Mrs. Bridge* (New York: Pocket Books, 1959, 1977).

2. See E. Ann Kaplan, *Motherhood and Representation: The Mother in Popular Culture and Melodrama* (London: Routledge, 1992), for a wide-reaching discussion of historical and cultural shifts in the representation of motherhood from the nineteenth century to the present period.

3. As Marianne Hirsch points out, the traditional focus of maternal ideology is not the mother, but rather the child, "that delicate and vulnerable organic being who required complete devotion and attention." Eighteenth- and nineteenth-century discourse on education and child development ultimately constructed the maternal role as "either the object of idealization and nostalgia or that which had to be rejected and surpassed in favor of allegiance to a morally and intellectually superior male world" (14). See *The Mother/Daughter Plot: Narrative, Psychoanalysis, Feminism* (Bloomington: Indiana University Press, 1989). For a materialist analysis of contradictory representations of women, see Juliet Mitchell, *Women: The Longest Revolution* (London: Virago, 1984); for social histories of motherhood, see Philip Aries, *Centuries of Childhood: A Social History of Family Life*, trans. Robert Baldick (New York: Vintage Books, 1962); and Ann Dally, *Inventing Motherhood: The Consequences of an Ideal* (New York: Schocken, 1982).

4. See all essays, but particularly, Linda Gordon, "Why Nineteenth-Century Feminists Did Not Support 'Birth Control' and Twentieth-Century Feminists Do: Feminism, Reproduction, and the Family," in *Rethinking the Family: Some Feminist Questions*, 2d ed., ed. Barrie Thorne and Marilyn Yalom (Boston: Northeastern

University Press, 1992), 140–54. For studies of maternity in a psychoanalytic frame, see Shirley Nelson Garner, Claire Kahane, and Madelon Sprengnether, eds., *The (M)other Tongue: Essays in Feminist Psychoanalytic Interpretation* (Ithaca, N.Y.: Cornell University Press, 1985); and Terry Brown, "Feminism and Psychoanalysis, a Family Affair?" in *Discontented Discourses: Feminism/Textual Intervention/Psychoanalysis*, ed. Marleen S. Barr and Richard Feldstein (Urbana: University of Illinois Press, 1989).

5. One might distinguish modern from early postmodern debates over maternity by considering that while modernism tended to regard representation as an expression of autonomous cultural agents, postmodernism's increasing emphasis on all agency as determined by representation suggests that the structural hegemony of popular discourses on maternity, the family, and the private sphere had itself become an arena of intensified public/political conflict. Consequently, theories of maternity, like theories of the family, have become predominantly marked by discourse sensitivity. See the essays in *Destabilizing Theory: Contemporary Feminist Debates*, ed. Michèle Barrett and Anne Phillips (Stanford, Calif.: Stanford University Press, 1992); Alice A. Jardine, *Gynesis: Configurations of Woman and Modernity* (Ithaca, N.Y.: Cornell University Press, 1985); Julia Kristeva, *Powers of Horror: An Essay on Abjection*, trans. Leon Roudiez (New York: Columbia University Press, 1982); and Patricia Yaeger, " 'The Language of Blood': Toward a Maternal Sublime," *Genre* 25 (Spring 1992): 5–24.

6. An understanding of American culture's mixed idealization and contempt toward Oedipal motherhood is usefully grounded in the Freudian image of the phallic mother. The trope of the phallic mother, a mature woman with breasts and a penis, has a long and complex history in myth, religion, literature, and psychoanalysis. Although—its full historicization goes beyond the scope of this book, I have relied on—and recommend—Marcia Ian's compelling analysis of the phallic mother's relevance to modern literary and psychoanalytic theories, which similarly deploy her as a figure of the "law of noncontradiction" (9), a model of the unified, autonomous self, and a representation of "certain eroticized ambivalences . . . that Freudian psychoanalysis was unable to 'own' " (59). In this sense, the phallic mother is not seen as a destabilizing force within the family, as some formulations would have her, but as a patriarchal idealization of principles of ultimate agency and autonomy, an idealization that structurally defers conflict and power differentials in favor of "a compulsion to resolve ambivalence by dissolving it into specious equivalence" (6). See *Remembering the Phallic Mother: Psychoanalysis, Modernism, and the Fetish* (Ithaca, N.Y.: Cornell University Press, 1993).

7. Rochelle Gatlin, *American Women Since 1945* (Jackson: University of Mississippi Press, 1987), 9.

8. Marynia Farnham and Ferdinand Lundberg, *The Modern Woman: The Lost Sex* (New York: Harper and Bros., 1947).

9. Philip Wylie, *Generation of Vipers* (New York: Farrar and Rinehart, 1942), 188–89.

10. Arguably, this ideal was exhausted even at its inception. For studies that problematize and historicize nineteenth-century gender roles, see Nancy F. Cott, *The Bonds of Womanhood: 'Woman's Sphere' in New England, 1780–1835* (New Haven, Conn.: Yale University Press, 1977); and Carroll Smith-Rosenberg, *Disorderly Conduct: Visions of Gender in Victorian American* (New York: Alfred A. Knopf, 1985).

11. The exhaustive list of "ills" for which mothers are apparently to blame according to postwar social critics such as Wylie would seem to qualify Freud,

by comparison, as a candidate for feminist sainthood. The fact is, however, that even feminists who encourage alternatives to the patriarchal nuclear family are not exempt from mom-bashing. For example, Juliet Mitchell, in *Woman's Estate* (New York: Pantheon, 1971), might be accused of blaming the victim when she attempts to answer the question "What does the family do to women?": "It produces a tendency to small-mindedness, petty jealousy, irrational emotionality and random violence, dependency, competitive selfishness and possessiveness, passivity, a lack of vision and conservatism. These qualities are *not* the simple produce of male chauvinism. . . . *They are the result of the woman's objective conditions within the family*" (italics Mitchell's) (162). Although Mitchell locates the problem within the oppressive family system—itself a result of sexist society— her catalog of faults attributable to women portrays them as monstrous perpetuators of a sickness they bring on themselves when they become part of a traditional family. As Nancy Chodorow and Susan Contratto have shown, mombashing, in this sense, has become a feature of a feminist psychoanalytic tradition as well. In "The Fantasy of the Perfect Mother" (in Thorne and Yalom, *Rethinking the Family*), the authors analyze the complex psychological themes that emerge from recent feminist work on mothering. What they find is that dramatic extremes—total blame or total idealization—seem always to describe the positions of feminist writings on mothering. This division stems from the nineteenth century, when we first saw "the growth of a sexual division of spheres that materially grounded mother-child isolation and bequeathed us a picture of the ideal mother who would guarantee both morally perfect children and a morally desirable world." Central to our understanding of motherhood is the inherited assumption that "what happens in the earliest mother-infant relationship determines the whole of history, society, and culture" (202). Consequently, our cultural ideology of motherhood maps onto images of mothers these extremes of blame and idealization. And there appears to be no synthesis of these emotional polarities: rage and joy, tenderness and fury. Even within very recent feminist discourse mothers are either denied their sexual drives, or the sexual aspects of motherhood are emphasized to the exclusion of all other aspects. As grown men and women, we either want to escape or fix our mothers. But why, many feminists ask, can't we just accept them as human beings? Ambivalence is, as Jane Lazarre argues, the only "eternal and natural" feature of motherhood (in Chodorow and Contratto, 199).

12. Linda J. Nicholson, *Gender and History: The Limits of Social Theory in the Age of the Family* (New York: Columbia University Press, 1986), 63; see also, Margaret Marsh, *Suburban Lives* (New Brunswick, N.J.: Rutgers University Press, 1990).

13. Frederick R. Karl, *American Fictions, 1940–1980* (New York: Harper and Row, 1983), 385.

14. Karl, *American Fictions*, 400.

15. Eve Kosofsky Sedgwick, *Epistemology of the Closet* (Berkeley: University of California Press, 1990), 4.

16. D. A. Miller, "Secret Subjects, Open Secrets," in his *The Novel and the Police*, quoted in Sedgwick, *Epistemology of the Closet*, 67.

17. Here, Joan Riviere's influential study, "Womanliness as Masquerade," is applicable to the unacknowledged performativity of the mother's role. The article is reprinted in *Formations of Fantasy*, ed. Victor Burgin, James Donald, and Cora Kaplan (New York: Methuen, 1986).

18. Sedgwick, *Epistemology of the Closet*, 3.

19. Sherwood Anderson, "A Story-Teller's Story," quoted in Alfred Kazin, *On*

Native Grounds: An Interpretation of Modern American Prose Literature (New York: Harcourt Brace Jovanovich, 1942, 1970), 213.

20. Kazin, *On Native Grounds,* 214.

21. Mitchell, *Woman's Estate,* 161.

22. My thanks to John Leo for this insight.

23. Carol A. Kolmerten and Stephen M. Ross, "The Empty Locus of Desire: Woman as Familial Center in Modern American Fiction," *Denver Quarterly* 17.4 (1983): 110. As they show, "Mother" functions as a complex sign within the family system, a central sign around which other meanings gather. Thus, while the father remains the moral center of the American family, "conventional novels isolate a symbolic female at the family's heart . . . some symbol of feminine redemptive potential" around which male characters "cluster" (109). Kolmerten and Ross continue to identify within the narrative structure of the contemporary family novel a formal parallel to this clustering phenomenon:

> At the level of the fiction's discourse, works about the family tend to reflect the structure and temporal ordering of a family. Every family has a present structure as a conjugal unit, a household, a collection of siblings, cousins, in-laws, and other relations. Every family also possesses a history extending back in time through progenitors and a potential future extending forward to descendants. . . . The narrative patterns in family novels—the points of view, the voices, the temporal ordering of events—almost without exception reflect the complexity inherent in the family structure. (110)

24. Annette Kuhn, "Structures of Patriarchy and Capital in the Family," in *Feminism and Materialism,* ed. Annette Kuhn and AnnMarie Wople (London: Routledge and Kegan Paul, 1978), 60.

25. See Linda Williams, "Something Else Besides a Mother: *Stella Dallas* and the Maternal Melodrama," *Cinema Journal,* 24, no.1 (Fall 1984): 2–27.

26. In *The Anti-Social Family,* 2d ed. (London: Verso/NLB, 1982, 1991), Michèle Barrett and Mary McIntosh look ahead to this mission, and they call for a more pluralistic affirmation of the diverse possibilities for family arrangements; the meanings we ascribe to 'the family' should be conditioned by its recognized status as "a constructed unity rather than a term on whose real referent or meaning we can agree" (95).

Chapter 5: Rules of the Game

1. Ludwig Wittgenstein, *Philosophical Investigations,* 3d ed., trans. G. E. M. Anscombe (New York: Macmillan, 1958), cf. 67.

2. Mary F. Robertson, "Anne Tyler: Medusa Points and Contact Points," in *Contemporary American Women Writers,* ed. Catherine Rainwater and William J. Scheick (Lexington: University of Kentucky Press, 1985), 119–41.

3. For a discussion of the interdynamics of feminism and deconstruction see Diane Elam, *Feminism and Deconstruction* (London: Routledge, 1994).

4. Robertson, "Anne Tyler," 139; 120.

5. Judith Butler, *Gender Trouble: Feminism and the Subversion of Identity* (New York: Routledge, 1990). Butler argues convincingly that categorical inversions fail to offer "a different set of terms" for feminist inquiry, but instead iden-

tify "the enemy as singular in form" thus constituting "a reverse-discourse that uncritically mimics the strategy of the oppressor" (13).

6. John Updike, "Family Ways," in *Hugging the Shore: Essays and Criticism* (New York: Knopf, 1983), 273–78; Mary Ellis Gibson, "Family as Fate: The Novels of Anne Tyler," *Southern Literary Journal* 16 (Fall 1983): 47–58.

7. Gibson, "Family as Fate," 48.

8. Frank Shelton, "The Necessary Balance: Distance and Sympathy in the Novels of Anne Tyler," *Southern Review* 20 (1984): 851–60.

9. Shelton, "The Necessary Balance," 851–52.

10. This and all subsequent references, unless otherwise specified, are drawn from Jean-François Lyotard and Jean-Loup Thebaud, *Just Gaming*, trans. Wlad Godzich (Minneapolis: University of Minnesota Press, 1985).

11. This and all subsequent quotations are taken from Tyler's *Searching for Caleb* (New York: Berkeley Books, 1975), 176.

12. See Jim Collins, *Uncommon Cultures: Popular Culture and Post-Modernism* (New York: Routledge, 1989), 43–49, for a well-historicized account of the distinctions that have defined intertextuality.

13. Harold Bloom, *The Anxiety of Influence* (New York: Oxford University Press, 1973).

14. Pierre Macherey, *A Theory of Literary Production* (London: Routledge, 1978).

15. Bill Readings, *Introducing Lyotard: Art and Politics*, (London: Routledge, 1991), 118.

16. Anne G. Jones, "Home at Last, and Homesick Again: The Ten Novels of Anne Tyler," *The Hollins Critic* 23.2 (April 1986): 6.

17. Readings, *Introducing Lyotard*, 116.

18. Jean-François Lyotard, *The Differend: Phrases in Dispute*, quoted in Readings, *Introducing Lyotard*, 116.

19. Which is not to undermine the cultural relevance of Bakhtin's explication of carnival as a popular means of displacing the boundaries that separate art and daily life. See Mikhail Bakhtin, *Rabelais and His World*, trans. Helene Iswolsky (Bloomington: Indiana University Press, 1984); for a feminist reading of Bakhtin's carnival that focuses on the image of the female grotesque, see Mary Russo, "Female Grotesques: Carnival and Theory," in *Feminist Studies/Critical Studies*, ed. Teresa de Lauretis (Bloomington: Indiana University Press, 1986).

20. Lyotard and Thebaud, *Just Gaming*, 100.

21. Jones, "Home at Last," 7.

22. Here, I am echoing Peter Stallybrass and Allon White in *The Politics and Poetics of Transgression* (Ithaca, N.Y.: Cornell University Press, 1986), 168.

23. In suggesting that Sulie ultimately becomes the central differend of the novel, I once again refer to Stallybrass and White, who show how the centrality of the maid as a figure of sexual knowledge and pleasure becomes written out of the Freudian family romance, in spite of the fact that Freud himself appeared at times more fixated on his own memories of his nurse than on his mother in the weeks before he discovered the Oedipus complex. "It is striking how Freud's patients . . . return as obsessively to their nurses as to their parents" (152). However, Freud's secondary revisions of his own dreams and fantasies about his nurse ultimately lead him back to the parents and to the family romance. The Oedipal "drama" is thus "played out in an imagined household where servants bear a symbolic part mainly as displacements of the biological parents" (153). Freud writes the domestic servant out of the scene so that "family romance could

be freed from the exogamous factors symbolically inscribed in the nurse" (163). His repetition of the family triad, the order of the law, or the symbolic order was his object of analysis. Thus, "he constructed a theoretical model which would indeed hold 'the members of a family . . . together permanently'" (163). As a result, Freud was able to naturalize the symbolic order, which was scientifically "placed in the immutable world of nature" (163).

Chapter 6: Father Trouble

1. Thomas W. Laqueur, "The Facts of Fatherhood," reprinted in *Rethinking the Family: Some Feminist Questions*, ed. Barrie Thorne and Marilyn Yalom (Boston: Northeastern University Press, 1992), 155.

2. For work that addresses, in diverse contexts, the advantages and disadvantages of the expansion of feminist methods, see Michèle Barrett and Anne Phillips, eds., *Destabilizing Theory: Contemporary Feminist Debates* (Stanford, Calif.: Stanford University Press, 1992); Marianne Hirsch and Evelyn Fox Keller, eds., *Conflicts in Feminism* (New York: Routledge, 1990); Gayle Greene and Coppelia Kahn, eds., *Changing Subjects: The Making of Feminist Literary Criticism* (London: Routledge, 1993); Linda J. Nicholson, ed., *Feminism/Postmodernism* (New York: Routledge, 1990).

3. An exception to this tendency is the collection of essays *Daughters and Fathers*, ed. Lynda E. Boose and Betty S. Flowers (Baltimore: Johns Hopkins University Press, 1989).

4. For example, Tania Modleski, in *Feminism without Women: Culture and Criticism in a "Postfeminist" Age* (New York: Routledge, 1991), argues that a "major conservative shift" has become discernible in the assumptions of a "postfeminist" culture. Male feminism, anti-essentialist extremism, and—in one particularly striking example—a contradictory reliance on familial metaphor in a *New York Times Magazine* article entitled "Literary Feminism Comes of Age" constitute strategies whereby women are restored to their proper prefeminist status as family servants, philosophical nonentities, and voiceless abstractions in the critical debates over representations of gender (3). In contrast, some would see Modleski's position as a distortion and would focus on the *expansion*, rather than the curtailment, of feminist methodologies. See Alice Jardine and Paul Smith, eds., *Men in Feminism* (New York: Methuen, 1987); Joseph A. Boone and Michael Cadden, eds., *Engendering Men* (New York: Routledge, 1990); see also John R. Leo's special issue of *American Transcendental Quarterly*, Series 5:3 (September 1991), which features work on nineteenth-century constructions of masculinity.

5. Jane Gallop, *Around 1981: Academic Feminist Literary Theory* (New York, Routledge, 1992), 242.

6. Gallop, *Around 1981*, 239.

7. Gallop, *Around 1981*, 243.

8. Jane Bakerman is one of the few academic commentators to acknowledge the scope and complexity of Smiley's fiction. See "Renovating the House of Fiction: Structural Diversity in Jane Smiley's *Duplicate Keys*," *Midamerica: The Yearbook of the Society for the Study of Midwestern Literature* 15 (1988): 111–20; also "Water on Stone: Long-term Friendships in Jane Smiley's *Duplicate Keys* and Charlaine Harris: *A Secret Rage*," *Clues: A Journal of Detection* 10.2 (1989): 49–63.

9. Another recent fictional work that attempts, less successfully than Smiley's,

a deconstruction of cultural myths of paternity is Mona Simpson's *The Lost Father* (New York: Vintage Books, 1993).

10. Sasha Torres, "Melodrama, Masculinity, and the Family: *Thirtysomething* as Therapy," *Camera Obscura: A Journal of Feminism and Film Theory* 19 (1988): 87–106.

11. Torres, "Melodrama," 87.

12. Torres, "Melodrama," 92.

13. Torres, "Melodrama," 91.

14. To be sure, the work of critics like Janice Radway and Henry Jenkins have rightfully challenged the Frankfurt School of thought by constructing consumers as active agents of intervention in the dynamic of textual production and reader consciousness.

15. See Lynn Spigel, "From Domestic Space to Outer Space: The 1960s Fantastic Family Sit-com," in *Close Encounters: Film, Feminism, and Science Fiction*, ed. Constance Penley, Elisabeth Lyon, Lynn Spigel, and Janet Bergstrom (Minneapolis: University of Minnesota Press, 1991).

16. I am very much aware of the current controversy surrounding the word "queer" and its affirmative reappropriation by gay, lesbian, bisexual, transgender, and transsexual activists. While "queer" represents power and subversion to some, to others it is a painful term, one that invariably retains its historical meaning as a weapon of intimidation, humiliation, and violence. My use of "queer" in this and all subsequent references speaks specifically to recent theoretical reevaluations of "queerness" that seek to signify the diverse and multiple subject positions possible within nonheterosexual contexts. I have chosen the term for its inclusionary value, although at times I retain the gender-specific terms "lesbian" and "gay" for the purposes of nuancing.

17. Stanley Fish, *Is There a Text in This Class?: The Authority of Interpretive Communities* (Cambridge, Mass.: Harvard University Press, 1980), 97.

18. Fish, *Is There a Text*, 97.

19. Fish, *Is There a Text*, 106.

20. Diane Elam, *Romancing the Postmodern* (London: Routledge, 1992), 5.

21. Fish, *Is There a Text*, 106.

22. Kaja Silverman, *Male Subjectivity at the Margins* (New York: Routledge, 1992) argues via Freud, Lacan, Althusser, and Laplanche for the plurality of masculine subjectivity. She demonstrates that the mid-twentieth century has witnessed a collapse of the discursive commensurability of the "phallus" and the penis, a commensurability on which dominant patriarchal history has fully depended. This breakdown, which, Silverman insists, has psychic as well as political implications, produces a variety of nonphallic masculinities, the diversity of which constitutes the representational crisis of the late twentieth century, a "crisis" that has powerful implications for the imaging of femininity and gender in general.

23. All quotations are taken from Jane Smiley, *The Age of Grief: Stories and a Novella* (New York: Alfred A. Knopf, 1987).

24. See Lynda E. Boose, "The Father's House and the Daughter in It: The Structures of Western Culture's Daughter-Father Relationship," in *Daughters and Fathers*, ed. Lynda E. Boose and Betty S. Flowers (Baltimore: Johns Hopkins University Press, 1989), 19–74.

25. For Silverman, in *Male Subjectivity*, "classic masculinity" is based in a sustained cultural alignment of structures of symbolic representation with structures of dominant historical "reality." This sustained connection and the invio-

lability of masculinity thus support and in return are supported by the unity of the family (15–16). In Silverman's words, "The survival of our whole 'world' . . . depends upon the preservation of two interlocking terms: the family and the phallus" (48).

26. For Freud, disavowal is primarily a defensive strategy on the part of the male child who, upon recognizing sexual difference, seeks to protect himself against knowledge of female castration. This disavowal becomes more difficult to sustain once the child enters the Oedipal conflict. See "Some Psychological Consequences of the Anatomical Distinction between the Sexes" (1925), in *Standard Edition*, vol. 19, ed. James Strachey (London: Hogarth Press and The Institute of Psychoanalysis, 1961, 1962, 1964), 248–60. For Lacan, "desire," the effect of which is language, assumes complex interconnections with structures of disavowal, as well as with the "ideal Father" who would "master" the neurotic's wish for the father to be dead. See Jacques Lacan, "The Subversion of the Subject and the Dialectic of Desire in the Freudian Unconscious," in *Ecrits: A Selection*, trans. Alan Sheridan (New York: W. W. Norton, 1977), 292–325.

27. Silverman, *Male Subjectivity*, 34. Unquestionably, Silverman's shorthand merits questioning, especially since Lacan's framework is notoriously unclear, and not even Lacanians agree on whether the phallus is always or ever coextensive with the father or reasserts meanings associated with masculine linguistic dominance. See Jacques Lacan, "The Signification of the Phallus," in *Ecrits: A Selection*, trans. Alan Sheridan (New York: W. W. Norton, 1977); in addition, Judith Butler's writing on Lacan offers an exacting analysis of these questions. See *Gender Trouble: Feminism and the Subversion of Identity* (New York: Routledge, 1990) and *Bodies That Matter: On the Discursive Limits of "Sex"* (New York: Routledge, 1993), 72–91. See also Jane Gallop, *Reading Lacan* (Ithaca, N.Y.: Cornell University Press, 1985); and Jane Flax, *Thinking Fragments: Psychoanalysis, Feminism, and Postmodernism in the Contemporary West* (Berkeley: University of California Press, 1990).

28. Both of these tropes are well inscribed within American and feminist literary traditions and their discussion. See Leslie A. Fiedler, *Love and Death in the American Novel*, rev. ed. (New York: Stein and Day, 1982). See also Sara Ruddick, "Thinking about Fathers," in *Rethinking the Family: Some Feminist Questions*, ed. Barrie Thorne and Marilyn Yalom (Boston: Northeastern University Press, 1992), 176–90.

29. Silverman, *Male Subjectivity*, 2.

30. Perhaps this is the dilemma historian Edward Shorter identifies when he remarks that today's family, unlike traditional families of the past, no longer insures that our names and memories will live on after we die, which makes the prospect of death all that much more terrifying. Apparently, "we have lost interest in the family lineage as a means of cheating death . . . and [parents] themselves are responsible for what their children become only to the point of seeing that they march into the future with straight teeth." *The Making of the Modern Family* (New York: Basic Books, 1977), 8.

31. Michel Foucault, *The History of Sexuality, Volume I: An Introduction*, trans. Robert Hurley (New York: Vintage Books, 1980).

32. Consider, for example, the male cyborg in such films as *The Terminator* and *Terminator 2: Judgment Day* (see Chapter 11).

33. Tony Tanner, *Adultery in the Novel: Contract and Transgression* (Baltimore: Johns Hopkins University Press, 1979), 16.

34. In "The Unconscious" (*Standard Edition*, vol. 14, ed. James Strachey [Lon-

don: Hogarth Press and the Institute of Psychoanalysis, 1957, 1962, 1964]), Freud describes projection as the externalization of internal anxiety, which allows the subject to react against it with "attempts at flight represented by phobic avoidances" (184). Although David's response to Dana could not properly be described as phobic, he is clearly in flight from any confrontation with her that might resolve the question of her fidelity. In this way, he avoids recognition of the internal nature of the self-betrayal taking place in his struggle with the Law of the Father, or cultural paternity. This concept is central to Lacan's thinking about masculine subjectivity and is suggested in his recourse to the term *meconnaissance*, a "failure to recognize" the self that is the condition of entry into the symbolic. See "The Mirror Stage," in *Ecrits: A Selection*, trans. Alan Sheridan (New York: W. W. Norton, 1977).

35. Joseph A. Boone, "Male Independence and the American Quest Genre: Hidden Sexual Politics in the All-Male Worlds of Melville, Twain, and London," reprinted in *Feminisms: An Anthology of Literary Theory and Criticism*, ed. Robyn R. Warhol and Diane Price Herndl (New Brunswick, N.J.: Rutgers University Press, 1991).

36. Similarly, in the family romances that Tanner considers, the actual act of adultery remains for the most part an invisible deed, a deed marked by gaps and silences that gradually spread throughout the text.

37. Judith Butler, "Imitation and Gender Insubordination," in *Inside/Out: Lesbian Theories, Gay Theories*, ed. Diana Fuss (New York: Routledge, 1991), 28.

38. Butler, "Imitation," 28.

39. Silverman, *Male Subjectivity*, 69. In her reading of the film *The Best Years of Our Lives*, Silverman points out that female characters in the film come rushing in to stabilize or resolve the gender conflicts that permeate the narrative. Instead, she argues, the film "sustains the correlation of masculinity and castration until the very end" (69). Similarly, *The Age of Grief* proposes no resolution, defying traditional narrative closure within the family romance. In its place, a space is left open for consideration of paternity's reinscription within the family plot.

40. Modleski, *Feminism Without Women*, 7.

Chapter 7: "A Possible Sharing"

1. Amy Tan, *The Joy Luck Club* (New York: Ivy Books, 1989), 331. All subsequent quotations are taken from this edition.

2. Marina Heung, "Daughter-Text/Mother-Text: Matrilineage in Amy Tan's *Joy Luck Club*," *Feminist Studies* 19.3 (Fall 1993): 597–616. Heung locates Tan's novel within the feminist revisionary tradition of maternal-centered family romance. While she acknowledges the incongruence between Oedipal structures and Chinese mother-daughter romance and the displacements that Tan's text necessarily enacts on these structures, Heung's reading seeks resolution in "mutual identification(s)," "sisterly" unity, and "mothering reciprocity." While such an interpretation draws attention to those aspects of the novel that nurture feminist community-building, my sense is that more emphasis could be placed on the hegemonic complexities of novels such as Tan's, the multiple readings that may admittedly occur even in feminist environments.

3. By "maternal family romance," I am referring to the kinds of narratives explored, most recently and comprehensively, by Marianne Hirsch, "feminist"

narratives that invert the traditional Freudian Oedipal romance by placing relations between mothers and daughters at the center of the family plot. See *The Mother/Daughter Plot: Narrative, Psychoanalysis, Feminism* (Bloomington: Indiana University Press, 1989).

4. Trinh T. Minh-ha, *Woman, Native, Other: Writing Postcoloniality and Feminism* (Bloomington: Indiana University Press, 1989), 8.

5. Minh-ha, *Woman, Native, Other*, 2.

6. Suzanne Juhasz, "Maxine Hong Kingston: Narrative Technique and Female Identity," in *Contemporary American Women Writers: Narrative Strategies*, ed. Catherine Rainwater and William J. Scheick (Lexington: University of Kentucky Press, 1985), 173. In "alternating movements toward and away from the mother" (173), Juhasz observes that the daughter's moves to individuate and to connect both arise from her essential attachment to female ancestors. "Telling their stories. . . both frees her from them and binds her to them" (175).

7. However, as King-Kok Cheung points out, this late arrival of Chinese women meant that they had remained closer to the culture of origin and were therefore "frequently the transmitters of culture for the second generation." See *Articulate Silences: Hisaye Yamamoto, Maxine Hong Kingston, Joy Kogawa* (Ithaca, N.Y.: Cornell University Press, 1993), 10.

8. Rose Y. Hsiao, "Facing the Incurable: Patriarchy in *Eat a Bowl of Tea*," in *Reading the Literatures of Asian America*, ed. Shirley Geok-lin Lim and Amy Ling (Philadelphia: Temple University Press, 1992), 154–56.

9. Maxine Hong Kingston's *The Woman Warrior* (1976) and *China Men* (1980) are often discussed as two parts of a single vision, a project that entails the construction of Chinese American culture through the reclamation of both matriarchal and patriarchal myths and histories. See David Leiwei Li, "*China Men*: Maxine Hong Kingston and the American Canon," *American Literary History* 2.3 (Fall 1990): 482–502; Roberta Rubenstein, *Boundaries of the Self: Gender, Culture, Fiction* (Urbana: University of Illinois, 1987).

10. Minh-ha, *Woman, Native, Other*, 149.

11. See Walter Shear, "Generational Differences and the Diaspora in *The Joy Luck Club*," *Critique* 34.3 (Spring 1993): 193–99.

12. The significance of "owing" or reciprocity is, as Shirley Geok-lin Lim explains, "an idealized social construct in . . . Confucianist . . . societies." See "Asians in Anglo-American Feminism: Reciprocity and Resistance," in *Changing Subjects: The Making of Feminist Literary Criticism*, ed. Gayle Greene and Coppelia Kahn (London: Routledge, 1993), 240. Lim views her initiation into feminist theory—which occurred while she attended a gathering of feminist scholars at Barnard in 1987—as a paternalistic gesture. She sees this invitation as her "chance" to be trained in the importance of "centric positioning" within the feminist literary critical community, a community in which Anglo-Americans formulate theory and Asians consume it (249).

13. Lao-tzu (sixth century B.C.) was the philosopher who founded Taoism. He believed that the universe is composed of five elements: wood, fire, earth, metal, and water. They move in a circle in precisely this order. The ones situated next to one another are in good relationship. Every person has all of these elements. Good people have a balance of all elements, although you can work to correct an imbalance.

14. Shirley Geok-lin Lim, "The Ambivalent American: Asian American Literature on the Cusp," in *Reading the Literatures of Asian America*, ed. Shirley Geok-lin Lim and Amy Ling (Philadelphia: Temple University Press, 1992), 22.

15. Julia Kristeva, *About Chinese Women*, trans. Anita Barrows (New York: Urizen Books, 1974, 1977).

16. Kristeva, *About Chinese Women*, 56.

17. Kristeva, *About Chinese Women*, 57, 58. In the Chinese language, mother and father, private and public merge in an "absence of clear-cut divisions between the order of things and the order of symbols" (56); while in the West, the patriarchal erasure of the semiotic suggests a polarization of spheres, the kind of polarization the practice of deconstruction challenges.

18. Kristeva, *About Chinese Women*, 58; she writes, "Not only has Chinese writing maintained the memory of matrilineal pre-history (collective and individual) in its architectonic of image, gesture, and sound; it has been able as well to integrate it into a logico-symbolic code capable of ensuring the most direct, 'reasonable,' legislating—even the most bureaucratic—communication: all the qualities that the West believes itself unique in honouring, and that it attributes to the Father" (57). In other words, the Chinese father has not succeeded in erasing the mother's disruptive presence in language, in history, in culture. The Western daughter is thus bound to the father in ways that Chinese women are not, particularly as a result of difference in language systems.

19. In Chinese writing and in Chinese women themselves, Kristeva seems to locate a way around the binary that ironically structures both her encounter with the East *and* the text of *About Chinese Women* itself. The text is broken up into two parts, the first providing her critique of women within patriarchal Judeo-Christian monotheism, a critique that positions Kristeva as Westerner, "On This Side." The second section, "Women of China," treats the particular historical conditions of women in the East. Indeed, Kristeva's discussion of language difference between East and West has value insofar as it affords a glimpse into the intricate interweaving of culture, gender, language, and kinship structure; however, her findings, based on her visit to China, have been sharply criticized, most notably by Gayatri Spivak, for its alleged ethnocentrism. See "French Feminism in an International Frame," reprinted in *Other Worlds: Essays in Cultural Politics* (New York: Methuen, 1987); also reprinted in Mary Eagleton, *Feminist Literary Criticism* (New York: Longman, 1991), 83–109.

20. Sau-Ling Cynthia Wong, "Ethnicizing Gender: An Exploration of Sexuality as Sign in Chinese Immigrant Literature," in *Reading the Literatures of Asian America*, ed. Shirley Geok-lin Lim and Amy Ling (Philadelphia: Temple University Press, 1992), conceptualizes the "ethnicizing of gender" in Chinese immigrant literature as the mirror response to the "gendering of ethnicity," or the process by which "white ideology assigns selected gender characteristics to various ethnic Others to create a coherent, depoliticized, and thus putatively self-explanatory mythic account of American social institutions and operations" (111). By turning the tables on this stereotyping practice, Chinese writers denaturalize the categories of ethnicity as defined by cultural hegemonies and reveal the socially constructed nature of both ethnic and gender categories. I am grateful to Wong, from whom my phrase, "familializing ethnicity" is drawn.

21. Minh-ha, *Woman, Native, Other*, 103.

22. Minh-ha, *Woman, Native, Other*, 104.

23. Rey Chow, *Woman and Chinese Modernity: The Politics of Reading between West and East* (Minneapolis: University of Minnesota Press, 1991), 159.

24. Chow, *Woman and Chinese Modernity*, 160.

25. See King-kok Cheung, *Articulate Silences*; see also "Imposed Silences in *The Color Purple* and *The Woman Warrior*," *PMLA* 103.2 (1988): 162–74.

Chapter 8: Reconstructing Kin

1. Deborah E. McDowell, "Reading Family Matters," in *Changing Our Own Words: Essays on Criticism, Theory and Writing by Black Women,* ed. Cheryl A. Wall (New Brunswick, N.J.: Rutgers University Press, 1989), 78.

2. Marianne Hirsch, *The Mother/Daughter Plot: Narrative, Psychoanalysis, Feminism* (Bloomington: Indiana University, 1989), 9.

3. I refer here to information provided by Erlene Stetson in her essay "Studying Slavery: Some Literary and Pedagogical Considerations on the Black Female Slave," in *All the Women Are White, All the Blacks Are Men, but Some of Us Are Brave: Black Women's Studies,* ed. Gloria T. Hull, Patricia Bell Scott, and Barbara Smith (New York: The Feminist Press, 1982), 71. For a more complete historical account of the black family under slavery and during the Reconstruction era, see Herbert G. Gutman's *The Black Family in Slavery and Freedom, 1750–1925* (New York: Pantheon, 1976); see also Carol B. Stack, *All Our Kin: Strategies for Survival in a Black Community* (New York: Harper and Row, 1974).

4. In their spurious effort to contain all social and emotional exchange within the family unit, Sethe, Denver, and Beloved in some ways resemble family groupings depicted in other works by Morrison; for instance, the Breedloves from *The Bluest Eye,* who, Roberta Rubenstein argues, "survive at the very fringe of society, where the 'hem' begins to unravel," and where "economic destitution and psychic abjection undermine the very bonds that attach family members to one another and form the basis for community." In *Boundaries of the Self: Gender, Culture, Fiction* (Urbana: University of Illinois Press, 1987), 129.

5. Hirsch, *The Mother/Daughter Plot,* 3.

6. Mary Helen Washington, introduction, *Memory of Kin: Stories about Family by Black Writers* (New York: Anchor Books/Doubleday, 1991), 1.

7. Deborah Horvitz, for example, has painstakingly described the novel's exploration of "matrilineal ancestry and the relationships among enslaved, freed, alive, and dead mothers and daughters." See "Nameless Ghosts: Possession and Dispossession in *Beloved,*" *Studies in American Fiction* 17.2 (1989):157.

8. Horvitz sees Beloved as symbolic of black women's collective memory. For her, Beloved speaks across generations of Africans and African slaves in the United States, thus creating "the crucial link that connects Africa and America for the enslaved women. She is Sethe's mother; she is Sethe herself; she is her daughter." See "Nameless Ghosts," 163–64. Similarly, Rebecca Ferguson holds the opinion that *Beloved* is centrally concerned with women's role in maintaining the continuity of family life, however in a much broader sense, "through the protection of their children, their men and the community." Consequently, for Ferguson, Beloved is more than the specific link between generations of women: "Beloved *is* above all a connection," she claims, "the reconnection with and restoring of all that was lost when [Sethe] was driven to kill her." See "History, Memory and Language in Toni Morrison's *Beloved,*" in *Feminist Criticism: Theory and Practice,* ed. Susan Sellers (Toronto: University of Toronto Press, 1991): 112, 114.

9. Washington, introduction, *Memory of Kin,* 7.

10. All quotations are from Toni Morrison, *Beloved* (New York: NAL, 1987).

11. Karen E. Fields, "To Embrace Dead Strangers: Toni Morrison's *Beloved,*" in *Mother Puzzles: Daughters and Mothers in Contemporary American Literature,* ed. Mickey Pearlman (New York: Greenwood Press, 1989), 163.

12. Michael Holquist, prologue, in *Rabelais and His World*, by Mikhail Bakhtin, trans. Helene Iswolsky (Bloomington: Indiana University Press, 1984), xxi.

13. Ferguson, "History, Memory, and Language," 113.

14. Washington, introduction, *Memory of Kin*, 3.

15. See, for example, Peter Kolchin's *American Slavery, 1619–1877* (New York: Hill and Wang, 1993).

16. Fields, "To Embrace Dead Strangers," 165–66.

17. Quoted in Rubenstein, *Boundaries of the Self*, 153.

18. Valerie Smith notes that literacy has long served as an instrument of cultural and social control in the West. See her introduction in *Self-Discovery and Authority in Afro-American Narrative* (Cambridge, Mass.: Harvard University Press, 1987).

19. McDowell, "Reading Family Matters," 79.

20. Washington, introduction, *Memory of Kin*, 5.

21. Ralph Ellison, *Invisible Man* (New York: Random House, 1947), 13.

Chapter 9: "Family" Romance

1. Donna Minkowitz, "Family Values? No Thanks," *The Advocate* (June 16, 1992): 17.

2. The problematic phrase "out is in" appeared on the front cover of the premier issue of *Out* magazine, a slick publication geared toward a professional, monied class of urban lesbian and gay consumers. Arguably, *Out* is one of many recent cultural indications–alongside mass-distributed films such as *Longtime Companion* and *Philadelphia*, cable television programs such as *In the Life*, a lesbian and gay variety show, and specialty shopping catalogs like *Shocking Gray*—that a post-Stonewall generation of "out" gays and lesbians has earned a modicum of return on its investment in cultural capital.

3. Diana Fuss, ed., *Inside/Outside: Lesbian Theories, Gay Theories* (New York: Routledge, 1991), 3.

4. Judith Butler, "Imitation and Gender Insubordination," in *Inside/Out: Lesbian Theories, Gay Theories*, ed. Diana Fuss (New York: Routledge, 1991), 14.

5. Eve Kosofsky Sedgwick, *Epistemology of the Closet* (Berkeley: University of California, 1990), 7–9.

6. James Baldwin, quoted in Dorothy Allison, *Bastard out of Carolina* (New York: Plume/Penguin Books, 1992). Subsequent quotations are from this source.

7. Alexander Doty, *Making Things Perfectly Queer: Interpreting Mass Culture* (Minneapolis: University of Minnesota, 1993), 3.

8. Again, see Doty, *Making Things Perfectly Queer*, 1–16.

9. I recognize that not all feminisms or feminists, for that matter, view sex as the origin of women's oppression. Feminism in the 1990s is becoming increasingly sex-friendly, especially since the pornography debates and the lesbian/feminist "sex wars" of the 1980s brought to light the exclusionary practices and facile assumptions about sexuality that inform much of earlier feminist theory. See *Cross Purposes: Lesbian Studies, Feminist Studies, and the Limits of Alliance*, ed. Dana Heller (Indiana University Press, forthcoming) for a range of essays exploring the interrelationships of lesbianism and feminism.

10. David Leavitt, *Equal Affections* (New York: Harper and Row, 1989), 85.

11. My thanks to John R. Leo for this observation.

12. Absent from this perspective is sufficient recognition of the deeply intertwined relations of homophobia and misogyny that are understood to be supported by the nuclear family and its ideological foundation in compulsory
heterosexuality.

13. William Hoffman's proclamation, abstracted from his review in *Vogue*, appears on the front jacket cover of the 1989 Harper and Row paperback edition
of Leavitt's *Equal Affections*.

14. Tania Modleski, *Feminism without Women: Culture and Criticism in a "Postfeminist" Age* (New York: Routledge, 1991), 12.

15. Modleski, *Feminism without Women*, 7.

16. The dichotomous relation between male homosexuality and homosociality is, of course, historically specific and culturally diverse. For an analysis that
seeks to locate this dichotomy along a continuum, see Eve Kosofsky Sedgwick,
Between Men: English Literature and Male Homosocial Desire (New York: Columbia
University, 1985).

17. David Leavitt, *Family Dancing* (New York: Knopf, 1984), 182–83.

18. Carol Iannone, "Post-Countercultural Tristesse," *Commentary* 83.2 (1987):
58.

19. This and all subsequent references are from David Leavitt, *The Lost Language of Cranes* (Toronto: Bantam Books, 1986), 173.

20. Joseph A. Boone, "Male Independence and the American Quest Genre:
Hidden Sexual Politics in the All-Male Worlds of Melville, Twain, and London,"
reprinted in *Feminisms: An Anthology of Literary Theory and Criticism*, ed. Robyn
Warhol and Diane Price Herndl (New Brunswick, N.J.: Rutgers University Press,
1991), 961–87.

21. It is interesting to note that in the recent PBS film version of the novel
Philip tucks Owen in, a loving and maternal gesture nowhere present in the
original text.

22. See Marjorie Garber, *Vested Interests: Cross-Dressing and Cultural Anxiety* (New
York: Routledge, 1992); see also Esther Newton, *Mother Camp: Female Impersonators in America* (Englewood Cliffs, N.J.: Prentice Hall, 1972).

Chapter 10: The Lesbian Dick

1. Marcia Ian, *Remembering the Phallic Mother: Psychoanalysis, Modernism, and the
Fetish* (Ithaca, N.Y.: Cornell University Press, 1993), 28n.

2. Judith Butler, "The Lesbian Phallus and the Morphological Imaginary,"
in *Bodies That Matter: On the Discursive Limits of "Sex"* (New York: Routledge,
1993), 90.

3. Paulina Palmer, "The Lesbian Thriller: Crimes, Clues, and Contradictions,"
in *Outwrite: Lesbianism and Popular Culture*, ed. Gabriele Griffin (London: Pluto
Press, 1993), 101.

4. Stephen Heath, *Questions of Cinema* (Bloomington: Indiana University Press,
1981), 127.

5. Teresa de Lauretis, "Sexual Indifference and Lesbian Representation," *Theater Journal* 40.2 (1988): 155–77.

6. Here, de Lauretis expands on the analysis put forward in Laura Mulvey's famous essay, "Visual Pleasure and Narrative Cinema," which appeared in 1975 in
Screen. In its early incarnation, the essay masculinized and essentialized the male
spectator position. Mulvey later modified her articulation of the "male gaze"

to acknowledge that women (and nonheterosexual men) might also derive distinctive, albeit contradictory, pleasure as agents of the gaze, and that males as well as females were potential objects of the gaze. See "Afterthoughts on 'Visual Pleasure and Narrative Cinema' Inspired by King Vidor's *Duel in the Sun* (1946)" in Mulvey's *Visual and Other Pleasures* (Bloomington: Indiana University Press, 1989), 29–38.

7. *Internal Affairs*, dir. Mike Figgis, Paramount Pictures, 1990.

8. Interestingly, Metcalf's character, Jackie, worked as a police officer early in the series. More recently, since the series installed recurring gay and lesbian characters (played by Martin Mull and Sandra Bernhard, respectively) and began dealing with queer themes, Jackie's dyke-like demeanor has been the subject of several offhand jokes.

9. On television, there was the short-lived character C. J. Lamb, a bisexual lawyer on *L.A. Law*. In Hollywood film, there was Debra Winger's Justice Department investigator in *Black Widow*. In *Silkwood*, Cher played an environmental/moral detective as Meryl Streep's roommate and coworker.

10. Jim Collins, *Uncommon Cultures: Popular Culture and Post-Modernism* (New York: Routledge, 1989), 30.

11. David Glover and Cora Kaplan, "Guns in the House of Culture," in *Cultural Studies*, ed. Lawrence Grossberg, Cary Nelson, and Paula Treichler (New York: Routledge, 1992), 213–24.

12. Lorraine Gamman, "Watching the Detectives: The Enigma of the Female Gaze," in *The Female Gaze: Women as Viewers of Popular Culture*, ed. Lorraine Gamman and Margaret Marshment (Seattle: Real Comet Press, 1989), 8.

13. Gamman, "Watching the Detectives," 19.

14. A substantial body of scholarship exists that addresses the image of the lesbian as outlaw. See, for example, Andrea Weiss, "Lesbian as Outlaw: New Forms and Fantasies in Women's Independent Cinema," *Conditions* 12 (1985): 117–31.

15. Judith Butler, *Gender Trouble: Feminism and the Subversion of Identity* (New York: Routledge, 1990), 75–76.

16. Gayle Rubin, "The Traffic in Women: Notes on the 'Political Economy' of Sex," in *Toward an Anthropology of Women*, ed. Rayna R. Reiter (New York: Monthly Review Press, 1975), 157–210.

17. De Lauretis, "Sexual Indifference," 155.

18. Eve Kosofsky Sedgwick, *Epistemology of the Closet* (Berkeley: University of California Press, 1990), 22.

19. Sedgwick, *Epistemology*, 8.

20. Butler, *Gender Trouble*, 87.

21. Quoted in Robert L. Caserio, "Supreme Court Discourse vs. Homosexual Fiction," *The South Atlantic Quarterly: Displacing Homophobia*, ed. Ronald B. Butters, 88.1 (1989): 268.

22. Caserio, "Supreme Court Discourse vs. Homosexual Fiction," 268, 270.

23. De Lauretis, "Sexual Indifference," 173.

24. John R. Leo, "The Familialism of 'Man' in American Television Melodrama," in *The South Atlantic Quarterly: Displacing Homophobia*, ed. Ronald B. Butters, 88.1 (1989): 36.

25. Kate Adams, "Making the World Safe for the Missionary Position: Images of the Lesbian in Post-World War II America," in *Lesbian Texts and Contexts: Radical Revisions*, ed. Karla Jay and Joanne Glasgow (New York: New York University Press, 1990), 269.

26. Adams, "Making the World Safe," 269.
27. De Lauretis, "Sexual Indifference," 159.

Chapter 11: Home Viewing

1. *Terminator 2: Judgment Day,* dir. James Cameron, Live Home Video, 1991.
2. Andrew Ross, "Families, Film Genres, and Technological Environments," *East-West Film Journal* 4.1 (1989): 6.
3. Ross, "Families," 18.
4. Patricia Mellencamp, "Domestic Scenes," *East-West Film Journal* 4.1 (1989): 136.
5. Sigmund Freud, "Family Romances," in *Standard Edition,* vol. 9, ed. James Strachey (London: Hogarth Press and the Institute of Psychoanalysis, 1959, 1962, 1964), 238.
6. Freud, "Family Romances," 238.
7. Fredric Jameson, *Postmodernism or, The Cultural Logic of Late Capitalism* (Durham, N.C.: Duke University Press, 1992), 286.
8. Jameson, *Postmodernism,* 285.
9. The forgetting of the present as past also holds important ramifications for the cultural redescription of masculinity and Oedipal fatherhood. For example, the father in Mike Nichols's recent film *Regarding Henry* forgets his entire history. Harrison Ford plays the father, a successful New York attorney who suffers amnesia when he is shot during a holdup. The brain damage that he suffers causes him to lose his memory and most of his adult, rational functioning. Subsequently, he can remember nothing of his own youth or his own parents. In this sense, the film is a Marcusean wonderland; Ford must rediscover his "inner child." He forgets about law; he forgets about the affair he was having. When he is locked into the corporate world, Henry is cruel, heartless, destructive. After he is brain-damaged, his wife seems happier, his kids can relate to him, and his secretary likes him better. In this way, the film suggests that corporate greed and blind consumption in the eighties made a moral wreck of the patriarchal family. The film celebrates a notion of freedom attainable through the acknowledgment of phallic insufficiency and a redescription of masculinity grounded in innocence. For example, before the accident, Henry lectures his children about the "work ethic." After the accident, his daughter reminds him of the importance of the "work ethic." "What's that?" he asks. She doesn't know. Through such forgetting, Henry becomes a more compassionate father and a nobler person. This cultural redescription of masculinity and paternity is consonant with a number of recent literary works (see Chapter 6). In *Regarding Henry,* the survival of the family depends on the father's ability to forget the past and enter a process of cognitive and ideological transformation. The forgetting of classic masculine subjectivity, as reinforced by the Oedipus, restores hope for the family.
10. See Margaret Goscilo, "Deconstructing *The Terminator,*" *Film Criticism* 12.2 (1987–88): 37–52, for a discussion of gender formulations in the film.
11. Worth considering, although beyond the scope of this essay, is the explicit anti-Semitism conveyed through this characterization.
12. Anne Balsamo, "Reading Cyborgs, Writing Feminism," *Communications* 10 (1988): 332. For a study of the modernist development of the body-machine complex, see Mark Seltzer's *Bodies and Machines* (New York: Routledge, 1992).
13. Mary Ann Doane, "Commentary: Cyborgs, Origins, and Subjectivity," in

Coming to Terms: Feminism, Theory, Politics, ed. Elizabeth Weed (New York: Routledge, 1989), 211.

14. Doane, "Commentary," 209.

15. Doane, "Commentary," 211.

16. Jean Baudrillard, *Simulations,* trans. Paul Foss, Paul Patton, and Philip Beitchman (New York: Semiotext(e), 1983).

17. Doane, "Commentary," 212; see also Donna Haraway, "A Manifesto for Cyborgs: Science, Technology, and Socialist Feminism in the 1980s," in *Coming to Terms: Feminism, Theory, Politics,* ed. Elizabeth Weed (New York: Routledge, 1989), 173–204.

18. Haraway, "A Manifesto," 191.

19. Haraway, "A Manifesto," 187.

20. Mellencamp, "Domestic Scenes," 137.

21. Arthur Kroker and Marilouise Kroker, eds., *Body Invaders: Panic Sex in America* (New York: St. Martin's Press, 1987), 21.

22. Laurie Schulze, "On the Muscle," in *Fabrications: Costume and the Female Body,* ed. Jane Gaines and Charlotte Herzog (New York: Routledge, 1990), 60–61.

Bibliography

Adams, Kate. "Making the World Safe for the Missionary Position: Images of the Lesbian in Post-World War II America." In *Lesbian Texts and Contexts: Radical Revisions*, ed. Karla Jay and Joanne Glasgow, 255–74. New York: New York University Press, 1990.

Allison, Dorothy. *Bastard out of Carolina.* New York: Plume/Penguin Books, 1992.

Aries, Philip. *Centuries of Childhood: A Social History of Family Life.* Trans. Robert Baldick. New York: Vintage Books, 1962.

Bakerman, Jane. "Renovating the House of Fiction: Structural Diversity in Jane Smiley's *Duplicate Keys*." *Midamerica: The Yearbook of the Society for the Study of Midwestern Literature* 15 (1988): 111–20.

———. "Water on Stone: Long-term Friendships in Jane Smiley's *Duplicate Keys* and *Charlaine Harris: A Secret Rage*." *Clues: A Journal of Detection* 10.2 (1989): 49–63.

Bakhtin, Mikhail. *Rabelais and His World.* Trans. Helene Iswolsky. Bloomington: Indiana University Press, 1984.

Balsamo, Anne. "Reading Cyborgs, Writing Feminism." *Communications* 10 (1988): 331–44.

Barr, Marleen S., and Richard Feldstein, eds. *Discontented Discourses: Feminism/Textual Intervention/Psychoanalysis.* Urbana: University of Illinois Press, 1989.

Barrett, Michèle, and Mary McIntosh. *The Anti-Social Family.* 2d ed. London: Verso/NLB, 1982, 1991.

Barrett, Michèle, and Anne Phillips, eds. *Destabilizing Theory: Contemporary Feminist Debates.* Stanford, Calif.: Stanford University Press, 1992.

Barth, John. *The Friday Book: Essays and Other Nonfiction.* New York: Putnam's, 1984.

Barthelme, Donald. *The Dead Father.* New York: Penguin, 1975.

Barthes, Roland. *The Pleasure of the Text.* Trans. Richard Miller. New York: Farrar, Straus and Giroux, 1975.

Baudrillard, Jean. *Simulations.* Trans. Paul Foss, Paul Patton, and Philip Beitchman. New York: Semiotext(e), 1983.

Bauer, Dale M. "The Politics of Collaboration in *The Whole Family*." In *Old Maids to Radical Spinsters: Unmarried Women in the Twentieth-Century Novel*, ed. Laura L. Doan, 107–22. Urbana: University of Illinois, 1991.

Bloom, Harold. *The Anxiety of Influence.* New York: Oxford University Press, 1973.

Bodroghkozy, Aniko. "'Is This What You Mean by Color TV?': Race, Gender, and Contested Meanings in NBC's *Julia*." In *Private Screenings: Television and the Female Consumer,* ed. Lynn Spigel and Denise Mann, 143–68. Minneapolis: University of Minnesota Press, 1992.

Boone, Joseph A. "Male Independence and the American Quest Genre: Hidden Sexual Politics in the All-Male Worlds of Melville, Twain, and London." Reprinted in *Feminisms: An Anthology of Literary Theory and Criticism,* ed. Robyn R. Warhol and Diane Price Herndl, 961–87. New Brunswick, N.J.: Rutgers University Press.

Boone, Joseph A., and Michael Cadden, eds. *Engendering Men.* New York: Routledge, 1990.

Boose, Lynda E., and Betty S. Flowers, eds. *Daughters and Fathers.* Baltimore: Johns Hopkins University Press, 1989.

Brower, Sue. "Fans as Tastemakers: Viewers for Quality Television." In *The Adoring Audience: Fan Culture and Popular Media,* ed. Lisa A. Lewis. New York: Routledge, 1992.

Butler, Judith. *Bodies That Matter: On the Discursive Limits of "Sex."* New York: Routledge, 1993.

———. *Gender Trouble: Feminism and the Subversion of Identity.* New York: Routledge, 1990.

———. "Imitation and Gender Insubordination." In *Inside/Out: Lesbian Theories, Gay Theories,* ed. Diana Fuss, 13–31. New York: Routledge, 1991.

Calhoun, Craig, ed. *Habermas and the Public Sphere.* Cambridge, Mass.: MIT Press, 1993.

Caserio, Robert L. "Supreme Court Discourse vs. Homosexual Fiction." *The South Atlantic Quarterly: Displacing Homophobia,* ed. Ronald B. Butters 88.1 (1989): 267–300.

Chase, Richard. *The American Novel and Its Tradition.* Baltimore: Johns Hopkins University Press, 1957.

Cheung, King-Kok. *Articulate Silences: Hisaye Yamamoto, Maxine Hong Kingston, Joy Kogawa.* Ithaca, N.Y.: Cornell University Press, 1993.

———. "Imposed Silences in *The Color Purple* and *The Woman Warrior.*" *PMLA* 103.2 (1988): 162–74.

Chodorow, Nancy. *The Reproduction of Mothering: Psychoanalysis and the Sociology of Gender.* Berkeley: University of California Press, 1978.

Chodorow, Nancy, and Susan Contratto. "The Fantasy of the Perfect Mother." In *Rethinking the Family: Some Feminist Questions.* Revised edition. Ed. Barrie Thorne and Marilyn Yalom, 191–214. Boston: Northeastern University Press, 1992.

Chow, Rey. *Woman and Chinese Modernity: The Politics of Reading between West and East.* Minneapolis: University of Minnesota Press, 1991.

Clover, Carol. "Her Body, Himself: Gender in the Slasher Film." In *Fantasy and the Cinema,* ed. James Donald. London: BFI, 1989.

Collins, Jim. *Uncommon Cultures: Popular Culture and Post-Modernism.* New York: Routledge, 1989.

Connell, Evan S. *Mrs. Bridge.* New York: Pocket Books, 1959, 1977.

Cooper, David. *The Death of the Family.* New York: Random House, 1970.

Cott, Nancy F. *The Bonds of Womanhood: "Woman's Sphere" in New England, 1780–1835.* New Haven, Conn.: Yale Univ. Press, 1977.

Coward, Rosalind. *Patriarchal Precedents: Sexuality and Social Relations.* London: Routledge and Kegan Paul, 1983.

Dally, Ann. *Inventing Motherhood: The Consequences of an Ideal.* New York: Schocken, 1982.

Degler, Carl N. *At Odds: Women and the Family in America from the Revolution to the Present.* New York: Oxford University Press, 1980.

de Lauretis, Teresa. *Alice Doesn't: Feminism, Semiotics, Cinema.* Bloomington: Indiana University Press, 1984.

————, ed. *Feminist Studies/Critical Studies.* Bloomington: Indiana University Press, 1986.

————. "Sexual Indifference and Lesbian Representation." *Theater Journal* 40.2 (1988): 155–77.

————. *Technologies of Gender: Essays on Theory, Film, and Fiction.* Bloomington: Indiana University Press, 1987.

Deleuze, Gilles, and Felix Guattari. *Anti-Oedipus: Capitalism and Schizophrenia.* Trans. Robert Hurley, Mark Seem, and Helen R. Lane. Minneapolis: University of Minnesota Press, 1983.

Doane, Mary Ann. "Commentary: Cyborgs, Origins, and Subjectivity." In *Coming to Terms: Feminism, Theory, Politics,* ed. Elizabeth Weed, 209–14. New York: Routledge, 1989.

Donzelot, Jacques. *The Policing of Families.* Trans. Robert Hurley. New York: Pantheon Books, 1979.

Doty, Alexander. *Making Things Perfectly Queer: Interpreting Mass Culture.* Minneapolis: University of Minnesota Press, 1993.

Eagleton, Mary. *Feminist Literary Criticism.* New York: Longman, 1991.

Ebert, Teresa. "Postmodern Politics, Patriarchy, and Donald Barthelme." *The Review of Contemporary Fiction* 11.2 (Summer 1991): 75–82.

Elam, Diane. *Feminism and Deconstruction.* London: Routledge, 1994.

————. *Romancing the Postmodern.* London: Routledge, 1992.

Ellison, Ralph. *Invisible Man.* New York: Random House, 1947.

Elshtain, Jean Bethke, ed. *The Family in Political Thought.* Amherst: University of Massachusetts Press, 1982.

————. *Public Man, Private Woman: Woman in Social and Political Thought.* Princeton, N.J.: Princeton University Press, 1981.

Ewen, Stuart. *Captains of Consciousness: Advertising and the Social Roots of the Consumer Culture.* New York: McGraw Hill, 1976.

Farnham, Marynia, and Ferdinand Lundberg. *The Modern Woman: The Lost Sex.* New York: Harper and Bros., 1947.

Felman, Shoshana. "Beyond Oedipus: The Specimen Story of Psychoanalysis." *MLN Comparative Literature* 98.5: 1021–53. Baltimore: Johns Hopkins University Press, 1983.

Ferguson, Rebecca. "History, Memory and Language in Toni Morrison's *Beloved.*" In *Feminist Criticism: Theory and Practice,* ed. Susan Sellers, 109–28. Toronto: University of Toronto Press, 1991.

Feuer, Jane, Paul Kerr, and Tise Vahimagi, eds. *MTM: "Quality Television."* London: BFI, 1984.

Fiedler, Leslie. *Love and Death in the American Novel.* Revised edition. New York: Stein and Day, 1982.

Fields, Karen E. "To Embrace Dead Strangers: Toni Morrison's *Beloved.*" In *Mother Puzzles: Daughters and Mothers in Contemporary American Literature,* ed. Mickey Pearlman, 159–69. New York: Greenwood Press, 1989.

Fish, Stanley. *Is There a Text in This Class?: The Authority of Interpretive Communities.* Cambridge, Mass.: Harvard University Press, 1980.

Flax, Jane. *Thinking Fragments: Psychoanalysis, Feminism, and Postmodernism in the Contemporary West.* Berkeley: University of California Press, 1990.

Foucault, Michel. *The History of Sexuality. Volume I: An Introduction.* Trans. Robert Hurley. New York: Vintage Books, 1980.

Fraser, Nancy. *Unruly Practices: Power, Discourse, and Gender in Contemporary Social Theory.* Minneapolis: University of Minnesota Press, 1989.

Freud, Sigmund. "'A Child Is Being Beaten': A Contribution to the Study of the Origin of Sexual Perversion." In *Standard Edition.* Vol. 17, ed. James Strachey. London: Hogarth Press and the Institute of Psychoanalysis, 1955.

———. "The Dissolution of the Oedipus Complex." In *Standard Edition.* Vol. 19, ed. James Strachey. London: Hogarth Press and the Institute of Psychoanalysis, 1961.

———. "Family Romances." In *Standard Edition.* Vol. 9, ed. James Strachey. London: Hogarth Press and the Institute of Psychoanalysis, 1959.

———. "Some Psychological Consequences of the Anatomical Distinction between the Sexes." (1925). In *Standard Edition.* Vol. 19, ed. James Strachey. London: Hogarth Press and the Institute of Psychoanalysis, 1961.

———. "The Unconscious." In *Standard Edition.* Vol. 14, ed. James Strachey. London: Hogarth Press and the Institute of Psychoanalysis, 1957.

Friedan, Betty. *The Feminine Mystique.* New York: W.W. Norton, 1963.

Frith, Simon. "Hearing Secret Melodies." In *High Theory/Low Culture: Analysing Popular Television and Film,* ed. Colin MacCabe, 53–70. New York: St. Martin's Press, 1986.

Fuss, Diana, ed. *Inside/Out: Lesbian Theories, Gay Theories.* New York: Routledge, 1991.

Gallop, Jane. *Around 1981: Academic Feminist Literary Theory.* New York: Routledge, 1992.

———. *Reading Lacan.* Ithaca, N.Y.: Cornell University Press, 1985.

Gamman, Lorraine. "Watching the Detectives: The Enigma of the Female Gaze." In *The Female Gaze: Women as Viewers of Popular Culture,* ed. Lorraine Gamman and Margaret Marshment, 8–26. Seattle: Real Comet Press, 1989.

Garber, Marjorie. *Vested Interests: Cross-Dressing and Cultural Anxiety.* New York: Routledge, 1992.

Garner, Shirley Nelson, Claire Kahane, and Madelon Sprengnether, eds. *The (M)other Tongue: Essays in Feminist Psychoanalytic Interpretation.* Ithaca, N.Y.: Cornell University Press, 1985.

Gatlin, Rochelle. *American Women Since 1945.* Jackson: University of Mississippi Press, 1987.

Gibson, Mary Ellis. "Family as Fate: The Novels of Anne Tyler." *Southern Literary Journal* 16 (Fall 1983): 47–58.

Gilbert, Craig. "Reflections on *An American Family, I*" and "Reflections on *An American Family, II.*" In *New Challenges for Documentary,* ed. Alan Rosenthal, 191–209, 288–307. Berkeley, Calif: University of California Press, 1988.

Glover, David, and Cora Kaplan. "Guns in the House of Culture." In *Cultural Studies,* ed. Lawrence Grossberg, Cary Nelson, and Paula Treichler, 213–24. New York: Routledge, 1992.

Goscilo, Margaret. "Deconstructing *The Terminator.*" *Film Criticism* 12.2 (1987–88): 37–52.

Greene, Gayle, and Coppelia Kahn, eds. *Changing Subjects: The Making of Feminist Literary Criticism.* London: Routledge, 1993.

Gutman, Herbert. *The Black Family in Slavery and Freedom, 1750–1925.* New York: Pantheon, 1976.

Habermas, Jürgen. *The Structural Transformation of the Public Sphere: An Inquiry into a Category of Bourgeois Society.* Trans. Thomas Burger with Frederick Lawrence. Cambridge, Mass.: MIT Press, 1989.

Haralovich, Mary Beth. "Sit-coms and Suburbs: Positioning the 1950s Homemaker." In *Private Screenings: Television and the Female Consumer,* ed. Lynn Spigel and Denise Mann, 111–42. Minneapolis: University of Minnesota Press, 1992.

Haraway, Donna. "A Manifesto for Cyborgs: Science, Technology, and Socialist Feminism in the 1980s." In *Coming to Terms: Feminism, Theory, Politics,* ed. Elizabeth Weed, 173–204. New York: Routledge, 1989.

———. "The Promise of Monsters: A Regenerative Politics for Inappropriate/d Others." In *Cultural Studies,* ed. Lawrence Grossberg, Cary Nelson, Paula Treichler, 295–337. New York: Routledge, 1992.

Heath, Stephen. *Questions of Cinema.* Bloomington: Indiana University Press, 1981.

Heller, Dana, ed. *Cross Purposes: Lesbian Studies, Feminist Studies, and the Limits of Alliance.* Bloomington: Indiana University Press, forthcoming.

———. *The Feminization of Quest-Romance: Radical Departures.* Austin: University of Texas Press, 1990.

Heung, Marina. "Daughter-Text/Mother-Text: Matrilineage in Amy Tan's *Joy Luck Club.*" *Feminist Studies* 19.3 (Fall 1993): 597–616.

———. "The New Family in American Cinema." *Journal of Popular Film and Television* 2.2 (1983): 79–85.

Hirsch, Marianne. *The Mother/Daughter Plot: Narrative, Psychoanalysis, Feminism.* Bloomington: Indiana University Press, 1989.

Hirsch, Marianne, and Evelyn Fox Keller, eds. *Conflicts in Feminism.* New York: Routledge, 1990.

Horvitz, Deborah. "Nameless Ghosts: Possession and Dispossession in *Beloved.*" *Studies in American Fiction* 17.2 (1989): 157–67.

Howells, William Dean, Mary E. Wilkins Freeman, et al. *The Whole Family.* New York: Ungar Co., 1986.

Hsiao, Rose Y. "Facing the Incurable: Patriarchy in *Eat a Bowl of Tea.*" In *Reading the Literatures of Asian America,* ed. Shirley Geok-lin Lim and Amy Ling, 151–62. Philadelphia: Temple University Press, 1992.

Hutcheon, Linda. *The Politics of Postmodernism.* London: Routledge, 1989.

Huyssen, Andreas. *After the Great Divide: Modernism, Mass Culture, Postmodernism.* Bloomington: Indiana University Press, 1986.

Ian, Marcia. *Remembering the Phallic Mother: Psychoanalysis, Modernism, and the Fetish.* Ithaca, N.Y.: Cornell University Press, 1993.

Iannone, Carol. "Post-Countercultural Tristesse." *Commentary* 83.2 (1987): 57–61.

Jackson, Kenneth T. *Crabgrass Frontier: The Suburbanization of the United States.* New York: Oxford University Press, 1985.

Jameson, Fredric. "Cognitive Mapping." In *Marxism and the Interpretation of Culture,* ed. Cary Nelson and Lawrence Grossberg, 347–57. London: Macmillan, 1988.

———. *Postmodernism or, The Cultural Logic of Late Capitalism.* Durham, N.C.: Duke University Press, 1992.

Jardine, Alice A. *Gynesis: Configurations of Woman and Modernity.* Ithaca, N.Y.: Cornell University Press, 1985.

Jardine, Alice, and Paul Smith, eds. *Men in Feminism.* New York: Methuen, 1987.

Jenkins, Henry. *Textual Poachers: Television Fans & Participatory Culture.* New York: Routledge, 1992.

Jones, Anne G. "Home at Last and Homesick Again: The Ten Novels of Anne Tyler." *The Hollins Critic* 23.2 (April 1986): 1–13.

Juhasz, Suzanne. "Maxine Hong Kingston: Narrative Technique and Female Identity." In *Contemporary American Women Writers: Narrative Strategies*, ed. Catherine Rainwater and William J. Scheick, 173–89. Lexington: University of Kentucky Press, 1985.

Kaplan, E. Ann. *Motherhood and Representation: The Mother in Popular Culture and Melodrama.* London: Routledge, 1992.

Karl, Frederick R. *American Fictions, 1940–1980.* New York: Harper and Row, 1983.

Kazin, Alfred. *On Native Ground: An Interpretation of Modern American Prose Literature.* New York: Harcourt Brace Jovanovich, 1942, 1970.

Kingston, Maxine Hong. *China Men.* New York: Vintage/Random House, 1980.

———. *The Woman Warrior: Memories of a Girlhood Among Ghosts.* New York: Vintage/Random House, 1975, 1976.

Kolchin, Peter. *American Slavery, 1619–1877.* New York: Hill and Wang, 1993.

Kolmerten, Carol A., and Steven M. Ross. "The Empty Locus of Desire: Woman as Familial Center in Modern American Fiction." *Denver Quarterly* 17.4 (1983): 109–20.

Kristeva, Julia. *About Chinese Women.* Trans. Anita Barrow. New York: Urizen Books, 1974, 1977.

———. *Powers of Horror: An Essay on Abjection.* Trans. Leon Roudiez. New York: Columbia University Press, 1982.

Kroker, Arthur, and Marilouise Kroker, eds. *Body Invaders: Panic Sex in America.* New York: St. Martin's Press, 1987.

Kuhn, Annette. "Structures of Patriarchy and Capital in the Family." In *Feminism and Materialism*, ed. Annette Kuhn and AnnMarie Wople, 42–67. London: Routledge and Kegan Paul, 1978.

Lacan, Jacques. *Ecrits: A Selection.* Trans. Alan Sheridan. New York: W. W. Norton, 1977.

Laing, R. D. *The Politics of the Family.* New York: Vintage Books, 1969, 1977.

Langbauer, Laurie. *Women and Romance: The Consolations of Gender in the English Novel.* Ithaca, N.Y.: Cornell University Press, 1990.

Laqueur, Thomas W. "The Facts of Fatherhood." Reprinted in *Rethinking the Family: Some Feminist Questions.* Revised edition, ed. Barrie Thorne and Marilyn Yalom, 155–76. Boston: Northeastern University Press, 1992.

Lasch, Christopher. *Haven in a Heartless World: The Family Beseiged.* New York: Basic Books, 1977.

Leavitt, David. *Equal Affections.* New York: Harper and Row, 1989.

———. *Family Dancing.* New York: Alfred A. Knopf, 1984.

———. *The Lost Language of Cranes.* Toronto: Bantam Books, 1986.

Leo, John R. "The Familialism of 'Man' in American Television Melodrama." *The South Atlantic Quarterly: Displacing Homophobia*, ed. Ronald B. Butters, 88.1 (1989): 31–52.

———, ed. *American Transcendental Quarterly.* Special issue on nineteenth-century constructions of masculinity. Series 5.3 (September 1991).

Lévi-Strauss, Claude. *The Elementary Structures of Kinship.* Revised edition. Trans. James Harle Bell and John Richard von Sturmer. Ed. Rodney Needham. Boston: Beacon Press, 1969.

Li, David Leiwei. "*China Men*: Maxine Hong Kingston and the American Canon." *American Literary History* 2.3 (Fall 1990): 482–502.

Liebman, Nina C. "Leave Mother Out: The Fifties Family in American Film and Television." *Wide Angle: A Film Quarterly* 10.4 (1988): 24–41.

Lim, Shirley Geok-lin. "The Ambivalent American: Asian American Literature on the Cusp." In *Reading the Literatures of Asian America,* ed. Shirley Geok-lin Lim and Amy Ling, 13–32. Philadelphia: Temple University Press, 1992.

———. "Asians in Anglo-American Feminism: Reciprocity and Resistance." In *Changing Subjects: The Making of Feminist Literary Criticism,* ed. Gayle Greene and Coppelia Kahn, 240–52. London: Routledge, 1993.

Lipsitz, George. "The Meaning of Memory: Family, Class, and Ethnicity in Early Network Television Programs." In *Private Screenings: Television and the Female Consumer,* ed. Lynn Spigel and Denise Mann, 71–110. Minneapolis: University of Minnesota Press, 1992.

Lyotard, Jean-François, and Jean-Loup Thebaud. *Just Gaming.* Trans. Wlad Godzich, Minneapolis: University of Minnesota Press, 1985.

Macherey, Pierre. *A Theory of Literary Production.* London: Routledge, 1978.

Marc, David. *Demographic Vistas: Television in American Culture.* Philadelphia: University of Pennsylvania Press, 1984.

Marsh, Margaret. *Suburban Lives.* New Brunswick, N.J.: Rutgers University, 1990.

Martin, Biddy, and Chandra Talpade Mohanty. "Feminist Politics: What's Home Got to Do with It?" In *Feminist Studies/Critical Studies,* ed. Teresa de Lauretis, 191–212. Bloomington: Indiana University Press, 1986.

Massumi, Brian. *A User's Guide to Capitalism and Schizophrenia: Deviations From Deleuze and Guattari.* Cambridge: MIT Press, 1992.

May, Elaine Tyler. *Homeward Bound: American Families in the Cold War Era.* New York: Basic Books, 1988.

McDermott, Alice. "Dark Domestic Visions? So What Else Is New?" *New York Times,* October 13, 1991, H32.

McDowell, Deborah E. "Reading Family Matters." In *Changing Our Own Words: Essays on Criticism, Theory and Writing by Black Women,* ed. Cheryl A. Wall, 75–97. New Brunswick, N.J.: Rutgers University Press, 1989.

Mellencamp, Patricia. "Domestic Scenes." *East-West Film Journal* 4.1 (1989): 135–67.

Minh-ha, Trinh T. *Woman, Native, Other: Writing Postcoloniality and Feminism.* Bloomington: Indiana University Press, 1989.

Minkowitz, Donna. "Family Values? No Thanks." *The Advocate* (June 16, 1992): 17.

Mitchell, Juliet. *Psychoanalysis and Feminism.* New York: Pantheon Books, 1974.

———. *Woman's Estate.* New York: Pantheon Books, 1971.

———. *Women: The Longest Revolution.* London: Virago, 1984.

Modleski, Tania. *Feminism without Women: Culture and Criticism in a "Postfeminist" Age.* New York: Routledge, 1991.

Moi, Toril. *Sexual/Textual Politics: Feminist Literary Theory.* London: Methuen, 1985.

Morrison, Toni. *Beloved.* New York: NAL, 1987.

Mulvey, Laura. *Visual and Other Pleasures.* Bloomington: Indiana University Press, 1989.

Newton, Esther. *Mother Camp: Female Impersonators in America.* Englewood Cliffs, N.J.: Prentice Hall, 1972.

Nicholson, Linda J. *Gender and History: The Limits of Social Theory in the Age of the Family.* New York: Columbia University Press, 1986.

———, ed. *Feminism/Postmodernism.* New York: Routledge, 1990.

Palmer, Paulina. "The Lesbian Thriller: Crimes, Clues, and Contradictions." In

Outwrite: Lesbianism and Popular Culture, ed. Gabriele Griffin, 86–105. London: Pluto Press, 1993.

Poster, Marc. *Critical Theory and Poststructuralism: In Search of a Context.* Ithaca, N.Y.: Cornell University Press, 1989.

———. *Critical Theory of the Family.* New York: Seabury Press, 1978.

Press, Andrea L. *Women Watching Television: Gender, Class, and Generation in the American Television Experience.* Philadelphia: University of Pennsylvania Press, 1991.

Pynchon, Thomas. *Vineland.* Boston: Little, Brown, 1990.

Radway, Janice A. *Reading the Romance: Women, Patriarchy, and Popular Literature.* Chapel Hill: University of North Carolina Press, 1984.

Rapping, Elayne. *The Movie of the Week: Private Stories/Public Events.* Minneapolis: University of Minnesota Press, 1992.

Readings, Bill. *Introducing Lyotard: Art and Politics.* London: Routledge, 1991.

Riviere, Joan. "Womanliness as Masquerade." Reprinted in *Formations of Fantasy*, ed. Victor Burgin, James Donald, and Cora Kaplan, 35–44. New York: Methuen, 1986.

Robbins, Bruce, ed. *The Phantom Public Sphere.* Minneapolis: University of Minnesota Press, 1993.

Robertson, Mary F. "Anne Tyler: Medusa Points and Contact Points." In *Contemporary American Women Writers*, ed. Catherine Rainwater and William J. Scheick, 119–41. Lexington: University of Kentucky Press, 1985.

Rorty, Richard. *Contingency, Irony, and Solidarity.* Cambridge: Cambridge University Press, 1989.

Ross, Andrew. "Families, Film Genres, and Technological Environments." *East-West Film Journal* 4.1 (1989): 6–26.

Rubenstein, Roberta. *Boundaries of the Self: Gender, Culture, Fiction.* Urbana: University of Illinois Press, 1987.

Rubin, Gayle. "The Traffic in Women: Notes on the 'Political Economy' of Sex." In *Toward An Anthropology of Women*, ed. Rayna R. Reiter, 157–210. New York: Monthly Review Press, 1975.

Schulze, Laurie. "On the Muscle." In *Fabrications: Costume and the Female Body*, ed. Jane Gaines and Charlotte Herzog, 59–78. New York: Routledge, 1990.

Sedgwick, Eve Kosofsky. *Between Men: English Literature and Male Homosocial Desire.* New York: Columbia University, 1985.

———. *Epistemology of the Closet.* Berkeley: University of California Press, 1990.

Seiter, Ellen. "Semiotics and Television." In *Channels of Discourse: Television and Contemporary Criticism*, ed. Robert C. Allen, 17–41. Chapel Hill: University of North Carolina Press, 1987.

Seltzer, Mark. *Bodies and Machines.* New York: Routledge, 1992.

Shear, Walter. "Generational Differences and the Diaspora in *The Joy Luck Club.*" *Critique* 34.3 (Spring 1993): 193–99.

Shelton, Frank. "The Necessary Balance: Distance and Sympathy in the Novels of Anne Tyler." *Southern Review* 20 (1984): 851–60.

Shorter, Edward. *The Making of the Modern Family.* New York: Basic Books, 1977.

Simpson, Mona. *The Lost Father.* New York: Vintage Books, 1993.

Silverman, Kaja. *Male Subjectivity at the Margins.* New York: Routledge, 1992.

Smiley, Jane. *The Age of Grief: Stories and a Novella.* New York: Alfred A. Knopf, 1987.

Smith, Valerie. *Self-Discovery and Authority in Afro-American Narrative.* Cambridge, Mass.: Harvard University Press, 1987.

Smith-Rosenberg, Carroll. *Disorderly Conduct: Visions of Gender in Victorian America.* New York: Oxford University Press, 1985.

Spain, Daphne. *Gendered Spaces.* Chapel Hill: University of North Carolina Press, 1992.

Spigel, Lynn. "From Domestic Space to Outer Space: The 1960s Fantastic Family Sitcom." In *Close Encounters: Film, Feminism, and Science Fiction,* ed. Constance Penley, Elisabeth Lyon, Lynn Spigel, and Janet Bergstrom, 205–35. Minneapolis: University of Minnesota Press, 1991.

————. *Make Room For TV: Television and the Family Ideal in Postwar America.* Chicago: University of Chicago Press, 1992.

————. "Television in the Family Circle: The Popular Reception of a New Medium." In *Logics of Television: Essays in Cultural Criticism,* ed. Patricia Mellencamp, 73–97. Bloomington: Indiana University Press, 1990.

Spigel, Lynn, and Denise Mann, eds. *Private Screenings: Television and the Female Consumer.* Minneapolis: University of Minnesota Press, 1992.

Spivak, Gayatri. "French Feminism in an International Frame." In *Other Worlds: Essays in Cultural Politics.* New York: Methuen, 1987.

Stacey, Judith. *Brave New Families: Stories of Domestic Upheaval in Late Twentieth Century America.* New York: Basic Books, 1990.

Stack, Carol B. *All Our Kin: Strategies for Survival in a Black Community.* New York: Harper and Row, 1974.

Stallybrass, Peter, and Allon White. *The Politics and Poetics of Transgression.* Ithaca, N.Y.: Cornell University Press, 1986.

Stetson, Erlene. "Studying Slavery: Some Literary and Pedagogical Considerations on the Black Female Slave." In *All the Women Are White, All the Blacks Are Men, But Some of Us Are Brave: Black Women's Studies,* ed. Gloria T. Hull, Patricia Bell Scott, and Barbara Smith, 61–84. New York: The Feminist Press, 1982.

Sundquist, Eric J. *Faulkner: The House Divided.* Baltimore: Johns Hopkins University Press, 1983.

Tan, Amy. *The Joy Luck Club.* New York: Ivy Books, 1989.

Tanner, Tony. *Adultery in the Novel: Contract and Transgression.* Baltimore: Johns Hopkins University Press, 1979.

Taylor, Ella. *Prime-Time Families: Television Culture in Postwar America.* Berkeley: University of California Press, 1989.

Thorne, Barrie, and Marilyn Yalom, eds. *Rethinking the Family: Some Feminist Questions.* Revised Edition. Boston: Northeastern University Press, 1992.

Torres, Sasha. "Melodrama, Masculinity, and the Family: *Thirtysomething* as Therapy." *Camera Obscura: A Journal of Feminism and Film Theory,* 19 (1988): 87–106.

Tyler, Anne. *Searching for Caleb.* New York: Berkeley Books, 1975.

Updike, John. "Family Ways." In *Hugging the Shore: Essays and Criticism,* 273–77. New York: Alfred A. Knopf, 1983.

van Boheemen, Christine. *The Novel as Family Romance: Language, Gender, and Authority from Fielding to Joyce.* Ithaca, N.Y.: Cornell University Press, 1987.

Washington, Mary Helen. Introduction. *Memory of Kin: Stories about Family by Black Writers.* New York: Anchor Books/Doubleday, 1991.

Weiss, Andrea. "Lesbian as Outlaw: New Forms and Fantasies in Women's Independent Cinema." *Conditions* 12 (1985): 117–31.

Weston, Kath. *Families We Choose: Lesbians, Gays, Kinship.* New York: Columbia University Press, 1991.

White, Hayden. *Tropics of Discourse: Essays in Cultural Criticism.* Baltimore: Johns Hopkins University Press, 1978.

Whyte, William. *The Organization Man.* Garden City, N.Y.: Doubleday, 1956, 1957.

Williams, Linda. "Something Else Besides a Mother: *Stella Dallas* and the Maternal Melodrama." *Cinema Journal,* 24.1 (Fall 1984): 2–27.

Wittgenstein, Ludwig. *Philosophical Investigations.* 3d edition. Trans. G. E. M. Anscombe. New York: Macmillan, 1958.

Wong, Sau-Ling Cynthia. "Ethnicizing Gender: An Exploration of Sexuality as Sign in Chinese Immigrant Culture." In *Reading the Literatures of Asian America,* ed. Shirley Geok-lin Lim and Amy Ling, 111–30. Philadelphia: Temple University Press, 1992.

Wood, Robin. "An Introduction to the American Horror Film." In *Movies and Methods, II,* ed. Bill Nichols. Berkeley: University of California Press, 1985.

Wylie, Philip. *Generation of Vipers.* New York: Farrar and Rinehart, 1942.

Yaeger, Patricia. "'The Language of Blood': Toward a Maternal Sublime," *Genre* 25 (Spring 1992): 5–24.

Yudice, George. "Marginality and the Ethics of Survival." In *Universal Abandon: The Politics of Postmodernism,* ed. Andrew Ross, 214–36. Minneapolis: University of Minnesota Press, 1988.

Index

This book was set in Baskerville and Eras typefaces. Baskerville was designed by John Baskerville at his private press in Birmingham, England, in the eighteenth century. The first typeface to depart from oldstyle typeface design, Baskerville has more variation between thick and thin strokes. In an effort to insure that the thick and thin strokes of his typeface reproduced well on paper, John Baskerville developed the first wove paper, the surface of which was much smoother than the laid paper of the time. The development of wove paper was partly responsible for the introduction of typefaces classified as modern, which have even more contrast between thick and thin strokes.

Eras was designed in 1969 by Studio Hollenstein in Paris for the Wagner Type-foundry. A contemporary script-like version of a sans-serif typeface, the letters of Eras have a monotone stroke and are slightly inclined.

Printed on acid-free paper.